P9-EDI-907

FROMMER'S
1987–1988 GUIDE TO DUBLIN & IRELAND

by Susan Poole

Copyright © 1977, 1979, 1981, 1983, 1985, 1987
by Prentice Hall Press

All rights reserved
including the right of reproduction
in whole or in part in any form

Published by Prentice Hall Press
A Division of Simon & Schuster, Inc.
Gulf + Western Building
One Gulf + Western Plaza
New York, NY 10023

ISBN 0–671–62355-9

Manufactured in the United States of America

*Although every effort was made to ensure the accuracy
of price information appearing in this book,
it should be kept in mind that prices
can and do fluctuate in the course of time.*

CONTENTS

MAPS

Acknowledgments

Our heartfelt thanks go to all those people who pitched in and shared with us their time and knowledge to help get out this trim but fact-packed volume. Appreciation goes to everyone at Bord Failte, the Irish Tourist Board, the Regional Tourism Offices, Shannon Free Airport Development Company, and the Northern Ireland Tourist Board, who—in that eminently lovable Irish fashion—did everything in their power to oblige.

Dedication

To Stella and Charlie, who proved to be so joyfully Irish at heart if not by birth.

A Word About Prices

This is a guide to an experience—an involvement with a colorful race living in a lovely land. But it is an experience you can enjoy in your own personal style and within your own particular travel budget. Hotels, restaurants, tours—all are available in Ireland at prices ranging from truly low-budget (hostels, farmhouses, private home accommodations) to utter luxury (world-famed grande dame hotels, magnificent castles), with many moderately priced offerings in between. All three price categories have been covered in this book; pick one range or vary your mode. Whichever range you are considering, one thing we can guarantee: all places have been chosen specifically because they give you the best value for your money.

Ireland's government imposes certain price controls, and, therefore, we can assure you that all prices for accommodations listed in this book are the *maximum* prices that can be charged during the year 1987 (expect 1988 rates to be higher). Quoted here are only those tariffs that apply in high tourist season: that can range from the beginning of May to the end of October, or be as short, depending on the individual establishment, as two months, July and August. Throughout the rest of the year, prices for lodgings often descend to amazing lows—always query. While hotel rates have been established, in today's uncertain world food and fuel prices may well go up before the end of 1987 and will almost certainly increase in 1988. We've included those restaurant and transportation charges available at press time. Use them as a guide, but *please* don't consider them gospel.

Chapter I

MEET THE IRISH

Why Ireland?
Ireland: North and South

OVER THE LAST FEW YEARS, Ireland has emerged as a place where discriminating travelers are going. In 1956, Tourist Board statistics reported 805,000 visitors during the year. By 1975, the figure had reached 1,688,000, and visitors from North America alone had tripled in number. In 1985, the North American figure rose to 426,000!

Even the late President Kennedy noted this phenomenon on his visit in 1963 to the homeland of his eight great-grandparents. Addressing the Irish people on the subject of achieving nationhood, he said:

"In the years since independence, you have undergone a new, a peaceful revolution, an economic and industrial revolution, transforming the face of this land, while still holding to the old spiritual and cultural values. You have modernized your economy, harnessed your rivers, diversified your industry, liberalized your trade, electrified your farms, accelerated your rate of growth and improved the living standard of your people . . . other nations in the world in whom Ireland has long invested her people and her children are now investing their capital as well as their vacations in Ireland . . . this revolution is not yet over."

What prompts this investment? Given 25 words or less, frankly, we couldn't tell you. Given the next 200 or so pages, we can try; even then we can only report what happens to ourselves and other visitors we've talked to in Ireland. You'll most assuredly be coming home with a whole different set of stories yourself.

THE FACE OF THE LAND: Many a good writer has tried to portray in words the face of this land—but it's always the poets who come closest. Ireland's beauty is as chimerical as her people—and as

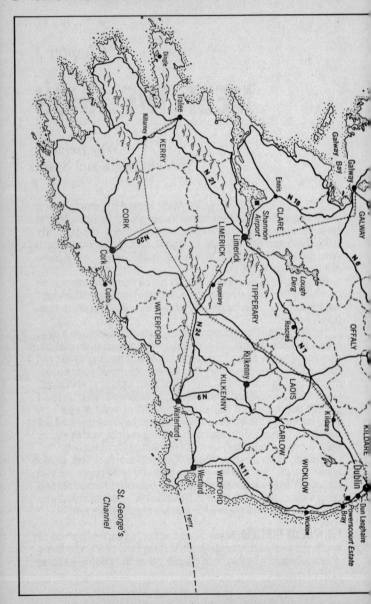

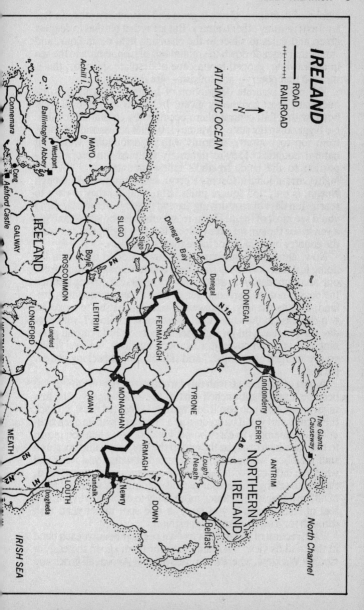

elusive of definition. Grass is grass and a stone is a stone in Ireland as it is in any other country. But grass that blushes to deepest green and pales to silver in the changing light of an hour, and stones that cascade down the mountains of Connemara to the sea in a sprawling, gapped moonscape of desolate splendor, this is the stuff that poetry—and tourism—are made of.

The most accurate description of Ireland's geography is the one that's most commonly given: Ireland is like an oval soup bowl, with a flat, central plain, encircled by coastal mountains. No bigger than the state of Maine (150 miles across and 315 miles from top to bottom), it brims with an astounding variety of natural bounties. They're delicately sculpted—in proper proportion to the land. Ireland's tallest mountain is 3,414 feet high (Carrantuohill in County Kerry), and her largest lake, Lough Neagh, is only 153 square miles. But, equally, they're easy to reach. Ten days of easy driving around the edge of the island and you'd see most of them. If you're in Dublin for breakfast and get a yen to see the sun set over Galway Bay that night, you can cross the country by train in not more than 3½ hours.

Now, although Americans are known around the world for doing just that, let me say right here that ten days of shifting from one accommodation to another every night and driving through the days is not my personal idea of how to see *any* country. Ireland, with its friendly, manageable size, lends itself to a one- or two-day base in the same hotel, guesthouse, or hostel, with easy day trips to reach major sightseeing spots. A little careful planning and you can cover just as much territory, see everything you've marked as a "must," and skip all that unpacking and repacking.

A host of bonuses go with this sort of travel. For one thing, you become a firmly entrenched part of the local scenery—the first night in any Irish pub you'll be a warmly welcomed guest: go back the second and you'll be greeted as a "regular" with an even richer holiday memory to carry home. For another, when you return to the same hearthside at the end of the day, you'll find hosts and staff members who are truly interested in where you went and what you did—and with *that* kind of conversational springboard, there's no telling where your second evening may wind up! Most of all, however, you're much more likely to catch the rhythm and feel of each region if you tarry in one spot rather than rush through for a series of one-night stands.

Each section of Ireland has its own peculiar beauty, each bend in the road its view. Take time to savor them all. In the east, in County Wicklow, where the waters meet at Avoca, all is rich and mountainy, quaint towns sheltered in steep canyons, a cool, crisp New England beauty of woods and hills and lakes. Along the southeastern coast, the sands are salt white and stretch for miles in undulating dunes. In the south and southwest, fishing villages cluster against the coastal cliffs—white-walled cottages peep through golden thatches like so many shaggy-haired schoolboys. The far west, where rock piles upon rock, is as stark as the bottom of a drained sea. The woods and fields of County Kerry are tangled and tropical with brilliant fuchsia blooms bursting through the high hedges that flank the roads. The fields of the midlands are flat and fertile and overrun by high-spirited, hard-muscled horses. Up north, in the highlands of Donegal, the cold northern sea pounds the high cliffs with all the froth-mouthed bad temper of a gouty old god—while vast, wild moors grope inland in a violet haze of heather. We have shivered on a 70-degree day at the terrible beauty of Donegal.

And the ultimate beauty is that all these beauties serve no practical purpose whatsoever. The Mountains of Mourne don't do double duty as a backdrop for soft-sell Volkswagen billboards. The Gap of Dunloe does not serve primarily as a setting for a Pizza–Tasty-Freeze–Hot-Dog (Pure Beef)–Souvenir stand. What a blessing to the visitor with a camera!

THE OLD SPIRITUAL AND CULTURAL: Living within this luminous little land of porter and chipped potatoes are 3,500,000 Irish people. And every one a potential drinking companion—whether tea, milk, or whisky. That the Irish are friendly is not the best kept secret of the century. Their peculiar brand of friendliness—that's what often comes as a surprise.

Like good hosts everywhere, the Irish don't intrude on you—they wait for you to make the first overtures. You won't exit from your plane to the strains of fiddles and a shower of shamrocks. But, coming in from the airport in a taxi one time, a visitor mentioned she was feeling chilly and hoped she'd brought warm enough clothes for the season (it was December), and the driver was ready to turn off the meter and take her home to the wife for the loan of a coat during her stay. On one of our own first days in Dublin we asked a gentleman standing in front of an appliance store for directions to the nearest post office. Walking away, we took a wrong turn and immediately heard him pounding down the pavement after us. He not only walked us to the post office, then he also helped us buy the stamps and pointed out the overseas mail slot. "Aren't we taking you away from your work?" we asked. "Ah, sure," he said, "there's nobody in Dublin today that's wanting appliances. I told the lad to look after the store or your folks would never be hearing from you, the way you were walking."

You can go your own way in Ireland and not speak to a soul: the Irish will certainly grant you your privacy. But you might just as well be sitting in the corner Trans-Lux watching a travelog of the country, with the Mormon Tabernacle Choir aah-ing rapturously in the background, for all the fun you'll have. Speak to almost any Irishman, present him with the simplest problem, and the outlines of your day begin to tremble like The Strange World of Mr. Mum. He'll burst upon you in huge, heaving rhythms of lovely words (the female of the species is gentler), taking your problem—and you—to the greatness of his bosom. He may not solve anything, but he'll rearrange the molecules of the situation just enough to afford you both ample satisfaction and invite you to tea with himself and the wife Sunday next, please God.

Long years ago when the Irish lived, for the most part, as peasants in huts, to turn away a stranger from your door while you had a potato to feed him and a warm fire within was to risk the heavy hand of heaven. The tradition still lingers. By definition, a stranger in Ireland is a person worthy of special favors. But a stranger with a problem—that's an irresistible combination to the expansive Irish ego. We'll never forget watching an elderly tourist approach a CIE bus driver on O'Connell Street one day and timidly ask for his help. He seemed to be echoing all Ireland when he extended his arms in one grand, outgoing gesture and replied, "Madam, I exist to make you happy."

By now, we imagine you're suspecting the truth about us—that we happen to be exceptionally vulnerable to the soul-feeding glories of the Irish countryside and warmth of the people, and we'll lay odds that you will return from the Emerald Isle with the same schmaltzy attitude!

Ireland: North and South

Green, fresh, and human it is—but what of the turmoil? There is not a reader or watcher of the news today who isn't aware of the violence which has been going on in Northern Ireland, the intractable sectarian warfare that has resulted in such tragic loss of so many lives. For impending visitors to Ireland, the violence is a major concern.

The reason lies in two words: *Northern Ireland,* which, since the much-disputed treaty of 1921, has remained an entity separate from the Republic in the south—a small, industrialized, six-county *British* province, operated under Westminster's wing. Although sharing the same small island with its southern brethren, the North's problems differ drastically, and its "troubles" have on very few occasions spilled over the border. While these troubles fester, the South watches on television—along with the rest of us—and mourns. But only once did the everyday southern citizens become actively involved. On January 30, 1972, British soldiers shot and killed 13 Catholics up North in Derry's Bogside—a day that has become known as "Bloody Sunday." In the South, the people of Dublin thronged into the streets, marched on Merrion Square, and set fire to the British Embassy. The police made no move to stop them.

Following the embassy burning, 15,000 people canceled their scheduled tours to Ireland. This is where the troubles have touched the Republic most directly. Tourism is Ireland's second industry, and its major market—despite the two countries' long history of struggle—is England. Fearful of their welcome, British tourists began staying away in droves. The Tourist Board imported English journalists to reassure their countrymen. After one such tour, British newsman Tony Dawe wrote: "Despite marked English accents and mannerisms, we met nothing but hospitality whether in shops, or bars, or boats, or beaches. The southern Irish might hold grievances against us collectively, but they seem pleased to greet us individually." The cross-Channel tourist figures which had slumped so badly in the summer of '72 plumped up happily in 1973.

Transatlantic traffic had also taken a nose-dive since the troubles started—but for a different reason. Unlike the British, Americans seem a bit vague on the geography of Ireland. Seen on the map, a mere dot in the ocean beside the vast continent of Europe, it looks so tiny people are convinced that the bombs going off in the center of Belfast echo through the back streets of Dublin. Not true. The road from Belfast to Dublin is 103 miles long and it is *not* traversed by armored cars. More likely it is jammed with northern tourists heading south for a bit of much-needed tranquility, a few weeks to "get away from it all."

For although the troubles may dominate news headlines and TV, they do not overly preoccupy the people of the South. If you want to discuss the subject, you will probably have to bring it up yourself. Not that the people of the Republic don't care. They do—they're simply all talked out. All the angles have been rehashed among friends for years, and everyone knows each other's opinions and prefers not to hear them again. The southern hope is for a united Ireland in the future; their present concerns are what they have always been—their own lives and development as a country.

This development took an important turn on January 1, 1973, when Ireland joined the new, nine-country European Economic Community. ("How does it feel to be a foreigner?" they asked each other on the day they "entered" Europe.) EEC membership has forced Ireland to look outward, possibly for the first time in its rather isolationist history. It has also forced up both prosperity and prices. Due to increased exports, Irish farmers have found their incomes suddenly enlarged; through industrial investment attracted during the first year of membership, projected new jobs went up a remarkable 60%. The present worldwide recession has again made unemployment a major Irish concern. In fact, Ireland still has one of the lowest economies of the countries in the Common Market and wrangles mightily in Brussels for more aid as an underdeveloped country. But even with its history of poverty, Ireland is no longer poor; there are very few people now who are not warmly dressed housed, and well fed. Providing more jobs to staunch further emigration, reducing the income gap, curtailing inflation, extending the social welfare program, giving a higher quality of public education—these are what southern Ireland is talking about today.

As for the North, the troubles go on, sometimes on a lowered scale, sometimes accelerated. As a visitor, however, you will probably never be exposed to violence during your stay. Indeed, not one tourist has been harmed because of the internal strife to date, despite the fact that some 45,000 Americans tour the province annually. True, the sight of armed patrols and military checkpoints are reminders of the situation, but they are not omnipresent, and on the whole do not overshadow a sojourn north of the border. From the people of Northern Ireland, you can expect a warm welcome, concern for your welfare as a visitor, and delight that you have come to experience their truly beautiful part of Ireland's magical landscape.

Chapter II

INTRODUCING DUBLIN

City on the Liffey

DUBLIN'S FAIR CITY—you've heard about it in song, story, and poetry long before your arrival. Maybe it's even your primary reason for traveling to Ireland in the first place.

Well, let me say that a very happy, memorable holiday is easily spent within the city limits with never a foot set out in the countryside. That's if you're a city person through and through. Of course, *Ireland* is much, much more than Dublin. You'll be cheating yourself if you think Dublin is the sum total of the country. But Dublin is an ancient, fascinating, lively, entertaining, and wholly unique European capital—Ireland may be Ireland, but it's not complete without Dublin. You'll come out on the short end of the stick if you don't plan at least a day or two in Molly Malone's hometown.

The city was founded as a trading port by the Danes in 841, conquered by Strongbow in 1171, and colonized the next year by Henry II, who peopled it with Normans from Bristol. From then until that day in 1916 when Padraic Pearse proclaimed the Irish Republic from the steps of the General Post Office in O'Connell Street, Dublin was essentially an English city and the seat of English government in Ireland. First the English erected Dublin Castle, and then high walls around the city to withstand the warring O'Tooles and O'Byrnes, who lived in the low, lush hills that circle the city. Much later, when Cromwell came, Dublin and its immediate surroundings constituted the Pale, and all of Ireland lay unprotected beyond.

In the 18th century, the English gave Dublin its most outstanding architectural features—the trim city squares and handsome rows of Georgian houses that account for much of its picturesque, chimney-pot skyline. In the early 20th century, the English were ushered out of Dublin in a blaze of idealism and rebel gunfire, and the city was finally relinquished to the devices of the warring O'Tooles and O'Byrnes. The Civil War ended in 1923. Dublin swept up the pieces, rebuilt its beautiful, 18th-century buildings, and began to take on—for the first time in history—the chores of an Irish capital in an Irish country.

That's where you'll find Dublin today—at the center of Irish politics, society, culture, and business, the largest city on the island (pop. 983,683) and the leisurely capital of a philosophic land. Leisurely, yes, but getting less so by the day, and less and less representative of its rustic environs and traditions. Over the last few years, certain phenomena have been reported in the streets of Dublin. People have been seen to "bustle." Businessmen have settled for occasional one-hour lunches, and traffic jams have been known to form both at morning and night. True, there are still a few horse carts stuck in that traffic; street vendors still roll baby carriages stocked with fresh fruit and flowers through the crowded thoroughfares. There's always time for the long, inquisitive greeting among friends—and in Dublin everyone a native meets either knows him or his second cousin—and time out for gossip is strictly sacrosanct. A New Yorker, walking down a "bustling" Dublin street, may get the distinct impression that he is caught up in the light-headed buoyancy of a slow-motion movie. Dublin has its brakes on—but there are sure signs that it's skidding.

As a visitor, you can make Dublin one of two things: a base from which to explore the country—there are green fields to hunt and fresh streams to fish only 20 minutes from O'Connell Street, and Galway is but a 3½-hour train ride away; or one long concentrated stop on a tour of the coast. Whichever you choose, there is really only one perfect way to see the capital itself—to dig under the city's skin and taste its singular blend of sweetness and acridity—and that is to walk through its streets and alleyways, peering into people's windows, as it were, and listening to the snatches of conversation that waft through pub doors at night. Dublin does resemble the rest of Ireland in one important respect: it lays its emphasis on people, rather than parks, monuments, and museums. But then, Dubliners have less need of the symbols; they are in themselves a matchless monument to the city and culture that created them—a wordy, often witty, congenial and contentious, self-perpetuating monument unto themselves.

Arriving in Dublin

Dublin Airport is seven miles due north of the city. Within the terminal you will find a **Tourist Information Desk** to make hotel bookings should you arrive without them (a chancy thing to do in midsummer). Also in the airport you can change your money, rent a car, eat cheaply at the snackbar, or dine more expensively at the grill. Airport coaches take you directly into the central bus station, **Busaras,** on Store Street, for £2.50 ($3.75) for adults, £1.25 ($1.88) for children. A taxi to the city center costs approximately £10 ($15).

Before delving into the details of life in Dublin City, a few words pertaining equally to Ireland as a whole—

THE CURRENCY: The Irish pound (or "punt") is divided into 100 pence, which comes in coins of ½, 1, 2, 5, 10, and 50 pence pieces. All banks get daily quotations of value and make exchanges accordingly.

Always change your money at a bank or American Express. Some of the big department stores call the banks daily to ascertain the pound's value, but many hotels and shops just take a "spread" over the week, sticking to a rate which could be higher than you need pay. You also get a better rate of exchange on traveler's checks than you do cash.

With the dollar fluctuating all over the place, it is difficult to give you a pound equivalent for conversion purposes. However, the chart below is based on the pound/dollar ratio at press time: $1.50 to the pound.

1p	$ .02	£1	$ 1.50
5p	$ .08	£2.50	$ 3.75
25p	$ .38	£3	$ 4.50
50p	$ .75	£4.50	$ 6.75
75p	$1.13	£10	$15.00

THE CLIMATE: You can't help teasing the Irish about their weather —they take it all so tragically. Especially the people working in tourism, who—unlike the Irish poets—see the romantic, and perpetual, mists that shroud their island as some sort of infernal subversion aimed at undermining the best laid plots of semistate tourist bodies to make a proper showing on the year-end report to the nation.

But if the Irish weather keeps the Tourist Board humble, it also helps protect a lovely little country, literally untouched up to now by uncaring human hands, from being littered bay-to-bay with yellow Kodak wrappers and 20-Afton cartons. It deters the indifferent hordes—and the no-taste land developers who follow the indifferent hordes—who ask for nothing more than a sunbeam to bask in, and don't care how the place looks after they've basked. It leaves Ireland—God bless the perverse Irish weather—green and sweet-smelling and to the devices of the true travel sophisticates.

It also does one other thing: it helps keep the prices down. Even though Ireland suffers (like the rest of the world) from inflation, it is still a good travel buy, and that's why we hesitate to say anything that might change the status quo. Let's none of us tell the Irish, but their weather, while it's something a visitor has to prepare for (that is, bring a raincoat), is nothing we're going to write home complaining about. It rains often, that's all, and Ireland's not the place to come for a suntan.

If anything, the cool, fresh Irish climate comes as a distinct relief to midsummer refugees from American heat waves. The climate in Ireland is moderate—all year round. The warmest months of the year are July and August, and they average between 58 and 60 degrees in temperature. The coldest month is February, when the average ranges between 40 and 42 degrees. The sunniest month in the north, west, and midlands is usually May, with from five to six hours of bright sunshine per day, while June is the sunniest month in the rest of the country. There's more rainfall in the mountains than the flatlands and in the west than the east—and snow is a thing seen mainly on Christmas cards.

What this means to you as a prospective visitor is that you must come equipped with moderately warm clothes and rain gear, plan your vacation around the possibility of patches of rain, and then be pleasantly surprised when you get more sun than you expected. The summer rain seldom splatters down from morning to night. Rather, the Irish weather seems to be controlled by two playful poltergeists with bad coordination. We've seen it change from sun to showers 12 times on an August day—and overlap four times in between.

A Note to British Readers: Ireland can often yield up sun when Great Britain has none—notably around the virginal beaches of the southeast (near Wexford and Waterford), which might prove a bit chilly to thin-blooded Americans but are very popular holiday venues for the hardier British beach fans.

Average temperatures vary throughout the country. The following chart represents those measured (in degrees Fahrenheit) in Dublin in recent years.

January	43.2	July	58.8
February	41.4	August	59.5
March	43.7	September	56.1
April	45.3	October	49.1
May	51.6	November	43.9
June	58.1	December	41.4

WHAT TO PACK AND WEAR: Poets may eulogize it, old men in Connemara may curse it, but a tourist has to pack for it. So the first thing you do before reaching for your duffel bag is read the section above on the Irish climate, and adjust.

The fine art of packing for economy and mobility has one cardinal rule. A little goes a long way, and less than that will take you every bit as far—much easier and cheaper. The best travelers in the world are those who go into a country unencumbered by either prejudice or luggage. With a maximum of one lightweight suitcase and a bulging hip pocket or shoulder purse, you need never waste precious moments unpacking and repacking, or precious pennies hiring porters to take you from train to taxi, from hotel room back to train. Once you've checked your suitcase out of the airport, you're on your own. You can swing along from guesthouse to hotel, picking out the place you want to stay without crumpling up on the first couch you see out of sheer exhaustion at the thought of toting your effects on up the block. Remember that variety is not really necessary in a travel wardrobe, as nobody you meet has ever seen your last year's outfit before, and tomorrow you'll meet somebody else who also hasn't. If variety is a psychological necessity for you, choose separates and try to sublimate your need in the diversity of experiences you'll receive on your travels. If you bring a variety, you have to carry that variety.

As for what to wear during your stay in Ireland, be practical and prepare for showers and coolness. Springweight clothes are perfect for summer and heavier clothes for the rest of the year. The Irish aren't prudes about clothing. Slacks and shorts are acceptable on women and so, lately, are bikinis. There was a marvelous incident reported in the Irish papers in recent years that shows how emancipated Irish thinking has become. A young and very pretty girl was wearing a two-piece and very tiny bathing suit on one of the white strands of the southern coast one day, when a mortified priest sent a note over the dunes to her, requesting that she "modify her bathing costume." The note was respectfully returned to the priest with the answer, "Certainly, Father, which part do you suggest I remove?"

Irish men wear sportsclothes and bulky knit sweaters in the country but almost always show up at the hotel dining table or in restaurants wearing a suit and a tie. It's another tribute to the genuine democracy that is practiced everywhere in Ireland: a man may work as a modest laborer by day, but he can eat at the next table to a minister of the Dail by night; if he looks and acts the part of a gentleman, he is accepted and treated as a gentleman. And the same holds true for tourists.

The best advice we ever received on packing for a journey is: set aside everything you feel you absolutely must take, and then ruthlessly put two-thirds of it back in the dresser drawers. Don't ever panic about leaving a necessity behind. The Irish use toothbrushes, too, and you can find the equivalent of an American Woolworth's on almost any Irish corner. If you can possibly take drip-dry clothes with you, they travel best, of course. But if you don't own any, don't rush out and make any major investments —quick-service cleaners exist in every major Irish town.

Dublin City Layout

Small and compact as capital cities go, Dublin is not a difficult city to grasp and get around; a few minutes spent poring over the map on page 16 should set you off in the right direction.

Note first that the **River Liffey,** peat-brown and musky with the smell of brewer's yeast, flows from west to east, slicing the city in two. On the western side of the city is Dublin's resplendent, 2,000-acre municipal playground, **Phoenix Park.** On the eastern side, the Liffey empties into Dublin Bay. Now locate **O'Connell Bridge;** we'll use this wide and busy central bridge as our point of reference in the following chapters.

Running to the north of O'Connell Bridge is **O'Connell Street,** Dublin's broad main street, a somewhat disappointing morass of ice-cream parlors, major movie houses, penny arcades, shops, statues, aluminum flagpoles, the fluted columns of the General Post Office, and stately 19th-century office buildings and hotels. O'Connell Street is one of the few places in Ireland where traffic tie-ups are a daily fact of contemporary life.

Cross the bridge, and O'Connell Street is continued to the south as **Westmoreland Street,** which leads one block to **College Green**—not an actual green but a wide intersection with more statues and more traffic. The entrance to Trinity College (wherein the *Book of Kells*) is on College Green. **Grafton Street,** Dublin's chic and narrow shopping street, starts a slow and interesting climb from College Green that ends at the corner of **St.**

Stephen's Green, which is a genuine green, this time: 22 acres of grass, trees, fountains, flowers, duck ponds—and no traffic.

The **city center** is the almost mile-long stretch from Parnell Square at the northern end of O'Connell Street to the St. Stephen's Green at the southern end of Grafton Street, with the cramped and busy streets on either side of these main thoroughfares.

Getting Around Dublin

Once you understand how the city works, you'll have little difficulty in navigating. Public transport is good, taxis are usually easy to locate (and the highly verbal drivers quite often worth waiting for), but driving can be difficult, especially during morning and evening rush hours, when O'Connell Street can come to a virtual standstill. Central Dublin has a rather remarkable one-way street system, newly devised to help speed the crosstown traffic. We'd suggest you look at the map and determine the point you wish to reach—then head in that general direction as per the one-way street arrows. Eventually, we've always found, one attains the goal. When driving into the city for shopping or sightseeing, it's best by far to park the car in a garage or lot for the duration and hoof it or use the buses. Most central streets have metered parking.

LOCAL BUSES: Dublin's bus service is both efficient and cheap. Operated by **CIE,** the national transport company that also runs the country's long-distance (called "provincial") buses and trains, it crisscrosses the city and its suburbs with 120 routes. Service starts at 6:30 a.m. weekdays, 9:30 a.m. on Sunday, and continues until 11:30 p.m. (For late nights, you'd require a taxi.) Most city buses start their run from O'Connell Bridge. Some lines start a block to the south at either Fleet Street or College Street, or north on O'Connell Street near Lower Abbey, North Earl Street, or Parnell Square. CIE starters, stationed at each point, are willing dispensers of information. Or you can phone 787777 to find out how to get there from here. When heading into town from the outskirts, take any bus marked **An Lar.** That's Gaelic for "the center." Fares are charged according to distance traveled and range from 45p (68¢) to 85p ($1.28) for adults, 25p (38¢) to 45p (68¢) for children under 16.

There are several bus bargains. Special **shopping fares** are offered between 10 a.m. and 4:30 p.m. on weekdays, for the center-city area bounded by Parnell Square and St. Stephen's

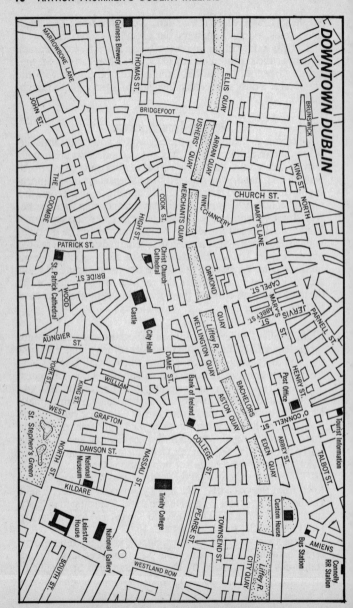

DOWNTOWN DUBLIN

Green. During those hours you can hop on and off buses at 25p (38¢). For those on a longer visit to Dublin, the monthly commuter ticket might be useful. This ticket gives unlimited travel on Dublin city buses and suburban trains, handy if you're staying outside the city and traveling in to sightsee. You can purchase commuter tickets at CIE's main ticket office, 59 Upper O'Connell St. Also pick up the free brochure, "Dublin by Bus," and a "Dublin District Bus and Train Timetable" for 40p (60¢). While at the office, inquire about sightseeing tours by coach and train leaving Dublin. Ask for the **Day Trip** brochure.

COMMUTER RAIL: CIE operates high-frequency electric commuter train service extending from Bray in the South around the soft curve of Dublin Bay all the way to Howth at the northern end. Trains will run every fifteen minutes (every five minutes during peak traffic hours), from 7 a.m. to midnight daily, with fares graduated according to distance traveled. Stops are made at Connolly, Tara Street, and Pearse city center stations as well as Dun Laoghaire (handy if you're coming or going by car ferry) and other suburban points. Some suburban bus lines will feed into the rail line to shorten the journey into town. This opens up accommodation options considerably, since it will now be possible to travel in and out of the city while enjoying the delights of a seafront base. You can get full details on this service by ringing 787777.

TAXIS: Taxis are numerous and reasonably priced but cannot be hailed on city streets. You either phone for a cab (small extra charge) or walk to the nearest cab rank and take the first driver on line. Ranks are located outside train and bus stations and at the airport. In the city center, you will also find them in O'Connell Street, on College Green, and on the north side of St. Stephen's Green. To phone a cab, look under "Taxicab Ranks and Shelters" in the telephone book for the rank closest to you (meters start as soon as the cabby takes off), or try one of the radio cab companies at: 01-761111, 683333, 766666, or 507777. The minimum fare within ten miles of the city center is £1.45 ($2.18). There is a 40p (60¢) charge for each extra passenger, and a baggage charge of 40p (60¢) per piece, plus a 40p (60¢) surcharge between 8 p.m. and 8 a.m.; 10% of the fare is the usual tip. For journeys outside the ten-mile radius, negotiate directly with the driver.

RENTAL CARS: You can rent a car in Ireland on a valid U.S. license.

Different companies have certain age stipulations applicable to their more expensive types of vehicles. For some cars you have to be over 26 and under 70 years of age. Rental rates are governed by seasons: high, economy, and low. During low season (November to April), it is possible to rent a small car for as little as £130 ($195) a week, with unlimited mileage. In summer, however, it is essential that you book a car ahead and put a deposit on it in order to avoid disappointment: the fleets are comparatively small.

The following Irish firms are known for reliability and service; all will deliver to either Shannon or Dublin Airport free of charge, and offer weekly as well as daily rates. Best to request brochures and choose the deal appropriate to your plans. If you are staying any length of time, the weekly rate with unlimited mileage *always* saves money.

Johnson & Perrott, 12a S. Leinster St., Dublin 2 (tel. 01-767213). This highly trustworthy company actually dates back to 1810—it was building horse carriages before the horseless ones appeared—and offers free car delivery to airports and city hotels in Dublin, Limerick, and Cork. J. & P. has an exceptional shoulder-season bargain: a Ford Fiesta costs only £130 ($195) per week (plus 10% tax), unlimited mileage, and basic insurance. This price is applicable May, June, mid-September, and October. In summer the same car costs £175 ($262.50), plus 10% tax, all mileage included. In addition to the Fiesta, they have many other models to choose from. Finally, a special deal in May and October—one free day for rentals of one week or more.

Dan Dooley Rent-a-Car, Knocklong, County Limerick (tel. 062-53103), is a family-run business, begun back in 1971. They have one of the largest fleets of rental cars in Ireland, with desks at Shannon, Cork, and Dublin airports as well as an office in Dublin city center. If your party is a large one you will be glad to know they also offer 9-passenger mini-buses and 4-berth camper vans. Timid drivers will find automatic-shift cars available. In 1986 rates ranged from £21 ($31.50) per day to £64 ($96) per day, with weekly rates ranging from £100 ($150) to £348 ($522). All rates include unlimited mileage.

Murray's Europcar, Baggot Street Bridge, Dublin 4 (tel. 01-681777), and 24 Upper O'Connell St., beside the Gresham Hotel (tel. 01-743937), offers free delivery and collection within five miles of a local company office. Other offices are at Shannon, Cork, Galway, Wexford, and Rosslare. They have a wide variety of sizes and models. Weekly rates in low season start at £126 ($189) with unlimited mileage, and peak season rates in July and

August are about 25% higher. Murray's also operates as official car-rental contractor to Aer Lingus and is the Irish agent for National Car Rental and Tilden of Canada.

Cahills, 36 Annesley Pl., Northstrand, Dublin 3 (tel. 01-747766), also with an office at Cork on Glanmire Rd. (tel. 021-506744), has favorable rates, and special long-term rates are available for periods over one week.

Hertz is in Upper Leeson Street, Dublin 2 (tel. 01-767476; toll free in the U.S., 800/654-3131), and at Dublin, Cork, and Shannon Airports, as well as Rosslare and Dun Laoghaire Ferry ports, with free delivery and collection within five miles of any branch office. **Avis** is at 1 Hanover St., E., Dublin 2 (tel. 01-776791), also with offices at major airports.

HANSOM CABS: "Horses hoofs and creaking wheels" and shades of Martin Cunningham, Leopold Bloom, Simon Dedalus, and Mr. Power seeing their friend, Paddy Dignam, off at Glasnevin Cemetery—if you really want to tour Old Dublin in proper style, you can rent a wonderful, turn-of-the century hansom cab and be drawn through the streets and the Georgian squares in "knee-jogging" splendor. A few of the old horse-drawn cabs that were prevalent in Joyce's day have been restored and reintroduced to service, and you can hire them by contacting **Paddy Sarsfield,** 5 Lower Kevin St. (tel. 01-755995). They seat from one to four persons, and where you go is a matter for discussion between you and the driver. If you want to take the most atmospheric route, suggest the Georgian squares and old streets on the south side of the Liffey.

Tourist Information and Aids

If there is a tourist board in the world more generous with assistance to visitors than the **Irish Tourist Board** (in Gaelic, *Bord Failte*—"Board of Welcomes"), we have not yet come in contact with it. Not only will the board provide you with free, detailed, and very helpful literature for planning your holiday, it is also able and willing to answer the most obscure questions you may have—or at least direct you to someone who can.

The Irish Tourist Board has offices in New York, San Francisco, Chicago, Toronto, Paris, Frankfurt-am-Main, Amsterdam, Brussels, Milan, London, Manchester, Birmingham, Glasgow, and Belfast, with representatives stationed in Sydney and Auckland. Any of them is capable of supplying you with literature and helping you plan special-interest tours. Among the literature you should request are: their official guides to hotels, guesthouses, and farmhouses, which list amenities and legal rates for the year; a map of Ireland; the year's **Calendar of Events;** a holiday planner called **Ireland: The Unexpected Pleasures** (sumptuously illustrated); the booklet listing free attractions in Ireland; fishing booklets giving details on boat hire, baits, licenses, and the best spots to drop your line; **The Open Forest,** a guide to national parks; and the list of **Tourist Information Offices** throughout the country. Addresses to write in the States are:

757 Third Ave.
New York, NY 10017
(tel. 212/418-0800)

230 N. Michigan Ave.
Chicago, IL 60601
(tel. 312/726-9356)

625 Market St.
San Francisco, CA 94105
(tel. 415/957-0985)

In Ireland, the main office is at Baggot Street Bridge, Dublin 2 (tel. 01-765871).

TOURIST INFORMATION OFFICES: Working in conjunction with the Irish Tourist Board are seven **Regional Tourism Companies,** each dealing with a particular area of the country and operating several local offices within each region. Each office is set up to provide you with both local and national information—and handle with solicitous Irish care any travel problem you might encounter. Get the list of offices from the board and use it faithfully to find out what's going on where you happen to be. Offices are open from 10 a.m. to 5:30 p.m. daily, but often extend their hours far into the bright evenings during heavy tourist months.

One of the finest services the regional offices offer is their **Room Reservation Service.** Through any office, you can book accommodations in every price range, from farmhouses to castles, locally or elsewhere in the country. There is a small charge for the service and you pay the cost of the telephone call plus in some cases a deposit to be applied against the charge for your room. There are desks at both Shannon and Dublin Airports to make bookings, provide maps, and give directions.

IN DUBLIN: Dublin's centrally located tourist office is north of the Liffey at 14 Upper O'Connell St. (tel. 01-747733). **Dublin and Eastern Regional Tourism** is invaluable to the city visitor. The charmingly patient staff will answer questions, give advice, book theater tickets and banquets, provide free brochures on local attractions, and sell guidebooks, timetables, and Ordnance Survey road maps. A very useful publication to purchase is the *Dublin Official Guide* (includes maps) at a nominal charge. An attractive giftshop in the basement sells souvenirs and craft items at competitive prices, and they can mail purchases for you.

Chapter III

DUBLIN: WHERE TO STAY

Accommodations at All Prices

WHEN IT COMES TO VARIETY, Dublin's accommodations offer an amazing range. Take your pick from: a castle, a Victorian mansion, something straight-walled and modern, or a structure lavishly adorned with plasterwork and heralded by torch-bearing iron maidens.

When it comes to price, the scope is equally wide. You can stay comfortably in a modest room with bath down the hall where the tariff, including a full, cooked Irish breakfast, would come to only about £9 ($13.50) per person. Or you can opt for gilt-and-crystal elegance at £86 ($129) double, cooked breakfast *not* included. In between rock bottom and the extravagant top are any number of well-priced possibilities. We should point out, however, that price, in Ireland, isn't necessarily the measure of value. Some of the least expensive places actually offer the most charming experiences.

All Irish hostelries have certain things in common. There are two distinct types: guesthouses and hotels. Guesthouses are not licensed to sell "spirits," but may be allowed to serve wine to residents. They are only required to serve breakfast but many offer other meals if they wish. They are not required to feed casual comers. Hotels, on the other hand, are licensed to sell all types of alcoholic beverages and must provide three meals daily to resident and nonresident alike. People staying in hotels should be able to purchase drinks 24 hours a day.

Amenities in most Irish hotels are not as extensive as those in America. Irish hotels are never equipped with air conditioning, nor will you feel its absence since there's an abundance of Mother

Nature's own air conditioning. Central heating is universal but nowhere near as intense as that to which North Americans are accustomed. (Extra heaters and electric blankets are usually kept on tap for thin-skinned transatlantics.) Many Irish hotels still offer rooms without bath (a very inexpensive way to stay in some of the most luxurious older inns). Many private bathrooms have tubs only, although shower-tubs are rapidly being installed. Good-quality hotels have phones and radios in all rooms and 24-hour switchboard service. Guesthouses seldom have either, but provide guests with the use of a hall phone and a key to the front door at night. There is no such thing as the 24-hour coffeeshop in Ireland (there is one open 23 hours in Dublin's Jurys Hotel), but night porters are quite adept at preparing small sandwiches and tea for ravenous tourists. As to Irish service—it is usually willing, but not always brisk. Relax, and repeat the ancient Irishism: "When God made time, He made a lot of it."

The following list of accommodations has been compiled after a thorough combing of Dublin's stock. All tariffs given are given in 1987 ranges (expect increases at both ends in 1988). Discounts for children refer only to those sharing a room with adults. Where the price is given for a full, cooked Irish breakfast, continental-style breakfasts are also available at little more than half that charge.

LUXURY HOTELS
£50 ($75) to £130 ($195) Double

The Westbury Hotel, Grafton Street, Dublin 2 (tel. 01-791122)

The Westbury, newest member of the Doyle Hotel Group, is tucked away just off Grafton Street right in the heart of the city center. Not only is it one of the most luxurious hotels in Ireland, it is without doubt one of the most beautiful. Its white marble entrance leads into a lower foyer carpeted in pale pink, and that same Navan/Youghal carpet leads up a sweeping staircase of cream marble and brass to the upper foyer, lobby, dining room, and other public spaces. Soft shades of peach, lots of marble, walnut panels, peach-silk wall coverings, oil paintings, valuable artifacts, wingback Chinese Chippendale chairs mixed companionably with modern furniture—all these are tastefully combined to create an atmosphere of spacious elegance. The upper foyer Terrace provides soft music throughout the evening and for afternoon tea; the Russell Room's peach-and-mint-green decor is the setting for fine dining; the Seafood Restaurant/Bar features shellfish from Dublin Bay; and the Polo Bar is hung wall to wall with hunting prints.

Guest rooms and suites all are furnished in mahogany and brass, have canopies over beds, marble bathrooms, built-in hair dryers and bathrobes for guests. They're also among the most spacious I've encountered in Ireland, and there are even some suites with Jacuzzis.

Rates are £75 ($112.50) single, £90 ($135) double, plus 15% service charge.

The Shelbourne Hotel, St. Stephen's Green (tel. 01-766471)

When Thackeray stayed at this hostelry back in 1843, he remarked that it was "magnificently conducted." Although the hotel has been extensively modernized since then, its reputation for service par excellence has remained unimpaired. With a wonderfully picturesque red-and-white façade overlooking St. Stephen's Green—and adorned with those iron, torch-holding maidens—(ask for one of the front rooms with a view of the park), the Shelbourne now blends a variety of styles and periods in its old and new portions. Both parts, of course, are in the deluxe bracket.

Some of the hotel's restaurants and bars are institutions in their own right. The Hunting Lodge restaurant is noted for its superb carving/buffet table with smoked fish and roast ribs of beef. In the elegant Shelbourne Restaurant the emphasis is on haute cuisine with an Irish flavor, and the Lord Mayor's Lounge is a favorite meeting place among Dubliners for afternoon tea. The Constitution Room, now a private meeting chamber, is so named because the Constitution of the Irish Free State was drafted there in 1922. The Horseshoe Bar is enthusiastically endorsed in Chapter V.

Of the 177 bedrooms (not counting the 8 private suites), all feature TV, radios, telephones, excellent bed lights, and private baths. The furnishings are delightfully varied, ranging from 19th-century period styles (with inlaid writing tables, gold-wreathed mirrors, and chandeliers) to pastel-hued, plush-carpeted modernity. The hotel also has a men's hairdresser and a smart little boutique on the premises. Rates range from £85 ($127.50) to £95 ($142.50) single, £100 ($150) to £130 ($195) double, with Irish breakfast priced at £8 ($12); add 15% service charge.

Jurys Hotel, Pembroke Road, Ballsbridge (tel. 01-605000)

If you're the kind of person who travels via Hiltons and Inter-

Continentals, this is the place for you. Because Jurys *is* the old InterContinental, abandoned by its American firm to an Irish one which has injected a far more Irish flavor.

Fittingly located close to the American Embassy, a short five-minute bus ride from the city center, the eight-story glass-and-cement hotel offers over 300 standardized rooms with shower-bath, direct-dial telephone (much sought after by businesspeople), color TV, and radio. Half are twins and half doubles, but the double rooms also include settees which can turn into single beds. Walls are soft pastels, carpeting to match; beds are amply sized, and two easy chairs flank a lamp. One of the Irish touches consists of framed Old Dublin prints, one to a room. The other is the lobby bar called The Dubliner, one of the handsomest hotel bars in the city.

In the 23-hour Coffee Dock Grill, you can purchase possibly the most decent hamburger in Dublin. The Embassy dining room provides international cuisine at lunch and dinner. A residents' lounge provides a friendly meeting place for after-hours drinking. A pavilion incorporates lounges, a sunken bar, indoor/outdoor pool, and a specialty fish restaurant, all under a 40-foot pyramidal glass roof. On the premises, too, are a newsstand/souvenir shop, a car-rental desk, airline desk, one-day laundry, beauty salon, and barbershop. The rather happily cornball Jurys Irish Cabaret is presented during summer in a vast ballroom hung with amazingly intricate brass cartwheel chandeliers. (See Chapter VII.) The 300-car carpark provides spaces for residents and visitors alike.

Prices range from £64 ($96) to £70 ($105) single, £72 ($108) to £78 ($117) double, plus 12½% service charge, with a one-third reduction for children under 12, free under 4. Take bus no. 5, 6, 7, or 8. Other Jurys hotels are located at Western Road in Cork and Ennis Road in Limerick.

Berkeley Court, Landsdowne Road, Ballsbridge (tel. 01-601711)

The Berkeley Court is one of Dublin's newest and most luxurious hotels. Set on four acres of landscaped grounds in the diplomatic embassy section of Dublin, the seven-story modern building has 200 bedrooms, all with private baths. Bedrooms tend to be a bit small, but are tastefully decorated with matching drapes and bedspreads, as well as attractive half-canopies over beds. TVs have remote controls so they may be operated from the bed, and telephones are all direct-dial. The huge lobby is adorned with marble pillars, plants, a fountain, wall hangings, and thick, bright Youghal carpeting. Comfortable, multicolored chairs and sofas are interspersed with antiques such as the lovely 18th-century Kingwood marquetry bombo commode. The bar and grill are all wood paneled, with etched glass and caned-back chairs, while the more formal dining room is in the Louis XIV style and features an international cuisine. You'll know you're in the lap of luxury from the moment you pull up to the Berkeley Court, for the elegant awning-covered car porch at its entrance can be closed off in bad weather. Rates are £75 ($112.50) for singles, £90 ($135) for doubles, with breakfast another £7 ($10.50).

Fitzpatrick's Castle Hotel, Killiney, County Dublin (tel. 01-851533)

One of Dublin's finest luxury hotels is actually about a 20-minute drive from the city on the outskirts of Killiney village. Set in nine acres of landscaped grounds, Fitzpatrick's was built in 1740, not as a fortification, but as the Manor House. It sits, however, on the site of a far more ancient building, for a huge stone fireplace unearthed in renovations (and now a prominent feature of the Dungeon Bar) proved to date from the 15th century. Its three turreted towers, white battlements, and hilltop location have, over the centuries, been the property of a British colonel, a captain, Lord Clonmel, the Chippendale family (of furniture-making fame), and the military (when it served as barracks from 1880 to 1950).

But it took Paddy Fitzpatrick to take what had become a veritable wreck and transform it into a charming luxurious establishment which manages to exude down-home friendliness in a baronial setting; even the suits of armor that greet you in the lobby seem endowed with a sort of aloof warmth. That special—and all-too-seldom found—graciousness no doubt stems from the fact that Paddy's lovely wife Eithne and their five grown children are all deeply involved in running the hotel, and their personal touches are felt by guests and staff alike. Testimony to the fact that I am not alone in this judgment are the large number of Dubliners who meet here for meals, the Irish from all sections of the country who make this their Dublin headquarters, and the locals from Killiney who crowd the popular bar in the evenings.

There are 86 bedrooms in the center building and its two flanking wings and seven luxury suites. Those facing the front boast little walk-on balconies set with a table and chairs for al fresco leisure, and those on the back are all fitted out with canopied beds. All have private baths with both tub and shower and all the facilities you expect in a luxury establishment. Both Jesters Restaurant (on the lower floor) and the beautiful lobby-floor Dining Room feature the freshest of local seafood, meats, and vegetables, and the Dungeon Bar has entertainment nightly. In addition to a popular nightclub, there's an indoor swimming pool, indoor squash courts, saunas, hairdressing salon, and a giftshop which stocks exceptional values in Irish tweeds, making this a complete resort hotel. For guests who want to dispense with Dublin driving, there are two courtesy runs to the city each day, and they'll also meet you at the airport, ferry, rail station, etc., if you make prior arrangements.

Adjoining the Castle, there's a block of modern time-sharing holiday homes (also in the luxury class) which may be rented by the week when owners are not in residence, providing self-catering facilities along with all the amenities of the hotel itself. (Contact the hotel for availability and rates.)

Rates range from £36 ($54) to £58 ($87) single, £49 ($73.50) to £82 ($123) double, plus a 12% service charge; suites go for more.

MODERATELY PRICED HOTELS
£34 ($51) to £60 ($90) Double

Buswell's Hotel, 25 Molesworth St., Dublin (tel. 01-764013)

A Dublin institution, Buswell's has hosted such Irish notables as Sir Roger Casement and Eamon de Valera over the years. Located just up from the Dail, it offers center-city convenience, superb accommodations at reasonable rates, and a dining room/pub-lunch/drinking clientele liberally sprinkled with politicians, leading Dublin businessmen, and colorful personalities. And small wonder, for since 1925 the hotel has been owned and operated by the Duff family with the sort of personal involvement which has led to possibly the lowest staff turnover in the city and an enviable guest list of "regulars" who return year after year. More and more conferences are being held here also, with the addition of several attractive meeting rooms.

Georgian elegance surrounds you in the lobby, the Leinster Room Restaurant, and the Georgian Bar, while the Tudor-style Molesworth Cellar Bar offers conviviality along with excellent lunch and evening snack selections. As for guest rooms, all 70 come equipped with private bath and shower, tea/coffee makers, hair dryers, direct-dial telephones, radios and color TV. Best of all, few are a "standard" size and shape, and each is individually decorated—there are quaint, old-fashioned rooms up under the eaves and others which are brightly modern. Rates run £40 ($60) single, £60 ($90) double, and £67 ($100.50) triple, with special winter weekend offers at considerable discounts.

P.V. Doyle Hotels (see addresses below)

P.V. Doyle was in the construction business when he became a hotelier in the mid-1960s, and his seven-hotel Dublin chain is a veritable paean to the utilitarian glories of cement and steel. At least three, however, fill a genuine gap in the Dublin hotel scene. All are within easy reach of the city center and provide modern, impersonal amenities at an exceptionally moderate price. In each of the following hotels, you will find: bright, spacious rooms with shower-baths; in-room TVs, radios, taped music, and telephones; central heating; a cocktail bar, grill room, and restaurant. The hotels differ only in size, shape, decor, and distance from the center. All charge a high-season rate of £30 ($45) single, £42 ($63) double, with a 25% reduction for children and a 15% addition for service. Full Irish breakfast is extra. Reservations for all Doyle hotels may be made through their Stateside office at 590 Fifth Ave., New York, NY 10036 (tel. 212/581-4486).

Tara Tower Hotel, Merrion Road (tel. 01-649666). Located ten minutes from the city center on the main road to Dun Laoghaire, this one has the nicest position, facing across the highway onto the Irish Sea. Ask for a front room with sea view, which will be done in brownish-yellow. The back rooms overlook only suburban homes and a distant golf course, and are decorated in blue. None is overdecorated; all have shag carpets and draped window walls. There are six floors, 83 rooms with bath, and parking for 80 cars in the lot out front. Oddly, the dining room does not face the sea but is sequestered with purple drapes at the murky rear of the lobby. Take bus no. 5, 6, 7, or 8.

Skylon Hotel, Upper Drumcondra Road (tel. 01-379121). The most central—only 1½ miles from O'Connell Bridge and ten minutes from the airport on the main Dublin–Belfast road—the Skylon has four straight-walled floors with 88 identically decorated rooms. All are twins or have one double and one single bed. TVs and radios are provided. Walls are white; rugs, bedcovers, and drapes are of striped orange. A hairdressing salon and giftshop are on the premises and a 250-car garage space is available at no extra charge. Manager Louis Langan promises good family rates and a high standard of 24-hour service. Take bus no. 3, 11, or 16.

Ariel House, 52 Lansdowne Rd., Ballsbridge, Dublin 4 (tel. 01-685512)

You can credit Michael O'Brien for the popularity Ariel House guesthouse enjoys with both Irish and foreign travelers. Michael (who spent several years in San Francisco working at some of America's finest hotels) has that unique ability to put himself in the traveler's shoes, see just what will make traveling easier, more comfortable and more fun, then proceed to furnish exactly that. He has complete sympathy for "the poor American who flies all night, then must get behind the wheel to drive on the wrong side of the road through a city as complicated as Dublin, just to find us in the first place." And he's waiting for each and every one with a warm and soothing welcome. When the time arrives to wend your way *back* through those complicated streets to the airport, he's been known more often than not to hop behind his own wheel to guide you to the point where you can't go wrong. In the interval between, he's a fount of information on Dublin sightseeing, entertainment, and dining out. Indeed, Michael's attitude towards his guests goes far beyond mere hospitality!

As for Ariel House itself, it couldn't be more conveniently located. Only five minutes from the city center, it is adjacent to Lansdowne Football Stadium, a major city bus route, and a rail stop for fast commuter service into town; a few minutes' walk from the American Embassy, Chester Beatty Library, the Royal Dublin Society, and both Jurys and Berkeley Court hotels.

More importantly, the century-old, red-brick main house and its modern garden extension out back combine the graciousness of a period parlor that transports you back to an earlier time with every modern convenience you could dream up in guestrooms. All have either twin beds or one double and one single bed, and two are large family rooms. Those in the main house are reached via a lovely old staircase, and have the high ceilings and tall windows of yesteryear plus the modern furnishings and private baths of today. In the extension looking out onto the garden, there's direct entrance from the back carpark (there's also off-the-street parking out front) to the ground-level rooms and a ramp for wheelchairs. All rooms have a built-in hair dryer, TV, telephone (soon to be direct-dial), and the best-designed clothes-and-luggage space I've seen anywhere.

Breakfast is served in a pleasant room (also accessible by wheelchair) on the ground floor overlooking the garden. In the evening, the dining room becomes a first-rate restaurant open to residents and non residents alike. Its pine ceiling, wooden tables accented by fresh flowers, red mats and soft candlelight make this the perfect setting for chef Marian Gary's gourmet cooking (see

Chapter IV). Pre-theater/cabaret dinners from 5 to 7 p.m., à la carte 5 to 9 p.m.

Rates (private bath and full Irish breakfast) range from £36.75 ($55.15) for singles to £42 ($63) for doubles. There's a 10% service charge.

The Clarence Hotel, Wellington Quay, Dublin 2 (tel. 01-776178)

The Clarence has been a Dublin landmark for years, a home-away-from-home for Irish businessmen and holidayers when they come to the city. Like its counterpart on the north bank (Wynn's, see below), it offers Grade A hotel facilities in a central-city location at prices designed to be as attractive as its facilities.

Centrally located on the south bank of the Liffey, it has a comfortable and homey atmosphere which has miraculously not been lost during recent extensive renovations. With a charming Regency decor throughout, its first-floor lounge is still a tranquil refuge from the city's hectic pace; a delightful Old World air still pervades its lounge bars; afternoon tea is still an event (often in the company of more Irish than tourists); its pretty restaurant—with tall windows adding an airy sense of light and space—still serves up what many call the finest steaks in Dublin; and its Grill Room still is a favorite with guests and city dwellers alike for inexpensive dining.

Rooms, while not elegant, are attractively decorated and comfortable. Those on the Liffey side offer fascinating views of river traffic, while others overlook city streets. Rates, among the most reasonable to be found for such quality and convenience, range from £24 ($36) to £28 ($42) for singles and £34 ($51) to £37 ($55.50) for doubles, plus a 15% service charge. Ask about weekend and winter specials.

Wynn's Hotel, 35/39 Lower Abbey St., Dublin 1 (tel. 01-745131)

Wynn's is a sister hotel to the Clarence (see above), and just as beloved to Irishmen around the country. Located on the northern bank of the Liffey, it, too, is just a short walk away from all center-city attractions. My first introduction to Wynn's came by way of afternoon tea in the lounge, which I shared with Dubliners seeking a respite from shopping, a smattering of priests and nuns relaxing from city streets, and Irish faces reflecting a distinct "country" glow. The few visitors from abroad were obviously as happy to be a part of this harmonious group as I.

Exploring further, I found the lounge bar to be every bit as convivial, with a teak and mahogany bar and a clientele of theatergoers, young couples and guests. The first-floor restaurant proved a happy solution of the where-to-eat question for any meal of the day, and the ultra-modern Grill Room offered eating at bargain prices. As for the staff, everyone I encountered made me feel, within minutes, as though I were a longtime and valued friend.

Like the Clarence, Wynn's rooms make no pretension to elegance. They do, however, exude a homey comfort seldom found in less-than-luxury hostelries. Furnishings and decor are attractive as well as comfortable, and both exceed reasonable expectations for the prices. Rates are £24 ($36) to £28 ($42) for singles; £34 ($51) to £37 ($55.50) double. As at the Clarence, ask about special rates for weekends and winter months.

Dalkey Island Hotel, Coliemor Harbour, Dalkey, County Dublin (tel. 01-850377)

If city-center lodgings leave you cold, if you want to enjoy coastal scenery and tranquility, yet be within easy reach of Dublin's attractions, then the Dalkey Island is just the place. Perched right at the water's edge, the hotel, only twenty minutes from the city center, looks out to Dalkey Island and Dublin Bay. Boats at the adjacent harbor are available to take you for an off-shore outing. Its Island Lounge features nightly entertainment during summer months, and the charming Sorrento Restaurant features fresh seafood on its limited, but very good, menu. Both have marvelous sea views and are popular gathering places for locals.

There are eight sea-front bedrooms, most with a terrace, and five with a glassed-in conservatory space for all-weather comfort. All guestrooms have private bath, telephone, color TV, and radio. Surprisingly low rates (including breakfast) range from £24 ($36) to £32 ($48) for singles, £42 ($63) to £47 ($70.50) for doubles, depending on the season. There's a 25% reduction for children and a 12½% service charge.

Good bus and rail transportation into Dublin.

Deer Park Hotel, Howth (tel. 01-322624)

Take the demesne of a working castle. Add a magnificent sea view, a 70-ton dolmen marking a neolithic tomb, an 18-hole golf course, 12-hole short course, 18-hole pitch-and-putt course, and a slope planted with 2,000 species of rhododendrons that H. G. Wells once described in bloom as "the finest view west of Naples." Now build a modern, chalet-style hotel, complete to bar and dining area, golf shop, and locker rooms. You've got luxurious amenities at top-grade prices, right? Wrong! Through some remarkable generosity of outlook, you have what is in our opinion certainly the most unusual economy hotel in the world!

Deer Park Hotel consists of a large A-line lounge-bar with deer heads mounted on the brick walls and windows framing the small island called Ireland's Eye, out on Dublin Bay. Extending back from this common room is a long corridor containing ten almost identical single rooms, each precisely eight feet by ten feet, with white walls and brown carpeting, all with pine-paneled ceiling, blue-striped spreads, and blue drapes. The closets are built in and the table doubles as a luggage rack. Single beds are extra long; double rooms have either one double bed or two single beds. An internal phone system connects you to the desk. All rooms have a private shower. This is the economy wing and prices (including plain breakfast) are: family room with three beds, £30 ($45); double, £26.50 ($39.75); single £17.50 ($26.25). For those wishing more luxurious accommodations, all with sea view, private bathroom, TV, and refrigerator, singles run £22.50 ($33.75), doubles £35.70 ($53.55). Add a 12½% service charge. A special here—on rentals of a full week, Deer Park gives you one free night.

Deer Park is best reached by car, as it is eight miles north of Dublin. The no. 31 Howth bus stops at the castle gates, but the hotel is half a mile within the grounds.

BUDGET ACCOMMODATIONS
Under £20 ($30) Double

YWCA Radcliff Hall, St. John's Road, Sandymount (tel. 01-694521)

The best low-budget place in town—almost phenomenal in its value—is the YWCA's Radcliff Hall, a thoroughly coed hostel geared to men, women, and/or children. Opened in 1968, Radcliff Hall is a renovated convent, including chapel, set in 2½ acres of lawns, apple trees, and flower gardens. In the main building, straight-walled and three stories high, there are 40 rooms, many of them singles, with built-in sinks and closets. This was the original habitation of the nuns and these rooms are high-ceilinged, very neat, and modestly proportioned. Across the lawn to the rear, 20 "chalets" have been constructed—all twins and all with private baths. These are similar to low-cost motel rooms, with paneled walls, narrow twin beds, two desks, and colorful curtains and bed throws. The decor is simple, an inspirational message adorns each wall, and the bathtubs are foreshortened "step" baths. But the block of chalets surrounds a beautifully kept rose garden that blooms gloriously in summer.

Meals are served in the main house in a modern white-and-coral dining room—in summer, on the picturesque patio just outside. Radcliff Hall takes guests throughout the year, and is also used as a conference center, but caters mainly to resident students during the school term. It is run precisely like a guesthouse in the summer—complete to the very helpful Mr. Chamney and Miss Brooks to see specifically to your tourist needs (sightseeing tips, tours, car rentals, etc.)—except for one minor item. While the staff serves the tables and keeps things clean and ship-shape, guests are required to make up their own beds. But this isn't much of a sacrifice when you consider the benefits: you have full use of a laundry room with iron, a recreation room with TV and table tennis, and a library. You are a 15- to 20-minute bus ride from O'Connell Street, but you are a two-block walk from the sea, and close to the RDS Show Grounds. And the prices are attractive—to say the least.

Bed-and-breakfast throughout the year is £12 ($18) per person in twin-bedded chalets with bath, £10 ($15) in single or double rooms without bath in the main house. Add 10% service charge to all rates. The half-board rate is £100 ($150) weekly, plus 10% service. Rooms are granted on a first-come, first-served basis—so write well in advance if you want one with bath, and a £10 ($15) deposit is required for every booking. Take bus no. 3 (which passes the door), 52, 6, 7A, 8, or 18.

Private Homes and Guesthouses

Unlike some countries, Ireland isn't all magnificent monuments, museum treasures, and natural glories—it's people. People make your Irish experience come alive, send you home hugging yourself to hold the warmth of it within you a little while. Collect Irish people in Ireland the way you would gemstones on a South Pacific beach. They are the true Irish treasure.

Meeting the Irish people is nowhere near as hard as meeting locals elsewhere. Many of them open their homes to guests, as much to put their natural talents for hospitality to work as to earn a few extra bob for the kids' school clothes. These homes are all inspected by the Irish Tourist Board for cleanliness and comfort, and town and country homes, as well as farmhouses, are listed in one accommodations booklet. Get this booklet from a Tourist Office and comb the possibilities. Amenities are noted. Some have only one or two rooms to let, while some have as many as 12; some come with hot and cold water in the rooms, some without. Many now offer private baths, but all have good bath facilities available (in some small homes you share the family bath). All are required to serve a full breakfast to guests and all include that in the very reasonable tariffs, which seldom top £11 ($16.50) per person in high season and can be as low as £7 ($10.50).

But the value lies not so much in what you pay as in what you get: a set of personal hosts who are almost always willing to talk about Irish life and politics (try and stop them!), and who will invite the good folk from America into their parlor for tea at night or to join with some friends who've dropped in for a bit of a sing-song. Being a paying guest in someone's home is a concept foreign to most American travelers, but one they cotton to very quickly once they give it a try. Don't be shy. Pick up the list. Ask a Tourist Office to find a room for you with someone nice, make a few phone calls yourself, or follow the lead of a friend. Just be warned that there is a hidden expense to the system: all those Christmas cards plus international postage you'll be sending back for years hence!

The following guesthouses and bed-and-breakfast homes are highly recommended and include locations outside the city center, but with good public transportation into the city.

Guesthouses: In the vicinity of the American Embassy, **Montrose House**, 16 Pembroke Park, Dublin 4 (tel. 01-684286), is just off Herbert Park. It's a two-story red-brick house fronted by a flower garden, furnished with antiques and lots of mahogany pieces, and presided over by Mrs. Catherine Ryan. The pretty, white-walled dining room looks out onto the garden through a bay window. All eight rooms are attractively done up and comfortable, and there's central heating. Depending on season, bed-and-breakfast rates are £15 ($22.50) to £20 ($30) per person. Take bus no. 10, 46A, or 64A to Herbert Park stop.

Just a ten-minute walk from St. Stephen's Green, **Kilronan House**, 70 Adelaide Rd., Dublin 2 (tel. 01-755266) is a four-story townhouse with 11 guestrooms. Mrs. Josephine Murray, its gracious owner/manager, has years of hotel experience, which are very evident in the smooth running of her attractive home. Tea and cookies are served each evening in the lounge, which has a TV and is a gathering point for guests, and breakfasts are highlighted by homemade brown bread and Mrs. Murray's homemade preserves. All guestrooms have telephones, and many have private baths with showers. Rates are £24 ($36) single, £36 ($54) double. There's a 25% reduction for children. A full Irish breakfast costs an additional £4.50. ($6.75). City buses no. 14, 15, 19, 20, and 46A are nearby.

Iona House, 5 Iona Park, Glasnevin, Dublin 9 (tel. 01-306855, 306217, and 306473), is in a charming Victorian section and is a lovely old red-brick house built around the turn of the century. Karen and Jack Shouldice provide such extras as perked coffee and American-style bacon (crisp, rather than thick, like the Irish bacon) to make visiting Yanks feel at home. There's a homey lounge and a private garden. Guestrooms (which tend to be on the small side due to the installation of private baths) are attractive and comfortable, with private shower, color TV, radio, and telephone. Central heating. Both German and French are spoken here. Seasonal rates range from £16 ($24) to £18 ($27) per person, with a 25% reduction for children.

Bed and Breakfast: Dolores and Tony Murphy are the delightful hosts at 14 Castle Park (off Guilford Park), Sandymount, Dublin 4 (tel. 01-698413). The modern, semi-detached house is brightly decorated and neat as a pin, and guests are welcome to sit in the sun in a small garden out back. There are three rooms with built-in wardrobes and sinks. You'll meet at least one or two of the Murphy offspring (two boys and two girls), who often help serve meals, and the entire family seems dedicated to making guests feel at home. Dolores will be glad to prepare the evening meal if you give her sufficient advance notice. Rates for bed-and-breakfast are £9.50 ($14.25).

Joe and Mary Mooney are hosts at **Aisling,** 20 St. Lawrence Rd., Clontarf, Dublin 3 (tel. 01-339097). Their graciousness is matched only by the beauty of their home, which is a period residence on a quiet street just off the Clontarf/Howth Road. Furnishings include antiques like the grandfather clock in the entrance hall and the lovely dining room is lit by a Waterford glass chandelier. Breakfast comes on beautiful china set on linen tablecloths, with Galway crystal stemware and sterling flatware. In short, the Mooneys and their two teenaged daughters have a very special home that they happily share with guests. The four bedrooms are spacious and attractively decorated; all have sinks, one comes with private bath, and there's a family room with shower. Central heating. Rates for bed-and-breakfast are £10.50 ($15.75), with £1 ($1.50) per person extra for private facilities and a 10% reduction for children.

Strand House, Seafront, Bray, County Wicklow (tel. 01-868920), is a two-story, neo-Georgian house which faces the sea from its own, set-back grounds (with convenient off-street parking). Mrs. Maeve O'Loughlin is the charming, helpful hostess and her home is nicely decorated throughout. She keeps tourist literature on hand for guests and is quite knowledgeable about local restaurants, as well as sightseeing highlights. Breakfast comes atop linen tablecloths, with a selection of dishes and perfect little butter curls, all of which probably reflects her long hotel experience. There are five bedrooms, all with sinks, one with private bath and one rather small, cozy room overlooking the sea. Bed-and-breakfast costs £9.50 ($14.25), with £1 ($1.50) more per person for the room with private bath.

DUBLIN: WHERE TO EAT

The Best Meals for the Money

THE HAPPIEST THING that has ever happened to Irish restaurants has happened in the past few years. You picked a good time to come and dine in Dublin.

The Irish never were great eaters. *Big* eaters, yes; gourmets, no. Potatoes and buttermilk were the great staples before the famine, and in current, more prosperous, times the Irish have prided themselves on being meat-and-potato people—"nothing fancy"—with a great taste for thick slabs of brown bread and apple tart.

But entry into Europe, via holiday tours and Common Market interchange, seems to be revising all that. The Irish are finally learning to *dine,* and having—possibly for the first time—the income to do so. Small, continental-style, chef-owned restaurants are springing up in the prosperous Dublin suburbs—and not only surviving but attracting throngs. All are charmingly appointed, all serve meals that could vie in excellence with any quality restaurant in San Francisco or New York. And all are, needless to say, recommended in the pages that follow.

Eating in Ireland can be a thing of joy—or sorrow. Irish ingredients can be gorgeous. Shellfish from Dublin and Galway Bays have spoiled travelers for life when it comes to eating seafood elsewhere. The oak-smoked salmon is glorious, washed down with dark stout. The lamb is sweet, the steak plump, the new potato in season a revelation. But the Irish can commit some dreadful sins against food. Meat tends to be overdone, vegetables boiled to destruction. Not so in the best restaurants, of course. But even here, it is important to *communicate*. If you like your steak rare, make it very plain that you actually enjoy seeing the blood ooze out on the plate. (Irish waiters have difficulty believing that.) When you ask for a side salad, specify how you want it made. Irish side salads tend to consist of two lettuce leaves, two slices of tomato, and one slice of hard-boiled egg—unadorned. Tell the waiter you would like a bowlful of greens with a vinaigrette dressing plus a pinch of garlic or whatever. The commotion in the back kitchen might be considerable, but every effort will be made to please.

While Ireland has no specific national cuisine, there are several outstanding items to scan menus for: fresh-baked brown or soda bread, fresh farm eggs, homemade orange marmalade and jam, Galway oysters, Dublin Bay prawns, fresh-caught salmon and trout. Irish tea, especially served with hot scones, can be nectar.

Dublin has eateries to fit all pocketbooks, dining hours, and tastes. Late-night dining is not common, but possible. Breakfast spots are practically unknown, as everybody breakfasts at his guesthouse or hotel. Choose from the following according to your location and in-pocket cash. Each one is excellent within its price category.

In Ireland, taxes are included in the meal price, but service charges are always extra.

Luxury Restaurants

In the following places, count on spending at least £25 ($37.50) per person for four courses, including wine and service charge. In each place, be sure also to reserve a table well ahead.

The King Sitric, East Pier, Howth Harbour (tel. 325235 or 326729)

One of Ireland's best seafood restaurants is atmospherically situated in the old harbormaster's house on the edge of Dublin Bay in Howth, nine miles northeast of O'Connell Bridge. Arrive early enough for a stroll around the fishing harbor and new yacht marina before dinner. It is the perfect place to dine elegantly before proceeding to the lively ballad sessions held nearby at the Abbey Tavern (see Chapter VII).

The restaurant is owned and operated by Aidan and Joan McManus. You'll meet Joan in the dining room overseeing a friendly and efficient staff. Aidan, who trained in London, Guernsey, and Switzerland, does the cooking with a delicate and imaginative touch which reflects a decidedly French influence. Aidan purchases the seafood fresh from the trawlers which pull into Howth's small fishing harbor. Depending on the season, you will find brill, turbot, salmon, bass, plaice, sole, scallops, squid, prawns, and lobster featured, with any variety of sauces, or simply grilled in butter. The important thing here is to consult the waiter on what the day's catch involved and how it is prepared. Order the specialty of the night and you'll never be disappointed.

The converted house is Georgian in decor. You have a predinner drink (wine license only) in the two-room lounge on the first floor, charmingly decked out in antique red-plush chairs and couches, and solid captain's chairs. The four-room dining area is beautifully decorated to bring out its Georgian features with antique prints and original local paintings hung about.

Main dinner courses range from £8.50 ($12.75) to £14 ($21), with higher prices for lobster and seasonal rarities. There's also a set dinner at £16.50 ($24.75). Open Monday through Friday for lunch, 12:30 to 2:30 p.m.; dinner Monday through Saturday from 6:30 to 11:30 p.m. Take bus no. 31 to Howth.

The Grey Door, 23 Upper Pembroke St. (tel. 762935 or 766890)

The former lounge of an elegant guesthouse has been transformed into an exquisite dining room that has Dubliners flocking in for gourmet dinners served with efficiency tempered with graciousness. The room is small—it will accommodate only 35 diners at a sitting—and beautifully furnished in the Georgian style. The fireplace blazes with a cherry glow on cool nights, and candles and fresh flowers adorn the tables. Soft shades of brown add to the feeling of coziness. The menu has decided Russian and Scandinavian accents, and the dining room is presided over by the two personable owners, Barry Wyse and P. J. Daly. Despite the elegance of its decor and expertise of the staff, however, the Grey Door is anything *but* stuffy. Instead, you have the feeling you've been asked to dine in a warm, friendly Dublin home. And when the food arrives, aah, well, it's so beautifully served and perfectly prepared that you *know* you're an honored guest!

There is a sensible table d'hôte menu for lunch priced at £10 ($15) exclusive of taxes, with an extensive à la carte each evening. Dinner without wine will run about £18 ($27) and you should book in advance at this popular place. Dishes such as blinis, borscht, pelmini, steak Rasputin, chicken Kiev, salmon Severnaya, and galupsti sound like the food James Bond might eat in *From Russia with Love* and of course you can eat this sort of food at the Grey Door, but for those who might find the idea of a different type of cooking slightly daunting be assured that once you have tasted the splendid dishes at this restaurant you will be back.

About a year ago "Blushes" wine bar was opened downstairs at the Grey Door, offering a more moderately priced lunch and dinner menu in more informal surroundings.

Service throughout is as elegant as the setting and often there is a guitarist on hand softly strumming his native folk music. All major credit cards are accepted. Hours are 12:30 to 2:15 p.m. for lunch (both restaurants) and 6 p.m. to midnight (Blushes), 7 to 11 p.m. (Grey Door). Closed Saturday lunch, Sunday, and bank holidays.

Le Coq Hardi, 35 Pembroke Rd., Ballsbridge (tel. 689070 or 684130)

Lovers of classic French cuisine will find it at its best in this charming ground-floor restaurant with its lovely basement cocktail bar and lounge. Owner-chef John Howard has created a warm, inviting atmosphere in which to present his award-winning dishes. The Georgian building features rosewood and brass interiors, inviting relaxation from the moment you enter the place, and one look at the menu tells you a culinary treat is in store.

The sophisticated menu features both classic and creative dishes with many seafood delicacies prepared with delicious sauces in innovative blends of herbs, cream, and wine as well as a marvelous selection of beef, veal, and chicken entrées. Outstanding, as you might expect, is the coq hardi—breast of chicken stuffed with mashed potato, mushrooms, and magic seasonings, wrapped in bacon, and baked and flamed with Irish whisky at your table. Mouthwatering! Even the humble French onion soup is done with special flair here, and vegetables are fresh and a delight.

Lunch is served from 12:30 to 3 p.m., dinner from 7 to 11 p.m., and reservations are essential. Also, don't show up in jeans—this is definitely a tie-and-jacket kind of place. The table d'hôte lunch is £14 ($21) and dinner prices average about £30 ($45) for four courses, plus a 12½% service charge. Expensive, but worth it.

Johnny's, 9 St. James Terrace, Malahide (tel. 450314)

The village of Malahide lies eight miles northeast of O'Connell Bridge. You drive through the village, turn left at the police station, and three doors down you'll find the basement restaurant named after Johnny Opperman. The place opened in late 1973 and immediately scored a phenomenal local success. Johnny is the owner-chef, his wife Eileen the hostess. Together they took an old Georgian terrace home and restored the original stone walls of the wonderful kitchen that is now the restaurant. You'll see the original hooks used for curing bacon and the superb granite fireplace that now blazes nightly, just as it used to.

The restaurant is divided into two rooms with stone alcoves and antique tables lit by candles in globes. Johnny trained in London and Switzerland and was chef at both the illustrious Shelbourne and Gresham hotels. He works in full view of the guests, who wander into his realm occasionally to inquire "What's cooking?" And he wanders out at intervals to inquire how they like it. They do! The food is continental—and great. The specialties are duckling prepared in many different ways and steak dishes in a variety of sauces. Eileen makes the finest wholemeal scones in Dublin. They come out of her oven every night at 7:30 sharp and go straight and hot to your table.

The menu is unique insofar as there is no service charge. The main courses range from £10.50 ($15.75) to £14 ($21) and the restaurant serves wines only, no spirits. Open five nights a week from 7:30 p.m. till 12:30 a.m. Closed Sunday and Monday. The no. 42 bus from Eden Quay stops at the door.

The Lord Edward, 23 Christchurch Place (tel. 752557)

This restaurant bears the name of Lord Edward Fitzgerald, who led the United Irishmen in the futile rising of 1798 and whose head ended stuck on a pike in Dublin Castle. He now lies buried in St. Werburgh's Church, some 30 yards away. Dublin Castle stands 300 yards away.

All of which amounts to a rather grim introduction to a charming seafood restaurant—in fact, possibly the best marine eatery in the city center. The ground floor of the premises is occupied by a pub. One flight up you come to a quite delightful bar. Stop there for one of the excellent martinis and admire the open fireplace with the blazing turf chunks, the beamed ceiling, white stucco walls, and stained-glass inserts above the bar. Over your drink you study the menu. Then proceed one floor up into the dining room, a softly lit chamber with gold-fringed shades, velvet-covered chairs, and bay windows. Enchanting—but small. It seats only 36 diners, so advance booking is essential. But how many restaurants purchase their fish twice daily in order to serve it fresh for lunch and dinner?

The meal is leisurely and relaxed, and the range wonderful: some 8 styles of prawn dishes, 15 brands of appetizers, and 8 varieties of sole. Not to mention the coffee, which ranges from Irish to Cossack (with vodka) and Calypso (Tía Maria). There is a set lunch at £13 ($19.50) and a dinner for £20 ($30) as well as an à la carte menu on which dinner will run about £30 ($45) for starter, main course, two vegetables, dessert, and coffee —but the lobster comes higher. Lunch is served Monday to Friday from 12:30 to 2:30 p.m.; dinner, Monday to Saturday from 6 to 10:45 p.m. Closed Sunday, bank holidays, and Good Friday.

Restaurant na Mara, Marine Road, Dun Laoghaire (tel. 806767)

For fresh seafood on the south side of the city—precisely seven miles south by the coastal road in the beach town of Dun Laoghaire—the Restaurant na Mara makes an attractive choice. Extremely popular locally, the restaurant's success story is indicative of changing Irish tastes in dining. Although the waters around Ireland have always brimmed with succulent shellfish and finny creatures just awaiting the butter and broiler, the Irish have tended to consider fish meals a Friday penance. Thus when Dun Laoghaire held a seafood festival several years back, and the Great Southern Hotel was asked to open a fish restaurant that week in the railway station buffet, the crowds that came were received with both joy and surprise. Feeling that they had been handed a charter, the Great Southern renovated the high-vaulted Victorian buffet room into a warmly candlelit restaurant with salmon-pink walls and carpets of turf brown to serve only fresh, seasonal fish dishes. Today, 90% of their trade consists of regulars.

Everything served comes from Irish waters, so it is best to ask for the catch of the day. The na Mara's lobster bisque is reputedly the finest in Dublin. The most popular main dish is the poached sole filets in white-wine sauce with prawns. Lobster is served four ways (or a fifth, by request, simply boiled with drawn butter). The flambé crêpes for two make an elegant ending.

Service is solicitous and the atmosphere friendly. Main courses at lunch and dinner range from £11 ($16.50) to £14 ($21), with lobster priced higher. Also at lunch a set four-course seafood meal is served, priced at £11.75 ($17.65) and up. Open 1 to 2:30 p.m. and 7 to 10:30 p.m. Closed Sunday, Monday, Christmas, and Easter.

Moderately Priced Restaurants

The following listing includes many dining places that qualify as "luxury" if you purchase à la carte, but slip into the moderate section by dint of providing set-price dinners also. In all but the few very casual eateries at the end, it's imperative to reserve.

Rajdoot Tandoori, 26/28 Clarendon St. (tel. 01-791122, ext. 132)

Entering this lovely Indian restaurant, you pass beneath a huge, glittering, 200-year-old crystal chandelier that once graced a Maharajah's palace in India. That's a fitting introduction to the elegance in decor and excellence in cuisine that have been the trademark of Mr. Sarda, the Rajdoot's owner, since he opened his first restaurant in Chelsea back in 1966. He went on to open others in England to wide acclaim, and now he's brought his Indian and Nepalese chefs to Ireland with a wide variety of North Indian cuisine.

In a setting of subdued lighting, soft sitar music, brass tables, statues, and Indian prints, you'll find such tandoori specialties as pigeon breast, lamb, and fish, as well as a good selection of curries and kebabs. Those delicious Indian breads—nan, roti/chapati, paratha, etc—are all available, too. There's a set lunch (three courses) for £7.50 ($11.25), and on Saturday a Shoppers' Lunch for £6.50 ($9.75). Main courses on the à la carte menu (the same at lunch and dinner) range from £6 ($9) to £10 ($15). The Rajdoot is just off Grafton Street in the Westbury Center, and hours are noon to 2:30 p.m. for lunch, 6:30 to 11:30 p.m. for dinner; closed Sunday and public holidays.

The Unicorn, 12 Merrion Court, off Merrion Row (tel. 688552)

This bright, pleasant restaurant was a Bord Failte award winner in 1981, and specializes in quick Italian dishes like lasagne, escalope alla peperonata, etc., averaging around £6 ($9) for lunch, £10 ($15) for dinner. Among the attractions here are the espresso and cappuccino coffee of outstanding quality, something not very easy to find in Dublin. Lovers of Italian cuisine will revel in the homemade pasta and perfect sauces.

The Unicorn is open from 10 a.m. to 10 p.m. daily (except Saturday, when it closes between 3:30 and 6 p.m.). Closed Sunday.

Ariel Restaurant, 52 Lansdowne Rd., Ballsbridge (tel. 685512)

This intimate, pretty restaurant is located on the ground floor of the guesthouse by the same name (see Chapter III). Overlooking a garden resplendent with roses and other flowering plants, its wooden tables are brightened by red mats and candles surrounded by flower arrangements. Chef Marian Gary specializes in such delicacies as chicken scaloppine with lemon, rack of lamb persillé, plaice in dill and cucumber, and Liffey salmon. Outstanding among the starters are mushroom beignets and chicken and walnut terrine. Starters are all under £3 ($4.50), and main courses (which come with vegetables) range from £7.50 ($11.25) to £10 ($15). Marian uses only the freshest of ingredients and everything is cooked to order. Delicious! To put the icing on the cake (if you'll pardon such a blatant pun), Marian and Ariel House owner Michael O'Brien are always on hand to see that service is especially friendly and personal. In short, this is one of the most pleasant, relaxing places to dine in Dublin, and after many meals there, I've never been disappointed. Open Tuesday to Saturday, with a pre-theater/cabaret dinner from 5 to 7 p.m. and à la carte service from 5 to 9 p.m. Best to book ahead.

Kilmartin's Wine Bar & Bistro, 19a Upper Baggot St. (tel. 686674)

This small, attractive restaurant is located in what used to be a bookmaker's shop, and its exposed-brick walls are adorned with mementos of its former occupant. As you might expect, its wine list is excellent, but the menu of lasagne, moussaka, fish, steak, veal, etc., comes in a close second. Service is both efficient and friendly, and prices of £7 ($10.50) to £9 ($13.50) make it very good value, indeed. Open Monday to Saturday from noon to midnight, Sunday from noon to 10 p.m.

Nieve's, 26 Castle St., Dalkey Village (tel. 856156)

This family-run restaurant is located about twenty minutes from Dublin's city center in the seaside village of Dalkey. It's an intimate, informal place with personal service and a resident pianist. Fare is mostly traditional Irish, with fresh, fresh seafood dishes high on the list. There's a good wine list, and dinner will run from £13 ($19.50) to £15 ($22.50) plus 12½% service charge. Major credit cards are accepted, and hours are 6:30 p.m. to midnight. Closed Christmas Day and Good Friday.

Budget Restaurants

Eating inexpensively and well in Dublin can be something of a feat. In all Europe, the Irish spend the highest percentage of their incomes on food. There is, however, one time-honored ploy for cutting your dining-out costs to a minimum. Traditionally, the Irish ate their main meal in the middle of the day, leaving the evening dining hour strictly to the Anglo-aristocrats or Behan's "Horse Protestants." With increasing sophistication, Dubliners have shifted toward taking their dinner at night, but those with working-class or rural backgrounds still favor the four-course lunch and the lighter "high tea" at night. Many Dublin restaurants cater to this preference by providing set dinners at lunchtime that can cost as little as £5 ($7.50) from soup through semolina, and an optional high-tea menu (a grill, lashings of bread, butter, and tea) at night costing little more. Adjust yourself to a top-heavy day, with huge breakfast, hefty lunch, and a comparatively light supper, and your food costs will be as low as Dublin allows. One custom is almost inviolable: the main meal is taken midday on Sunday, after church and before football. Several top restaurants close down Sunday night, after providing a reasonably priced special Sunday menu for lunch.

A welcome event on the Irish restaurant scene is the arrival of special tourist meals under the Food Fare program, which began in 1981. Some of the leading restaurants in the country now offer hot, three-course meals for £5 ($7.50) to £7.35 ($11). The free Bord Failte Food Fare booklet lists some 47 in Dublin alone, and it should be the budget traveler's constant companion.

Bewley's Café, 78/79 Grafton St. (tel. 776761)

Not so much a café as a Dublin institution, Bewley's makes and sells the most magnificent coffee in town and fills the street with the aroma of roasting beans. There are five branches, all of them delightfully atmospheric with gleaming dark-wood walls and long shelves packed with tins of tea and coffee. It's one of the great gossip-cup rendezvous, equally conducive to chitchat and quiet contemplation of aching sightseers' feet. The only niggling complaint one may have is that they keep such short hours.

Although mainly a cup-and-snack spot, Bewley's also serves moderately priced midday meals. You can assemble a tasty three-course lunch for no more than £3 ($4.50). This might include lentil soup, stuffed liver and bacon, and trifle to finish. Followed, of course, by a cup of that famous house brew. Coffee and full breakfasts are served at the Grafton Street and Westmoreland Street branches.

Hours are 8:15 a.m. to 6 p.m. Monday to Saturday. Closed on Sunday.

Casper & Giumbini's, Wicklow Street (tel. 775122)

Located in the old Wicklow Hotel premises just across from Switzer's side entrance, this attractive bar and restaurant is replete with hand-carved mahogany, Tiffany-style lamps and stained-glass windows, and gleaming brass, and is a favorite gathering place for Dublin's young executives (male and female). There's a pianist for lunch and on weekends. In the bar section, you can order homemade soup, a lovely smoked salmon platter (also chicken or tuna), or hot dishes such as homemade Scotch egg, ham, salad and French roll, cottage pie or London-style bangers-and-mash at prices of about £2 ($3). A special bar attraction is the selection of exotic cocktails and American canned beers (maybe the only place in Ireland they're available). For heartier fare, the restaurant section, on a different level, offers a full menu of veal, chicken, lamb, seafood, and steaks, along with lighter dishes of quiche, pizza, and omelets in a price range of £3.50 ($5.25) to £8 ($12) à la carte. Table d'hôte menu at £8 ($9.60). From noon to 2:30 p.m. on Saturday and Sunday there's an excellent brunch for £5 ($7.50) with a Bloody Mary. Open every day noon to midnight. Major credit cards honored.

Timmermans Wine Cellar, Powerscourt House (use the South William Street entrance after 6 p.m.)

Located in the original cellar of Powerscourt town house and furnished with hand-carved booths from an old chapel, Timmermans is at once cozy and lively. Crowds are heaviest at the lunch hour, but are increasing for the popular musical evenings, which offer jazz, ballads, and folk performers on different nights of the week. There's a selection of over 50 wines (French, German, Italian, Spanish, Greek, California), as well as sherries and port. The menu includes a marvelous pâté and brown bread for £2 ($3) and salad platters which range from £4 ($6) to £6 ($9). Hot dishes run from £4 ($6). Open every day except Sunday and holidays, from 10:30 a.m. to 11 p.m.

Regency Fare Restaurants

The Regency Fare Group operates some eight value-for-money restaurants, six in center-city Dublin, two in Dun Laoghaire Shopping Center. Their avowed aim is to "provide a service to the public in the form of a very high standard of food at reasonable cost with emphasis on freshness, variety and quality." Well, they're certainly on target, and you'll be hard pressed to find better budget eating anywhere in the area.

"Variety" covers everything from the upstairs **P.J.'s** with traditional Irish dishes to **Only Natural** with its take-away or eat-in salads, sandwiches, etc., made only from natural ingredients, to the deli underneath P.J.'s that specializes in quick foods and self-service. At this writing, locations and opening times are those shown below, but with this enterprising firm, you may well find others by the time you read this. Rest assured that wherever it appears, the Regency Fare name *means* dependability and budget prices.

Regency Fare, 28 South Anne St., 8:30 a.m. to 6 p.m.

Graham O'Sullivan, 52 Dawson St., 8:30 a.m. to 6 p.m. (5:30 p.m. on Saturday)

Graham O'Sullivan, 21 Marlborough St. (back of Clery's, off O'Connell Street), 8 a.m. to 6 p.m.

Graham O'Sullivan, 11 Duke St., 9 a.m. to 6 p.m. (5:30 p.m. Saturday)

Only Natural, 12 Duke St., 9 a.m. to 6 p.m.

P.J.'s, 12A Duke St., 10 a.m. to 7 p.m. (6 p.m. on Saturday)

Graham O'Sullivan, Marine Road, Dun Laoghaire Shopping Center, 9 a.m. to 6 p.m.

Graham's Restaurant, Georges Street, Dun Laoghaire Shopping Center, 9 a.m. to 6 p.m.

Pub Grub

Another time-tested way to eat well on a limited travel allowance is to haunt the food-serving pubs. Pub grub is a relatively new concept in Ireland, unlike the Commonwealth countries where "counter lunch and tea" are almost always served up with the brew. In most Irish pubs you can usually purchase thin sandwiches with slivers of ham or cheese between roll halves, but for something more substantial you have to know where to go. Most of those serving food are in the city center and cater to local office staff, from stock boy to secretary to in-conference executives. All offer at least one hot dish (such as curried chicken or sausage and cabbage) as well as sandwiches and salad plates. Prices are in the £3 ($4.50) to £5 ($7.50) range.

Opposite Christchurch in The Liberties, the **Lord Edward** (Christchurch Place) offers five menu choices daily, including one hot dish, such as curried chicken, and a well-priced smoked salmon salad. Soup, cheese, and coffee are available. The pub is large, carpeted, and comfortable. A personal favorite is **Searson's** on Baggot Street, where the smoked salmon is lovely and the brown bread fresh. Oysters are served in season; washed down with properly pulled Guinness, they are a memorable treat. **Neary's,** on Chatham Street (off Grafton), is more central and serves identical fare. The **Stag's Head** on Dame Court dishes up hot platters of bacon or beef with two vegetables and jacket potatoes in a setting that dates back to 1770, with ceiling-high mirrors, gleaming wood, and stained glass.

Chapter V

DUBLIN: WHERE TO DRINK

A Pub Crawl Through Dublin

BY RIGHTS THE PUBS of Dublin—nearly 1,000 of them—deserve a volume instead of a measly chapter. In this space it's quite impossible to do more than hint at the social nuances and finely shaded degrees of pleasure these institutions generate. So please keep in mind that the following is merely a whiff—a token sample—of the world that constitutes Dublin pub life.

Definitions, Rules, and Rituals

First, let's note some peculiarities quite alien to the American bar concept. These definitions are somewhat enigmatic, insofar as they don't exist legally but very much so in practice. Thus, many (not all) Irish pubs are divided into the actual pub (which is the bar), cubicle-like snugs, and a "lounge." By hallowed tradition, women don't drink in the bar portion, but are very welcome to do so in the snugs. The lounges cater to men, couples, *and* women. Pubs which are only pubs—minus any of the above appendages—were long considered male territory only, but this is changing annually. There's sometimes a slight difference between bar prices and lounge prices, but a marked difference in decor. The lounges are almost invariably the most comfortable part of each pub, and you may pay a few pennies extra for the pleasure of reclining in chairs.

In the sophisticated metropolitan hostelries these distinctions tend to blur. But in the workingmen's drinkeries they're pretty cast iron. What is ironclad everywhere is the round-buying principle, which resembles a religious ritual. It applies only to men, but it applies rigorously. Each member of a group, says the

"Commandment," buys a round of drinks *in turn*. He must *not* hog the bill, no matter how loaded he may be, lest he be suspected of playing the Rich-American-Treating-the-Natives.

The lone tourist may feel that this group ritual is irrelevant to him, but that would be a major mistake. In Irish pubs groups seem to procreate by a kind of amoeba process. With about three casual words on the stranger's part, he is instantly surrounded by stalwart friends who have known him all his life—at least the last ten minutes of it.

With female tourists the process may be even faster. But don't get the wrong idea here: apart from much poetic banter, Irish pub drinkers rarely make advances toward lady imbibers. What's more, as a foreigner her virtue is very nearly sacrosanct. She would have to work fairly hard before the great engulfing wave of brotherhood around her changed into something more personal. An invitation after closing is more likely to mean "come home and meet the wife and kids" than a tête-à-tête.

All the above, of course, are broad generalities. Dublin pubs fall into a fascinating array of categories and these again come in subdivisions, each with its own subtly different mode of behavior, ambience, and clientele. They range from chrome and leather cocktail joints to chintzy and stolid Victoriana; from artists', writers', and admen's hangouts to caps-on workingmen's boozers; from Bohemian rendezvous and showbiz gossip exchanges to the stodgiest suburban establishments, redolent with cold drafts and plastic petunias.

In all of them, however, a pint of Guinness costs from £1.25 ($1.88) to £1.50 ($2.25), a nip of whiskey about £1.20 ($1.80). In summer the pub hours run from 10:30 a.m. to 11:30 p.m., in winter to 11 p.m. In Dublin and Cork, pubs also shut from 2:30 to 3:30 p.m. on weekdays, the so-called Holy Hour. Sunday hours all year are from 12:30 to 2 p.m., then from 4 to 10 p.m.

But these hard and fast hours don't really convey the concept of pub time. Most Dublin pubs are late starters—meaning they don't get rolling until around 9 p.m., when the customers stroll in after work, tea, and a couple of hours in front of the "telly." On the other hand, conviviality, once sparked, may continue long after official closing time. This is accomplished by someone in a group waving an expansive arm and suggesting everyone go over to his place. And that includes *everyone* in the group or within earshot. So you purchase another couple of bottles in a brown paper bag and prolong festivities in private, one or two hours after the barman has sounded "time"!

Before commencing our pubbing (which all this preliminary

jabber is leading up to), let us reiterate that the establishments mentioned are merely flecks in the froth, drops in the bucket, minnows in the ocean, or whatever other term exists to express a minute sampling from a very large pie. The immense rest you can partially discover by doing your own exploring, O Lucky Tourist. What follows, though, will give you a good start. Quite a proportion of folks will probably get no farther. A few may not get past the first.

Dublin's Pubs

South of the Liffey, **Toner's** is located in Baggot Street opposite the Williams Supermarket. This is still the favored hangout of Dublin's artists, poets, students, and the inevitable would-bes. The place is almost 200 years old, has an exceptionally handsome mahogany bar, and rates as one of the best instant-contact drinkeries in the country.

Across the road on the way to St. Stephen's Green is **Doheny & Nesbitt's.** With two good snugs ideal for discussing private manners or holding hands, it caters chiefly to the professional crowd —lawyers, architects, medicos, and such.

Farther on toward St. Stephen's Green is **O'Donoghues,** 15 Merrion Row. One of the great ballad pubs in the land, it attracts a vast assortment of youngsters, many of them clutching their own guitars. O'Donoghues has been held responsible for launching the ballad renaissance in Ireland and is something of an international mecca for the youth hostel set (no sleeping bags allowed) as well as older devotees of Irish music. The entertainment here is spontaneous, not planned, but can be downright wonderful—or woeful, if your luck is out. The decor doesn't matter, because most of the time you can hardly see it through the mass of bodies.

If the body crunch gets too much for you at O'Donoghues, there's good traditional Irish music just across Merrion Row at **Foleys Lounge Bar.** It's not one of Dublin's old-time pubs, but seems well on its way to establishing a music tradition of its own. Traditional musicians hold forth every night and at Sunday lunch, then it's jazz every Sunday night.

On St. Stephen's Green itself stands the fashionable Shelbourne Hotel, which houses the **Horseshoe Bar.** Some reputable authorities have called this the best hotel bar in the world. Small and intimate, it is decorated with massive mirrors reflecting some of the best dressed—and earning—young women and men in these regions. For Americans it holds the special attraction of serving excellent cocktails. Friday is the big night here, when the place positively glitters with elegance and the parking spots outside abound with Jaguars, Rollses, Daimlers, and Mercedes.

Off the Green and down Grafton Street, you'll find Chatham Street on your left. At No. 1 is **Neary's,** whose back door faces the stage door of the Gaiety Theater. Consequently it's the watering hole of stage people and their admirers, plus the nonstarving artists, playwrights, students, and theatrical entrepreneurs. Semi-Edwardian in style, with a pink marble bar and wrought-iron arms holding the light globes above the doorway, Neary's is Peter O'Toole's drinking spot whenever he drops into Dublin.

McDaid's, in Harry Street, with its ornate façade, is easy enough to find (the street is one block long). This used to be *the* writers' pub in Dublin, and the place where Brendan Behan knocked back his pints. Although the Borstal Boy's glory is no more, the air inside is still heavy with literature, the patrons mainly university professors, students, poets, and word-spinners.

Over to **Davy Byrne's,** 21 Duke St. This is the curiously subtitled "moral pub," where Joyce's immortal Mr. Leopold Bloom stopped to partake of a glass of burgundy and a piece of gorgonzola on June 16, 1904. The place today is chiefly the haunt of high-powered young executives and attractive secretaries. The back room has been transformed into a chic cocktail lounge, and the atmosphere is perfumed, cosmopolitan, and the closest you'll find to "singles joint." Ideal for lone tourists of either sex.

Davy Byrne's gets decided competition from **The Bailey,** just across the street. The clientele here is about the same, with an added sprinkling of writers and journalists. The Bailey has an additional claim to fame in owning the front door of No. 7 Eccles Street, where Leopold and Molly Bloom lived in *Ulysses*.

For a complete contrast you might try **The Old Stand,** on the corner of Exchequer Street (turn left from Grafton into Wicklow Street). A fine old pub, it attracts droves of hard-drinking, back-slapping rugby types and other team-sport participants in an atmosphere of turbulent good fellowship.

Around the corner, in Dame Court, stands one of the handsomest public houses in town, crammed with exquisite fittings, graced with a wonderful bar, which could well serve as a national monument—a sample of drinking decor for future generations. The **Stag's Head** dates from 1770 (its last refurbishing was in 1894!) and its ceiling-high mirrors, stained-glass skylights, gleaming wood, and wrought-iron chandeliers share the limelight with mounted stag's heads which look down on contented regulars mixing happily with those visitors lucky enough to find it. Its pub lunch is one of the best in town, and midafternoon it is one of my personal favorites for resting the feet, sipping a pint, and joining Dubliners who obviously see it as a welcomed respite from center-city shopping or a proper setting for an impromptu break from the office. Many of those same faces show up for after-dark imbibing.

Go down Georges Street, right into Dame Street, into College Green and Westmoreland Street, turn right down Burgh Quay, then first right into Hawkins Street, and left into Poolbeg Street. The reward for all this walking is **Mulligans,** where—again according to our unimpeachable authorities—the best pint in Dublin is drawn. Mulligans opened its doors in 1782 and many of the original trappings have survived, including 19th-century gaslights. The patrons are a wonderful mixture: newspapermen from the *Irish Press* offices, television as well as rugby stars, students from Trinity College across the way, dock laborers, and taxi drivers—what the Irish call "a rich bag" (James Joyce was a patron).

But for real antiquity you have to go down to the Quays, walk the south bank of the Liffey as far as 20 Lower Bridge St., and behold **The Brazen Head.** Reputedly the oldest pub in Dublin, it received its liquor license in 1666, during the reign of not-so-good King Charles II, who fancied Restoration comedies and buxom orange-vending girls about equally. The inn lies off a stone-paved courtyard and consists of a low-ceilinged room, dimly lit by brass-banded lanterns. It is decidedly not a rowdy place, frequented largely by the calm and polite elderly gentlemen who live in the hotel upstairs. Hard to believe that a revolution was hatched here, but it was. Patriot leader Robert Emmet met here with Wolfe Tone to plan the ill-fated rising that ended with the former being taken out and hanged, drawn, and quartered in Thomas Street.

Cross the River Liffey and head for **Madigans** in North Earl Street, off the middle of O'Connell Street. Decked in beautiful woodwork and stained glass, and equipped with an impressive marble bar, Madigans appeals strongly to the sporting crowd and features two television sets on which the numerous punters can follow the races. And afterward console themselves at that marble bar.

You'd have to go quite a ways to equal this final pub listing, which is absolutely unique. **John Kavanagh's** lies on the far north side, at No. 1 Prospect Square, at what was once the front gate of Glasnevin Cemetery. (Glasnevin is the Arlington of Ireland and harbors some of the greatest Irish martyrs, poets, and statesmen.) The pub opened in 1833, one year after the cemetery, and is still in the hands of the Kavanaghs. Bare of superfluous ornamentation, it has a delightful atmosphere and was used as background in several movies, such as *Quackser Fortune Has a Cousin in the Bronx*.

The above catalog, as already indicated, is filled with sins of omission. To coin an Irishism, you'd need 100 pages to list the pubs that aren't there!

Chapter VI

DUBLIN SIGHTS

What to See By Day

DUBLIN IS A CITY TO STROLL ABOUT, because Dublin is, essentially, a subtle city. Unlike such capitals as Paris and Rome, Ireland's major city does not leap out at you with glories at each bend. Rather, it sinks slowly into your consciousness with certain smells, a snatch of sound; a most common sense is one of déjà vu, as if sometime a century back you had strolled these streets wearing other costumes and walking with other folk. The trot of a dray horse adds to the illusion (the traffic jams detract). The Dublin fighting for its share of the European Community is very much a 20th-century city. But there are pockets that have yet, thankfully, not received the news.

Old and new have merged in Dublin—not always successfully —so there is no way to specify where one starts and the other ends. Explore and expect surprises. Duck down stone-arched alleyways, through brick-paved lanes. The oldest part of Dublin, where medieval walls still stand, is called **The Liberties.** Just south of the Liffey Quays and west of O'Connell Bridge, it incorporates Dublin Castle, Christ Church Cathedral, rows of weary tenements, and some of the saltiest characters in town. Eighteenth-century Dublin, when the English were in full sway, is well represented by the elegant **Georgian squares**—notably Merrion and Fitzwilliam Squares—a mile farther south. Wherever you walk details delight. A silver streetlamp inset with ornately wrought shamrocks glows softly against the rainlit sky. A miniature white horse stands firm in the clear fanlight topping an unpretentious doorway; fluted Doric columns frame those with more airs. Cast- and wrought-iron foot-scrapers, lamp-holders, door-knockers, and railings are embellished with the most remarkable variety of imaginative craftsmanship—from seahorses to clenched fists. Fourteen stone River Gods glare down on the

Liffey from the magnificent façade of the Custom House, only one—the Liffey itself—a lady god (Anna Livia).

For company on your walk, let us suggest an old friend of ours, Gordon Clarke, who is no longer with us but who left a nice legacy in his small "Tourist Trail" booklet, available at either of the Dublin Tourism offices for less than £1 ($1.50). The book includes easy-to-follow maps of a Dublin walking tour, with accompanying text. Signposts along the route help you find your way.

Sightseeing Tours

Before starting your stroll, it is an excellent idea to get an overview. This can be best accomplished by either joining a coach tour of the city or hiring your own personal driver/guide.

CIE operates a first-class **City Sightseeing Tour,** complete with chatty and well-informed courier. It leaves from Busaras, the central bus station on Store Street, weekdays from April to November and on Monday, Wednesday, and Saturday other months, at 10 a.m., returning at 1 p.m., and at 2:45 p.m., returning at 6:30 p.m. The tour takes in the city highlights and will get you nicely oriented to the whats and wheres of Dublin. The fare is £7 ($10.50) for adults, half price for children under 15. Advance bookings should be made at 59 O'Connell St. (across from the Tourist Office). While there, pick up a **Day Tours** folder, which describes all the tours running out of Dublin—to Powerscourt, Glendalough, the Boyne Valley, and points north, south, and west.

Gray Line Dublin City Tours, Tourist Office, 14 O'Connell St. (tel. 786682 or 766887), will collect you at your hotel for a full or half-day tour of Dublin for a charge of £9.50 ($14.25) or £14.50 ($21.75) per person, four people sharing. A wide variety of tours around the Dublin area include Powerscourt, Glendalough, Avoca, the Boyne Valley, Malahide Castle, and helicopter and special-activity tours at varying prices. Nightlife tours also offer great value. Call for reservations, exact times, itineraries, etc. Be sure to specify if you wish to be picked up at your hotel.

For a fascinating trip back in time there is "A Guided Walk into Old Dublin." The two-hour tour begins at Christchurch Cathedral, then visits the old city walls and wood quay, the original Viking settlement, St. Audoen and St. Patrick Cathedrals, the Brazen Head (the oldest pub in Ireland), the Tailors Guild Hall, and Marsh's Library (the oldest library in Ireland). For schedules, price, and booking contact **Old Dublin City Tours** (tel. 756701, ext. 5230).

Churches and Cathedrals

Christ Church Cathedral (off Lord Edward Street) is an awesome edifice. Founded in 1038, it contains the tomb of Strongbow, first Norman conqueror of Ireland, and relics of several highly historic occasions. It was at Christ Church that Richard II received the homage of the kings of Ireland in 1394, that King James II attended Mass en route to the Battle of the Boyne, and that King Billy offered up thanks for winning said battle. There are many exquisite and ancient architectural details to inspect, both within the sanctuary and below in the vaulted crypts. Hours: 10 a.m. to 5 p.m. Monday through Saturday and tours after services on Sunday at 12:45 and 4:30 p.m. from May to August. From September to April closed Monday, open Tuesday to Friday 10 a.m. to 12:45 p.m. and 2:15 to 4:30 p.m., Saturday 10 a.m. to 12:45 p.m. Open for services only on Sunday. Take bus no. 21, 21A, 54, 54A, 78, 78A, or 78B.

St. Patrick's Cathedral (St. Patrick's Street), equally antiquated and awe-inspiring, dates back to 1190, and is on the site where St. Patrick baptized converts. It is best known for the fact that Jonathan Swift—author of such satirical masterpieces as *Gulliver's Travels* and other works of "furious indignation," to steal a phrase from his own epitaph—was dean of the cathedral from 1713 to 1745. His tomb is marked by a golden plaque in the floor of the south aisle, with his faithful Stella buried beside him. Hours: 9 a.m. to 6 p.m. on weekdays, to 4 p.m. on Saturday. Take bus no. 50, 50A, 50B, 54A, or 56. The choral services, held on weekdays at 9:45 a.m. and 5:45 p.m., on Sunday at 11:15 a.m. and 3:15 p.m., are especially inspiring in the surroundings. You are expected to leave a 60p (90¢) contribution. The Cathedral closes immediately after services on Sunday, and 12:30 to 1:30 p.m. November to February on weekdays.

St. Michan's Church (Church Street) is a 17th-century building but its tower, left over from a former Norse church on the site, is pegged at 12th century. It's the crypt that's so remarkable here: due to some strange atmospheric quirk, the bodies interred in it do not decompose. Two of the mummified bodies on view are those of the Sheare brothers, who were executed for doing their anarchistic best during the Rebellion of 1798. All very eerie and fascinating. Hours: 10 a.m. to 12:45 p.m. and 2 to 4:45 p.m. on weekdays, 10 a.m. to 12:45 p.m. on Saturday; the vaults are closed on Sunday. Take bus no. 34, 34A; admission to the vaults is 80p ($1.20) for adults, 40p (60¢) for children.

Museums and Art Galleries

Ireland's **National Museum** (entrance on Kildare Street) is well worth a visit for its excellent and illuminating collection of Irish antiquities, which occupies most of the ground floor. Look for the delicately crafted Tara Brooch and the heavy silver Ardagh Chalice, both from the eighth century and indicative of Irish art during the Golden Age. Also see the impressive 12th-century Cross of Cong. Along one wall, you will find relics of a much older Ireland—prehistoric graves transferred in their entirety to the museum and encased in glass. In one, you can see a crouched skeleton and food vessel that date back to 1800 B.C. Adjoining the main hall is a large room containing a comprehensive study of the Rising of 1916 and including some heart-gripping farewell letters from those condemned to death after the Rising. In the second-floor gallery are cases of Irish silver, coins, and crystal, and displays of early Limerick and Carrickmacross lace. The Music Room on the second floor features traditional instruments such as the Irish harp and the uilleann pipes. The museum has another building (entrance on Merrion Street) which houses natural history exhibits and will be of special interest to the youngsters. And on Merrion Row, the museum occupies a third building (entrance near the Shelbourne Hotel) where items illustrate the Viking era and the Middle Ages in Dublin. Hours are 10 a.m. to 5 p.m. daily, including bank holidays, and 2 to 5 p.m. on Sunday. Closed Monday. Take bus no. 7A, 8, 9, 10, 11, or 13.

The **National Gallery** (entrance on Merrion Square West), Ireland's major art gallery, is a handy block away from the Natural History Museum and around the corner from the National Museum, so you might do all your museum going in one energetic spurt. The gallery has a representative collection of old masters, including works by Titian, Rubens, Rembrandt, El Greco, and Goya, with later works by Monet, Sisley, Cézanne, and Degas. But what it's noted for is its major collection of Dutch painters. The gallery displays a complete collection of works by Irish painters of the 18th and 19th centuries. The portraits of eminent figures in Irish history and art from the 16th century to today are also shown and the gallery has sculptures, miniatures, watercolors, and drawings, more than 2,000 from all periods. Hours: 10 a.m. to 6 p.m. weekdays, to 9 p.m. on Thursday, 2 to 5 p.m. on Sunday. Free guided tours every half-hour on Sundays. There's a cafeteria and a very good bookshop.

Back to the theme of Irish antiquities: Make sure you drop by **Trinity College** (entrance on College Green) to see the renowned

Book of Kells. Stop first at the porter's office on the left of the arched entranceway to the campus and he will direct you to the Old Library. The *Book of Kells* is a copy of the four gospels handwritten in Latin by the monks in the early ninth century and found in the monastery at Kells. The detail is incredible, the designs sweeping. The book is now bound in four volumes. Two are displayed in glass cases and pages are turned daily to expose a new spread to view and to the light. Several other illuminated manuscripts are on display in the oaken-walled library, as is an ancient Irish harp reputed to have seen combat duty with the bold Brian Boru. There is a small admission charge to see the *Book of Kells.* Showing hours are 9:30 a.m. to 4:45 p.m. on weekdays, 9:30 a.m. to 12:45 p.m. on Saturday, closed Sunday and public holidays. All the cross-city buses pass Trinity. A stroll through the campus, surrounded by stately 18th-century buildings, makes a peaceful center-city interlude.

In one of the last poems written in his lifetime, W. B. Yeats issues this invitation to come to Dublin's Municipal Gallery of Modern Art (now renamed the **Hugh Lane Municipal Gallery of Modern Art),** Parnell Square (tel. 01-741903).

> *You that would judge me, do not judge alone*
> *This book of that, come to this hallowed place*
> *Where my friends' portraits hang and look thereon;*
> *Ireland's history in their lineaments trace;*
> *Think where man's glory most begins and ends,*
> *And say my glory was I had such friends.*

The portraits of the poet's friends—John Synge, Augusta Gregory, Roger Casement, Griffith O'Higgins, and Hazel Lavery—still form part of the Dublin Municipal Collection, which is actually one of Dublin's most handsome Georgian houses, Charlemont House. There is a fine collection of continental paintings bequeathed to the city of Dublin by Sir Hugh Lane in an unwitnessed will discovered after he went down with the *Lusitania* in 1915. The lack of witnesses has caused no end of controversy between London's National Gallery (which had the pictures) and Dublin's Municipal Gallery (which wanted them). A compromise has been worked out which provides that 31 pictures remain in Dublin, eight in London, for seven years; then they are exchanged for a further seven. The collection includes works by Rénoir, Degas, Manet, Monet, Corot, Daumier, Ingrès, and others. The gallery's permanent collection includes paintings of the modern continental schools and contemporary works by Irish artists. Hours: 9:30 a.m. to 6 p.m. Tuesday through Saturday, from 11 a.m. to 5 p.m. on Sunday. There's a very good restaurant open during gallery hours. Take bus no. 11, 12, 13, 16, 16A, 22, or 22A.

Right across from the gallery is the **Garden of Remembrance,** which was opened in 1966 to commemorate all who gave their lives in 1916. It makes a pleasant place to rest museum-weary feet.

Impressive Buildings

Dublin Castle (Cork Hill, just off Lord Edward Street) was founded by the Normans in the 13th century and provided a seat of government for the British while they were in Ireland. There are only two towers and part of a curtain wall left from the original structure, but there is still much of interest to see within the castle yards. The state apartments which housed the British viceroys have recently been restored to their pre-Treaty opulence and are open to the public Monday to Friday from 10 a.m. to 12:15 p.m. and 2 to 5 p.m., on Saturday, Sunday, and bank holidays from 2 to 5 p.m.; there is a small admission charge. In the upper castle yard are the Genealogical Office and the Heraldic Museum, where you can obtain information on your Irish ancestry. In the lower castle yard stand the Record Tower, with walls 16 feet thick, and the small and lovely Church of the Most Holy Trinity, formerly the Chapel Royal. Among the many carved heads on the chapel walls are all the kings and queens of England—with Brian Boru and St. Patrick lending a little perspective. Also within the castle walls is the headquarters of the Gardai (police). Outside the main gate, where the heads of rebellious Irish kings were spiked in years gone by, stands a memorial to the men who fought and were killed attacking Dublin Castle during Easter Week, 1916. The castle yards are open from 8 a.m. to 6:30 p.m. Monday to Friday, and open to visitors daily; Mass is held in the church on weekdays at 8:45 a.m. and on Sunday at 10 a.m. Take bus no. 21, 21A, 50, 50A, 50B, 54, 54A, or 56.

There are two buildings set on the Liffey quays that will linger in your Dublin memories for a time—especially if you see them late at night, lit up and sparkling across the leaden water to fuse gloriously with your postpub haze. Closest to the bay is the **Custom House** (Custom House Quay), the domed and columned building that is considered Dublin's finest public edifice. It was designed by James Gandon, finished in 1791, and completely gutted by fire during the Troubles in 1921. The interior has been carefully restored. Farther up the river is the **Four Courts** (Inns Quay), also designed by Gandon and begun in 1785. It, too, was almost completely destroyed by fire in 1922, with a fantastic loss of records, was restored, and now houses the Irish Law Courts.

Across from Trinity College on College Green is the **Bank of Ireland,** housed in the distinctive building that was Ireland's House of Parliament before the Act of Union. The major distinction is that, while the architecture of the building is of the Ionic order, the columns are Corinthian—it was Gandon's attempt to harmonize this building with those of the college across the green. The original House of Lords is still intact, preserved as it was before 1800 and containing fine tapestries of the Battle of the Boyne and the Siege of Derry. You can view the House during banking hours by asking any uniformed attendant on duty to guide you.

The present meeting place of Ireland's Parliament (*Dail Eireann)* is **Leinster House** in Kildare Street, which you may visit only when the House is not in session, from 10 a.m. to 12:30 p.m., and from 2 to 4:30 p.m., Monday through Friday. Take bus no. 7A, 8, 9, 10, 11, or 13; it's in the same block as the National Museum and Gallery.

Then there's the **General Post Office** in the center of O'Connell Street. Originally built in 1818, it served as headquarters for the rebel forces during the 1916 Rising. It was from between the pillars of this portico that Padraic Pearse proclaimed the Irish Republic to the people of Ireland. During that week, the building was almost completely destroyed by heavy fire from a British gunboat stationed nearby on the Liffey and afterward had to be completely rebuilt. In the central hall, there is a statue of the dying Cuchulain—Ireland's most valiant warrior of ancient myth, who held off hordes of armed men single-handedly by tying his wounded body to an upright stake and fighting till he died. The statue commemorates all those who gave their lives within this building in 1916. Take any cross-city bus.

The Parks and Zoo

One of the loveliest places in the city center for a pause between museums or stores—or to have a sandwich in the sun on a summer day and throw the crusts to the ever-eager swans—is **St. Stephen's Green** at the top of Grafton Street. One of the oldest open squares in Europe (it dates from 1690), it has formal flower beds, an artificial lake with waterfall and arched stone bridge, trees, and statues. The gates are open from 8 a.m. weekdays, 10 a.m. on Sunday, to dark. Take bus no. 10, 11, 13, 14, 14A, 15, 15A, 15B, or 20.

Farther out, but even lovelier, are the **Botanic Gardens** in Glasnevin. These occupy what was once the demesne of the Thomas Tickell family (he was secretary to the lord lieutenant of Ireland). Sheridan, Jonathan Swift, and Charles Stewart Parnell are among the men who have strolled through these gardens, and Parnell and O'Connell are among those buried at the cemetery nearby. James Joyce often visited the gardens and some references to its more exotic plants appear in his works. Tickell's house is presently the home of the director of the gardens. There are 50 acres of varied plants and trees, a rose garden, lily pond, mill race, and extensive ranges of greenhouses. The gardens are open in summer from 9 a.m. to 6 p.m. on weekdays, from 11 a.m. to 6 p.m. on Sunday; in winter, from 11 a.m. to 4:30 p.m. Take bus no. 13, 19, 34, or 34A.

Phoenix Park is Dublin's back garden—a great expanse of green, almost 2,000 acres in size. Within the park—which, we would agree with Dubliners, is one of the most beautiful in Europe—are the elegant residences of the American Embassy, the Papal Nunciature, and the president of Ireland. By day, the park is frequented by walkers and birdwatchers, polo players, equestrians, Gaelic footballers, and small boys who wear drooping knee pants and carry formidable hurleys. By night, its pastures are grazed by herds of cattle and its groves are roamed by deer. On Saturday afternoons, the park brims with Irish sportsmen in pursuit of weekend exercise and lovely, green-eyed girls in pursuit of the Irish sportsmen.

At the northern end of the park is the **Phoenix Park Racecourse,** an equally excellent place to meet the sportsmen and their coterie. At the southern end, near the Parkgate Street entrance, are the idyllically peaceful **People's Flower Gardens.** Between the two lie the **Zoological Gardens,** one of the oldest and certainly most charming zoos in Europe. It won distinction as early as 1857 for breeding the first lion cubs in captivity and has since bred over 700 lion cubs as well as the first Himalayan bears in Europe. All manner of wildlife is represented, and the moated enclosures and two natural lakes are attractively landscaped. In one corner, there's a small **Children's Zoo,** where your youngsters can play with tame billy goats and make a wish while seated upon the Wishing Seat. The glass-enclosed **Treetops** fast-food restaurant provides high-quality fast food at inexpensive prices, and the **Pride of Lions' Coffee Shop** and the **Lakeside Ice Cream Parlour** have outdoor umbrella-table service. Adults pay £2.50 ($3.75) admission to the zoo, children from 3 to 14 give £1.20 ($1.80), and children under 3 are admitted free. During the summer months hours are 9:30 a.m. to 6 p.m. on weekdays, from 11 a.m. on Sunday. In winter, the zoo closes at sunset. Take bus no. 10, 14, 14A, 25, or 26.

The Guinness Brewery

Dublin's Guinness Brewery is the largest of its kind in Europe. It occupies 60 acres on the south side of the Liffey in the western part of the city, employs about 2800 people, produces 3½ million glasses of good dark stout per day, and exports more beer than any brewery in the world!

It was also one of the most enthusiastically visited breweries ever open to tourists—or should we say pilgrims?—Because of an extensive modernization and reconstruction program, there are no tours of the plant at present, but you are cordially invited to call by the Guinness Hop Store (it's clearly signposted and just around the corner from the Brewery front gate), where you'll be warmly welcomed from Monday to Friday between 10 a.m. and 3 p.m., except on bank holidays. The historic four-story building—which, as its name suggests, was once used to store the hops used in brewing Guinness—has been carefully refurbished and restored, and you'll see a film about the brewing process, sample a glass or two of the dark stuff in a traditional-style bar, and browse through the Brewery Museum (which includes interesting sections on coopering and transport.

If this is your first taste of the "wine of Ireland" and you don't react with immediate enthusiasm to the first glass, may we suggest you simply push on to the second. Stout can be an acquired taste—one very enjoyably acquired.

Take bus no. 21 from College Green or no. 78 from Fleet Street to Visitors' Centre in Crane Street beside the brewery.

Kilmainham Jail Historical Museum

If you have a free Sunday afternoon in Dublin, there's something we think you may want to do. Go out to Kilmainham and take the guided tour through the jail. It's no longer used as a jail; it was abandoned in 1924, after expelling its last prisoner, the late president of Ireland, Eamon de Valera. But in 1960, a group of volunteers began restoring the dilapidated fortress to the general condition it was in in May 1916, when 14 men calmly entered the stone-breakers' yard to give their lives in "excess of love" for Ireland. There, as the shots resounded in the courtyard and the bodies crumpled against the wall, a passion quivered through Ireland that solidified in one final and desperate determination to be free. There that brilliant moment of transcendence occurred that was chronicled by the poet Yeats:

> *MacDonagh and MacBride*
> *And Connolly and Pearse*
> *Now and in time to be,*
> *Wherever green is worn,*
> *Are changed, changed utterly:*
> *A terrible beauty is born.*

Kilmainham was operated as a jail in 1787 and received its first political prisoners in 1796—and what prisoners it housed since that day! After the Rebellion of 1798, the jail was packed; the brothers Sheares, whose bodies lie in the crypt at St. Michan's, were taken from Kilmainham to be executed. Robert Emmet—the patriot who cried from the dock, after sentence of death had been pronounced, "When my country takes her place among the nations of the earth, then, and not till then, let my epitaph be written!"—spent the night before his execution at Kilmainham. His faithful friend and assistant in the cause of freedom, the 21-year-old Anne Devlin, was kept at Kilmainham in a below-ground-level cell for four years and was so mistreated that she emerged white-haired and as withered as an old woman, but still faithful. The Rising of 1848 and the Fenian Rising of 1867 restocked the cells. Charles Stewart Parnell operated the boycott tactics of the Land League from Kilmainham. In 1883, 26 of the Invincibles took up residence at the jail; five were hanged and are buried there. But it was after the Easter Week Rising of 1916 that the cells were filled to overflowing with the men and the women who had been involved in the brave attempt. Ninety-seven of these (de Valera among them) were court-martialed and sentenced to death under British law; 14, including all who had signed the Proclamation, were executed; the sentences of the rest were commuted to life. As political power shifted in the ensuing years, these prisoners were pardoned. But in 1921, de Valera opposed the Treaty and was back in Kilmainham along with many of his associates, to be freed again when the jail was closed in 1924.

The tour is conducted by a member of the volunteer restoration committee who will show you into the induction room of the jail, the room where Parnell was imprisoned for seven months, the corridors and cells in which the rebels of 1798 and 1916 were lodged, the stone-breakers' yard where the tricolor of Ireland flies proudly over a memorial to the men who earned it that night, the restored chapel where Joseph Mary Plunkett married Grace Gifford hours before his 1916 execution, and, finally, into the Main Compound, where an excellent museum of the fight for liberty has been established. Not that Kilmainham can be considered just another museum: to the Irish it is more than that—it is a shrine, their Eternal Flame. To Irish people all over the world— Kilmainham is hallowed ground.

The jail is open on Sunday afternoons from 3 to 5 p.m., but tours for visiting groups may be arranged for weekdays by reservation (phone 01-755990). Admission is 40p (60¢) for adults, 20p (30¢) for children. Take bus no. 21, 78, 78A, 78B, or 79.

Irish Sports

There's a legend that at some point during World War II, Adolf Hitler thought of invading Ireland. He sent two secret agents into the country, but changed his mind when they returned with their report. "The Irish," they announced, "spend Sunday afternoons murdering each other for the fun of it. We'd better invade some other country."

What the agents would have watched was an amiable bout of the sport known as **Gaelic football**—and a much gentler version than they would have seen had they come spying in 1884, when the Irish form of football got its first uniform set of rules.

Gaelic football today is by far the most popular field sport in all of the 32 counties. At the All-Ireland finals at Dublin's Croke Park, crowds of up to 90,000 fervent fans pack the stands, rocking the sky with yells of "Galway Forever," "Up Cork," or "Come on the Kingdom," depending on who's battling whom. Entire towns in the provinces lie half-deserted because everybody who can has gone to the Big Smoke to watch the finals. You won't find any lukewarm neutrals on the subject. Everybody seems to have his or her team—and all are ready to lay down their lives for it.

Gaelic football will be quite familiar to visitors from a score of other countries that play similar games. But that's more than can be said about Ireland's second great sporting passion—**hurling.** This is a unique national game and takes a bit of studying. It's played with camans or hurleys—hip-high sticks with a spoon-like tip—and a small leather ball that travels so fast that you frequently can't see it fly.

Both the football and the hurling finals are played, year after year, at Croke Park. It's as eternal as the rhythm of the seasons. The first Sunday in September is hurling, the last is football. But whichever game you catch, you'll see a patch of the finest grass carpet ever grown on a sports ground and watch Irishmen—and women—at their most enthusiastic. Not to mention the precision marching of the Artane Boys' Band, who spell out the initial letters of the teams on the green field with their bodies.

Spectators at the **racecourses** may be a little more sedate, but their fervor runs at least as high. The Irish seem to drink a love of horseflesh with their mothers' milk, and few other countries can offer an equal variety and quality of racing events.

The Big Four among the Turf Classics (of a total 180 meetings each year) are the **Leopardstown Steeplechase** in February, the **Irish Grand National** at Fairyhouse on Easter Monday, the **Punchestown Steeplechases** at the end of April, and the **Galway Races** on the last two days in July.

Within the Dublin area, **Phoenix Park** and **Baldoyle** provide a magnificent background for horse events. Listening to a Dublin bookie chaffing with the losers and encouraging the winners is something of an educational experience—providing you can follow his lingo.

Special Events

If you happen into Dublin during the first week of May or August, don't happen out again till you've made at least one stop at the Royal Dublin Society's showgrounds in Ballsbridge (take bus no. 5, 6, 7A, or 8 from O'Connell Street). The occasion in May is the society's annual **Spring Show,** which is billed as "the shop window of Irish Agriculture and Industry." What it really is is a monster-size, national country fair with all manner of prize-winning stock on display, lots of exciting horse-jumping competitions during the days, and much mingling of Irish and cross-Channel farm folk done up in their Sunday best and come into Dublin for the fortune and fun. A whole lot of that fun, by the way, is going on back in the center-city pubs.

In August, the occasion is far more sophisticated and rates as Ireland's top social and sporting event of the year: the **Dublin Horse Show.** The Horse Show is a colorful event, attracting up to 150,000 international horse-lovers annually. During the day, there are continual jumping events—recognized as among the finest in the world. Auction sales are conducted in the Sales Ring, and Irish traditional music can be heard on the band lawn. The Army Bands give daily concerts. A gorgeous display of flowers is presented by the Royal Horticultural Society. There's an Irish arts-and-crafts exhibit, where you are sure to find a bargain or two. On Friday, international teams compete for the Bank of Ireland Nation's Cup and the Aga Khan Trophy, and on Saturday the International Grand Prix of Ireland is held, one of the richest in the world. For information on tickets and applications for seat reservations (by no means necessary), write the Ticket Office, Royal Dublin Society, P.O. Box 121, Ballsbridge, Dublin 4 (tel. 680645).

The **Dublin Theatre Festival** takes place during the last week of September and the first week of October and is a unique theatrical celebration that incorporates all of Dublin's theaters and spreads onto the streets and university campuses and community halls, in a series of first nights which offer innovative Irish drama and major overseas theater and dance companies. Great Irish playwrights such as Behan, Leonard, Friel, and Murphy have been represented, and the Festival has been the originator of classics like *Da, Philadelphia, Here I Come!, The Importance of Being Oscar, Translations,* and *The Morning After Optimism,* which have gone on to grace the stages of the world.

The Festival specializes in presenting new Irish work and the central weekend of the Festival offers visitors to Dublin the opportunity to see nine new Irish plays over a period of three days. Other highlights are international theater and dance of the highest standard from places such as Sweden, South Africa, the United States, Britain, France, Germany, and many others representing all types of theater from comedy, classics, experimental theater, mime, and musicals. A Festival Club, where the theatergoers mingle with actors, directors, and international press, as well as workshops, exhibitions, and an international theater conference, all make this a very special celebration. For details during your visit, contact Dublin Theatre Festival, 47 Nassau St., Dublin 2, and it is a good idea to contact them well in advance.

For specific dates of the above events, check the Tourist Board's **Calendar of Events.** If you plan to be in Dublin during Horse Show Week, be sure to make hotel reservations well in advance and check the prices before committing yourself. Accommodations during that week can be filled right up to the least impressive rafters. And even the noblest hostelries tend to raise their prices.

In Search of Literary Greats

Ireland's greatest gift to the rest of the world may well be its writers, whose keen, sharp-witted, and uniquely phrased insights into the foibles of those who walk this earth are timeless and universal. From this sparsely populated little island have sprung an enormous proportion of civilization's greatest wordsmiths, and of them, a good many were born, lived, or died in Dublin. While some of the landmarks they left behind have disappeared and others have changed since they figured in their lives, the following will surely bring you closer to those whose legacy of such a wealth of words has prodded the minds and hearts of the rest of us.

The house at 7 Hoey's Court where **Jonathan Swift** was born is now gone, but it stood very near St. Patrick's Cathedral, where he was its most famous Dean, serving 32 years, and where he was laid to rest. Listen for his footsteps, too, at Trinity College, where he was a student. Poet **Thomas Moore** also studied at Trinity, and you'll find his birthplace at 12 Aungier St. Both **George Bernard Shaw** and **Oscar Wilde** began their tumultuous lives in Dublin in the year 1854, Wilde at 21 Westland Row and Shaw at 33 Synge St. **W. B. Yeats's** birthplace was 5 Sandymount Ave., and 42 Fitzwilliam Square was his residence from 1928 to 1932.

James Joyce was born in Rathgar at 41 Brighton Square West, and from his self-imposed exile mapped the face of his native city in unremitting detail. The martello tower he occupied with Oliver St. John Gogarty in 1904 is now a Joyce museum (see Section 3 of this chapter), and his devoted followers can trace the Dublin meanderings of his Leopold Bloom as unerringly as if Joyce had written a guidebook rather than his masterpiece *Ulysses*. This is such an intriguing pasttime for visitors that the Tourist Board has prepared a "Ulysses Map of Dublin" of the book's 18 episodes, which is yours for a small charge.

Brendan Behan captured the heart and soul of modern Dublin in words that his countrymen sometimes agonized over but never denied. He was born in Dublin in 1921 and remained its irreverent, wayward son until the early end of his life in 1964, when the President of Ireland led a huge crowd to Glasnevin Cemetery for the interment. His spirit no doubt still roams the city streets, reveling in the things that have changed and those that have remained the same.

While not a literary landmark, the Moore Street market was well known to Behan and no doubt to many another Dublin writer. It's just behind the G.P.O., and to go along Henry Street, then turn into the lively commerce of Moore Street is to walk into a never-changing bit of the kaleidoscope of color that characterizes this city and kept its writers busy. From 10 a.m. to 5 p.m. on weekdays, fishmongers and greengrocers and vendors of a dozen other wares gather to haggle, gossip, and contemplate the vagaries of Dublin life. Not a literary landmark, but surely a haunt of those with a literary bent!

Chapter VII

DUBLIN AFTER DARK

Ballads, Theater, and Cabaret

DUBLIN DOESN'T OVERWHELM its visitors with nightlife. But what it does offer can often be memorable. Theater and song in Dublin, whether formally on stage or in the costumed guise of a Georgian banquet, is Ireland entertaining at its best.

Pub life is more than active (see Chapter VI), and beyond that Dubliners enjoy a constant round of parties at home—any home: their own, that of a neighbor, or the evening's new pub acquaintance. The answer to the visitor in search of the true after-dark scene is to make contact with a Dubliner, establish a willingness to meet others, and let the gregarious Irish take it from there. Ten times out of ten they do.

But if you prefer a more proper introduction to an Irish home, take advantage of the following program:

Meet the Irish Program

This is a scheme aimed at giving visitors an opportunity to mingle with the locals. Not just any locals, but folks with similar business or professional backgrounds and/or similar interests and hobbies. You get a form from the Publicity Department of the Irish Tourist Board in Dublin and fill in a few details like your age group, profession, means of transport, and personal interests. They handle the rest and—as visitors report—handle it very nicely. But please note that this program isn't suitable for tourists in a hurry. It's hard to arrange social contacts when you only have, say, one particular night in Dublin to spare for socializing. These forms should be filled in at least three or four weeks before you leave home to allow enough time for a reply to be received. The program operates from April to September only; write the Irish Tourist Board, Baggot Street Bridge, Dublin 2.

Irish Theater

For Americans, one of the major surprises the Irish Republic springs is the sheer quantity of live theater. What's more, Irish theater, when good, is superlative. Which is not really astonishing in a nation of natural extroverts and instinctive self-dramatizers.

Yet the Irish stage owes its world fame to a relatively recent development. The national repertory company, created in 1898 through the genius and dedication of W. B. Yeats and his associates, tapped the immense reserve of original native talent against bitter opposition from the conservative classicists. It was via this company that audiences first met playwrights like J. M. Synge and Sean O'Casey. Their vehicle was the now hallowed **Abbey Theatre,** which propelled performers like Sara Allgood, Barry Fitzgerald, Siobhan McKenna, and Cyril Cusack to glory.

The old Abbey opened in 1904 and burned down in 1951. The New Abbey Theatre made its debut in 1966, as Europe's newest theater. For many first-timers it's a bit too new, soberly streamlined and sleek, without a trace of Edwardian curlicues. But it's a wonderfully comfortable structure with a spacious auditorium and a magnificently equipped stage. And it's still *the* Irish theater.

No summary of Irish stage spirit could ignore the work of Hilton Edwards and Michael MacLiammoir, a partnership of 50 years that ran the **Gate Theatre** until the latter's death in early 1978 and rivals the Abbey in quality. They combined the best of two worlds: Edwards is an Englishman who chose to live in Ireland; MacLiammoir was most floridly Irish.

Bookings for all theatrical productions should be made in advance directly through the theaters or at Brown Thomas or Switzer's agencies.

An excellent **Theatre-Go-Round** pass discounts tickets to nine of Dublin's leading theaters, plus eight others throughout the country. Inquire at the Tourist Office for details.

THE MAJOR THEATERS: Prices, programs, and times at Dublin's major theaters are as follows (all closed Sunday):

The **Abbey Theatre,** Lower Abbey Street (tel. 01-744505, 787179). Programs consist almost entirely of new plays by Irish authors interspersed with repertory revivals, including Yeats, Synge, O'Casey, Behan, and Beckett. Nightly at 8 p.m. Tickets run from £5 ($7.50) to £8 ($12).

The Peacock, downstairs in the Abbey (same phone). Provides the Abbey Players with an opportunity for experimental work. Features new and contemporary plays, poetry readings, Gaelic-language dramas, intimate theatrical evenings. Nightly at 8:15 p.m. with occasional lunchtime and late-night shows. Tickets are £5.50 ($8.25) to £6.50 ($9.75).

The Gate, Parnell Square (tel. 01-744045). Has always produced classics with a special accent on Irish writers of sophisticated comedy—Goldsmith, Sheridan, Shaw as well as the best of Irish, English, and American modern plays. It has done wonders with Wilde.

The Gaiety, S. King St. (tel. 01-771717). Features rollicking local revues showcasing Ireland's "house comedienne," Maureen Potter. Pantomimes yearly at Christmas. Also hosts visiting artists. Nightly at 8 p.m. and Saturday matinees at 3 p.m. Tickets vary but average £5 ($7.50).

Eblana, Store St. (tel. 01-746707). A small theater within the modern central bus station. Recently garnering acclaim for its productions of contemporary plays. Tickets are about £5 ($7.50).

THE "POCKET THEATERS": You'll find the more avant-garde work being done in the "pocket theaters" of Dublin. The **Project Arts Centre,** at 38/41 E. Essex St. (tel. 01-712321), is an artist's cooperative where anything might happen, from poetry readings, to rock musicals, to cinema, to Ibsen. Prices are kept at a bare minimum and at times lunchtime theater is presented to attract local shop and office workers. Tickets are priced about £3 ($4.50) to £5 ($7.50), with discounts for students and senior citizens. Watch the papers also for mention of **Focus,** evenings of Irish music and poetry at **Christ Church Cathedral,** puppet shows at the **Lambert Mews Theatre** (great for kids!), pub plays, and lunchtime productions at **Trinity College.**

THE NATIONAL CONCERT HALL: During just one month, the National Concert Hall, Earlsfort Terrace, Dublin 2 (tel. 01-711888), actually booked such diverse attractions as a fully staged performance of *The Merry Widow,* a series of jazz concerts, the Dresden Philharmonic Orchestra, a Folk Aid Concert for Ireland, the Johann Strauss Orchestra of Vienna, a recital by an international opera singer, and about a dozen others. It's an exceptionally fine hall used in an exceptionally imaginative manner. Be sure to check out what's on there when you're in Dublin.

Prices are in the £3 ($4.50) to £8 ($12) range, and occasionally there's a free attraction.

Traditional Irish Music

Ask Americans if they know an Irish song and nine out of ten —regardless of ancestry—will respond with "Galway Bay" or a similar Tin Pan Alley concoction about as Irish as hamburgers are German. It's difficult to express just how unfair this ignorance is to one of the greatest musical traditions on earth.

Irish music is quite fundamentally different from the plastic sugar of American imitations: wilder, more passionate, often atonal, with unfamiliar rhythm patterns and a depth of feeling that sounds startling to Top Twenty addicts. The traditional instruments are *not* those used by pop combos; fiddles, brass-strung harps, tin whistles, pipes, flutes, and one-stick *bodhran* drums stretched with goat skin produce sounds much more akin to Basque and Breton ensembles than to transatlantic orchestrations.

You can hear some of the true Gaelic lilt in the offerings of the Clancys (who conquered America before making a dent in Ireland), the Dubliners, the Abbey Singers, or in the Gaelic ballads soloed by Dolly MacMahon, Seamus Ennis, or Joe Heaney. The records they export contain mostly their catchy and rousing numbers in the conventional style, which give you no more than a hint of the strange melodic richness of Irish folk themes.

But you can capture the genuine core of the art by attending the functions of **Comhaltas Ceoltoiri Eireann** (C.C.E.). This is the national organization of traditional musicians and those interested in preserving Ireland's finest music. Their Dublin headquarters is at 32/33 Belgrave Square, Monkstown (tel. 01-800295). Each night sees sessions of traditional music, song, and dance; admission is £1 ($1.50). Also on the premises are a traditional music library, instrument workshop, and comprehensive advisory service. Visitors are welcome, but not essential: Comhaltas (pronounced Coalthus), like most truly artistic bodies, is quite self-sufficient.

A Ballad Club

This one *is* for visitors. If all Ireland at its joyous and sentimental best could be squeezed into the space of a single building, it would be the **Abbey Tavern.** Located in Howth, on the north shore of Dublin Bay, this grandest of ballad clubs boasts neither neon signs nor chromium fittings—just a bar, a small candle-gleaming seafood restaurant, and a barnlike hall in the rear. But that rather crude adjunct has probably spread more concentrated happiness than all the nighteries of the Western world combined.

You sit in a *sugan* chair close to an open turf fire with a pot hanging on the crane, sip your drink, and feel your heart opening and soaring while the Abbey Singers play. What they play is everything this nation has or wants to have—the pleasures, the sorrows, the jokes, the fights, the sadness, and the hopes. On their fiddles, spoons, pipes, and tin whistles they conjure up the past and serenade the present. They play so superbly and sing so hauntingly that you forget what brilliant instrumentalists they are —you seem to be playing yourself, even if only in the echoes of your mind. Singly or in chorus they roam the range of Irish balladry, prehistorically, almost eerily Gaelic to contemporary political, the sweet, deceptively simple voices of the girls alternating with the powerful male renditions. There's no telling what the Abbey Singers will perform on any particular night—they sing as the mood carries them. But we can give you one guarantee: you won't forget them.

During July and August you *must* book ahead (tel. 01-322006). Singing starts at 8:30 p.m. (and there's a superb new restaurant upstairs if you want a sumptuous dinner beforehand—more elegant and more expensive than the one below), and the club is closed on Sunday. Howth, where the Abbey stands, is nine miles northeast of Dublin; to drive, simply follow the coast. Bus no. 31 goes out from Lower Abbey and O'Connell Streets.

Irish Nights

For Irish entertainment in the cabaret style, try **Jurys Irish Cabaret,** held nightly except Monday from May to October at 8:20 p.m. in Jurys Hotel, Ballsbridge (tel. 01-605000). The price of £12.50 ($18.75) *includes* two drinks of your choice, and the level of production is fully professional. It's "export entertainment," as the Irish call it—which means "When Irish Eyes Are Smiling" and the "Rose of Tralee" and a lot of good, clean Irish sentimentality. It also means that the majority of the audience will consist of your own countrymen. You get a 2½-hour show, nicely staged with plenty of pretty young colleens in country costumes, black-haired baritones, and little, freckle-faced charmers to illustrate the step-dance. Six harpists join to play traditional tunes and a Seaneachai, an Irish storyteller, spins yarns full of parish priests, and fellows getting married at 50, and cracks about drinking—it was the Seaneachai who kept the villagers entertained before TV. The evening vibrates with Irish charm and goodwill, and don't be surprised if your throat catches just a little and the thought, "Gosh, I'm in Ireland," flits across your mind. It's meant to. Go along about 7:30 p.m. to get a good seat or to dine. With four-course dinner, the evening costs £23.90 ($35.85). Book ahead.

Another good bet for Irish cabaret is the **Braemor Rooms** at the County Club, Churchtown (tel. 01-988664, 981016, or 982308). Here, for an £18.50 ($27.75) all-inclusive charge, you'll enjoy a full, four-course dinner in a plush setting, followed by a 1½-hour program that changes frequently, but always features the best in national and international entertainment. After the show, there's dancing until after midnight.

Doyle's Irish Cabaret holds forth at the Burlington Hotel, Upper Leeson Street (tel. 01-605222). It's a two-hour show that in 1985 featured Noel V. Ginnity (billed as "The Leprechaun Himself"), Deirdre O'Callaghan and her Magic Harp, and singing star Des Smyth. A ballad group and the Rory O'Connor dancers completed the ensemble. You can come along at 7 p.m. for the dinner of cream of Tullamore soup, Galway Bay salmon, Mullingar heifer (fillet steak), colcannon, and Irish Mist soufflé plus the show for £21.95 ($32.93) or at 8 p.m. for just the cabaret, where you'll pay £12.50 ($18.75) for the show and two drinks.

Chapter VIII

DUBLIN SHOPPING SPREE

Top Buys in Irish Items

THE BEST WAY to conjure up Ireland on winter days when your vacation is but a misted memory is to take home a bit of the country with you. Irish crafts are a product of the soil and the sea. Wool from the sheep which crop the green fields is transformed by western farm families into tweeds the colors of gorse, sloe, and lichen. With symbolic stitches, fishing folk knit their stone walls, their twisted ropes, their winding cliff paths, creels, and sod huts into weather-resistant Aran sweaters. Rich green marble from the rock-strewn shores of Connemara is chipped into jewelry, rosary beads, paperweights. Turf dug from the bogs of County Donegal is pressed and molded into pendants and wall plaques of original Celtic design.

Some Background

Celtic design springs from the intricate patterns and glowing colors of the ninth-century *Book of Kells* created by artists who, as one expert put it, "did not display their skill for human eyes and applause but were imbued with the idea that the eyes of God would detect errors and worked solely to glorify Him." Today's Irish artists tend more toward pleasing tourists, but that's our gain. You'll find golden swirls ornamenting high-fashion garments, illuminated letters gleaming from hand-thrown and painted pottery plates. Worked into much of the jewelry and artwork of Ireland are ancient bards and warriors, the heroes and heroines of a country's dawn.

So many Irish craft items are individually made, often in isolated country cottages, that our cardinal rule for shopping in Ireland is: Buy what you like when you see it, for you may never see its like again. Specialties of the country include linen goods, crystal, hand-woven tweeds of all weights, hand-knits and crochet work, gossamer lace, pottery, and woven rushwork from the Rivers Shannon and Boyne. Among the most popular souvenirs are blackthorn walking sticks; shillelaghs; stuffed character dolls, including leprechauns: inexpensive copies of ancient jewelry, such as Tara brooches; turf molded into Celtic crosses and zoomorphic designs; family crests and coats-of-arms; and Claddagh rings—once exchanged at marriage by the insular fisherpeople in the Claddagh district near Galway City—which show two hands clasping a heart surmounted by a crown.

Many Irish shops are set up to mail packages to America; some will mail worldwide. American Customs regulations permit you to bring back up to $400 worth of retail purchases tax free. You may mail home, however, as many gifts as you wish, as long as no one gift exceeds $25 retail and not more than one package is sent to the same address on one day.

Some Shops

Before starting out on a shopping trek, pick up the Tourist Office's free booklet, **A Guide to Dublin Shopping.**

Dublin City boasts two major shopping districts. Low-cost clothing, furniture, and house goods sell along Henry Street, which runs off O'Connell Street at the corner of the G.P.O. and bisects the famed Moore Street market. The more elegant shopping street is Grafton, between College and St. Stephen's Greens, with small giftshops and boutiques in the arcades, lanes, and narrow streets that open off Grafton Street. Two of Dublin's three major department stores are located on Grafton Street: **Brown Thomas** and **Switzer's.** The third, **Clery's,** is on O'Connell Street. South Great Georges Street is also filled with shops of every description.

Be sure to set aside a good block of time when you visit the **Powerscourt Town House Centre,** on Clarendon Street in the heart of the city (it's signposted on Grafton Street at Johnson's Court, between Wicklow and Chatham Streets). The huge mansion was built for Lord Powerscourt in 1774 and is one of the finest in the country, with magnificent plasterwork ceilings which show the transition from rococo to neoclassical decoration. The refurbishment of the house and courtyard has managed to hold to original style while accommodating a collection of Ireland's finest boutiques and specialty shops, as well as an Antiques Gallery and members of the Craftsman's Guild who work in plain view fashioning fine shoes and boots, leather bags and other goods, jewelry, woven goods, and just about every other craft item you could mention. Boutiques feature men's and women's couture fashions, designer shoes and bags, Aran sweaters, Irish linen and lace, and Waterford glass. There's a hairdresser in residence, as well. The eight restaurants offer everything from gourmet French cuisine to hamburgers and pizza to traditional Irish meals, as well as inviting spots to rest feet and indulge in a light pick-me-up of pastry and tea. All in all, Powerscourt is a delightful place to visit, even if shopping is not your thing. It is that rare-to-nonexistent entity, a *tasteful* shopping center. Open 9:30 a.m. to 6 p.m., Monday through Saturday.

The following are those Dublin shops that we believe offer the highest quality Irish items at the most reasonable prices. Shops open between 9 and 10 a.m. and close between 5:30 and 6 p.m. six days a week, unless otherwise noted.

SOUTH OF THE LIFFEY: One of the brightest stars in Dublin's shopping firmament is the **House of Ireland,** 37/38 Nassau St. (tel. 01-777473, or 777949). Director Eileen Galligan has a keen eye for the best of Irish-made goods and has assembled one of the country's best selections. From Waterford glass to Belleek, Wedgwood, Aynsley, and Royal Tara china to fine tweeds, knitwear, and linens to Celtic jewelry to family crests right down to blackthorn walking sticks and quality souvenir items—you'll find an amazing array of them all, as well as a highly trained and helpful staff. One example of Eileen's expertise is the porcelain dolls she was among the first to merchandise. Made by Owencraft, of Ballyshannon, the dolls are exquisitely made and wear handmade costumes which illustrate the social history of Ireland. There's Molly Malone with her wheelbarrow of "cockles and mussels, alive, alive-O"; a Dublin flower vendor; a countrywoman dressed for Fair Day; and—of particular interest to us Yanks—an emigrant lady dressed in a homespun cape over her one good dress for the long journey to "Amerikay" and carrying a handwoven straw basket that holds a crocheted shawl and a tiny photograph of her loved ones. They make ideal reminders of Ireland to carry home and come packaged in sturdy carry-on cartons. However, if you don't want to take them back personally, as with all other purchases, the House of Ireland will gladly ship, and they give a £10 ($15) discount on purchases over £100 ($150). Start at College Green and head up Grafton Street, passing **Switzer's** on your right and **Brown Thomas** on your left. Check both for quality, expensive gifts. Groups of 30 or more who give 24 hours' notice can attend showings of Irish fashions at Brown Thomas, complete with harpist and free Irish coffee.

On your left, in Grafton Arcade, you'll find two good shops to explore:

Patricia's Irish Crafts, Grafton Arcade. Patricia York is a great authority on heraldry, about which she occasionally lectures. Consult her on a heraldic plaque bearing your family name. This is another one-room, well-stocked shop, with unusual small items, such as scenic pictures worked in tweed, miniature shillelaghs, Irish T-shirts, and the fine Taraware *Book of Kells* jewelry.

Monoghan's, Grafton Arcade, is the best place in town for men's, women's, and children's Aran cashmere, lambswool, and Shetland sweaters. The extremely helpful Mr. Monoghan is very careful about fit and insists you try on until perfectly suited. The ground floor is given over to sweaters; the basement contains men's jackets and shirts. The store offers worldwide shipping with greetings enclosed, and a mail-order catalog available.

Turn left at the corner of Brown Thomas, and now you have entered Duke Street. Cross over and inspect the shops in Creation Arcade.

The **Blarney Woollen Mills,** Creation Arcade, Duke St. (tel. 01-710068) is the Dublin branch of the famous woolen mills at Blarney and features the best of gifts from all over Ireland. There's a marvelous selection of Waterford glass and Belleek china as well as superb Pallas 100% linen dresses, skirts, and tops, and classic designs in Donegal tweed suits and coats from the country's top designers. They specialize in Irish sweaters and have good values in Aran hand-knit sweaters. They'll mail anywhere in the world, and you can pick up a copy of their helpful Personal Shoppers Guide when you call in.

Around the corner, walk to the bottom of Dawson Street, where you'll find:

Fergus O'Farrell, Norwich Union House, 62 Dawson St., which has marvelous creations of copper and wood. Designer Fergus O'Farrell is a law unto himself in Irish crafts, producing absolutely top-quality gift items, such as solid-brass door knockers designed and made in Ireland. Large figures out of Irish antiquity are available, as are attractive items incorporating Connemara marble, and silver jewelry. He closes at 1 p.m. on Saturday in winter.

Across from the National Museum are:

Cleo, 18 Kildare St. and at 2 Shelbourne St., Kenmare, Co. Kerry, a long-established shop in which to poke around and look for something a bit different: Munster cloaks, designer clothes in specially chosen tweeds and Irish linens, hand-knit sweaters with matching wool skirts, and men's authentic fishermen's waistcoats and fabulous caped overcoats.

Irish Cottage Industries, 44 Dawson St., a well-stocked, two-floor shop with shelves and shelves of richly hued tweeds. They carry some of the prettiest colors available in the city, many of which can be made up to order in boutique styles on display, with a vast range of hand-knitwear and accessories and men's jackets. It closes at 1 p.m. on Saturday in winter.

A half block up Dawson Street, turn right into South Anne and you reach, on the south side:

Kevin and Howlin, 31 Nassau St., at the bottom of Dawson Street, facing Trinity College, is a well-known men's shop with a terrific range of beautiful tweeds which can be tailor-made into jackets and suits, many from Donegal and exclusive, all hand-woven and tough as steel. There's also a huge range of ready-made jackets and suits, overcoats, tweed hats in fisherman and Sherlock Holmes styles, and tweed ties, all made from their own exclusive tweeds. The service is solicitous. This shop closes at 1 p.m. on Saturday November to June.

If you've eaten that terrific smoked Irish salmon until you're growing fins and feel you just can't go home without taking some along, the place to go is **McConnell and Nelson,** 38 Grafton St. (tel. 01-774344). Sean Nelson and his staff will help you select from their large stock, then seal it for travel, and best of all, their prices will be considerably less than you'd pay at the airport duty-free shops, once the only place salmon was available in packages designed for travel.

Fred Hanna Ltd., 27/29 Nassau St. (tel. 01-771255, 720797, or 771896), is Dublin's largest bookshop and carries a wide range of Irish-interest publications as well as secondhand books, maps, etc.

Greene & Co., 16 Clare St. (tel. 01-762554), began in 1843 as a lending library, and there's still something of that atmosphere in the large shop whose walls literally bulge with thousands of new and secondhand volumes. Browse through the sidewalk trays for unexpected treasures or ask them to search for some rare or out-of-print tome (which they'll do at no charge). But if you're a dedicated book lover, be warned: Don't go into Greene's unless you're prepared to spend lots of time—this is book-lover country, and you'll never be able to duck in and out quickly!

NORTH OF THE LIFFEY: The proper way to reach the following shops is to walk to O'Connell Bridge, turn left, and stroll up the quay until you reach the elegant arched Metal Bridge, built in 1816, and let that lead you to the:

Dublin Woollen Company, at Ha'penny Bridge, which was founded in 1888 by Mr. V. J. Roche, whose grandsons still personally operate the business. Once dispensing hand-woven tweeds and trimmings to the trade, the company now caters with tweeds, gifts, and Irish fashions to a wider clientele. The shop features an especially large range of Irish knitwear. The tweed selection is also extensive and the shop is stocked with delightful boutique items—capes, crocheted blouses, traditional Irish shawls, Aran sweaters, and kilts, many of them one-of-a-kind. Lovely mohair throws, scarves, and stoles are displayed in profusion. The staff is courteous and attentive, the shopping experience among the most pleasant available in Dublin.

Several shops worth considering along O'Connell Street:

Clerys, 26 Upper O'Connell St., is a department store, the largest and one of the oldest stores in Ireland. It offers a huge collection of Waterford crystal, excellent values in Belleek china, linen, tweeds, and furs, and incorporates a modern self-service restaurant.

Thomas Mullins, 36 Upper O'Connell St., also known as **Heraldic House,** excels in heraldic shields bearing family coats-of-arms. About 400 are in stock; others can be ordered. Maps are available showing origins of family names. The store does a huge mail-order business and also carries a wide range of mainly Irish souvenirs. Open until 6:30 p.m. from June through September.

Some specialty shops on the north side:

Waltons Musical Gallery, 2/5 North Frederick St., a continuation of O'Connell Street, north. This is the finest shop in the country for searching out Irish records, sheet music, and traditional instruments. Everything from tin whistles to harps is on sale—it is not unusual to be testing instruments alongside Ireland's best known musicians. In the sheet music selection, tunes date back four centuries; consult Niall Walton. In the record department, Peter Ryan is knowledgeable. LPs average £6 ($9) and you can purchase everything from unaccompanied Gaelic ballads to the gutsy renditions of contemporary protest songs by the Dubliners.

Coins and Medals, 10 Cathedral St., Dublin 1 (tel. 01-744033). Both shop and owner delight coin collectors from wherever. Mr. Emil Szauer started as a private collector but now buys and sells coins ranging from Greek and Roman times to early Irish days. His interest in and knowledge of numismatics are astounding; he belongs to at least seven numismatic societies and helped found the one in Ireland. Nor is Mr. Szauer shy on his subject— especially with fellow enthusiasts. He points out to the uninitiated that coin collecting is not just for the few but within every person's reach. War and commemorative medals are also on sale, as well as books dealing with such matters. Hours are 2 to 5:30 p.m. on Monday, 9:30 a.m. to 5:30 p.m. Tuesday through Saturday.

Dunnes Stores, 50 Henry St., is the Marks and Spencer of Dublin, the Alexander's of Henry Street. It's crowded and busy and of no charm, but a good place to pick up discount toothpaste and little necessities, such as cheap knickers and pantyhose.

Finally, two mementos you don't take with you but wait for and then enjoy throughout the year; the first is **Ireland of the Welcomes,** The Tourist Board's handsomely produced, bimonthly travel magazine. The photography is wonderfully evocative; the feature writers have included poets Yeats and Dylan Thomas, humorists Patrick Campbell and Art Buchwald. The artwork, incorporating old woodcuts and folk designs, can be witty and stylish. All in all it's the most consistently imaginative publication issued by any tourist body. But then wit and words *are* the Irish talents. Subscriptions: $12 one year, $20 two (the better deal). Mail checks to the Irish Tourist Board, Baggot Street Bridge, Dublin 2.

Inside Ireland is a quarterly newsletter, available only by subscription, which goes chiefly to the U.S. and Canada and covers what is happening in Ireland at the moment. For example, past issues have touched on the apartment scene (a fairly new development), the activities of a modern-day County Clare matchmaker, and the latest in racing and angling news. There's a "Roundup" column reporting on everything from politics to recent publications to current Irish humor. And if you have a hankering to find your Irish ancestors or are thinking of moving to Ireland, there's an Information Service which paid-up members can contact for answers to your specific questions. They've researched such topics as property purchase, dual citizenship, setting up a business, tax regulations, and retirement in Ireland. A Genealogical Supplement goes free to every subscriber, as does a Recommended Accommodations booklet which is periodically updated. (Every issue reviews one or more places to stay and dine, keeping you abreast of the newest restaurants, bed-and-breakfasts, etc.) They also publish *Property Ireland* for those interested in Irish real estate, and there's an informative *Irish Summer Schools Directory,* as well as a shopping discount service. You can get a sample copy by sending $1 to Inside Ireland, Rookwood, Ballyboden, Dublin 16 (tel. 01-907906 or 907359). Annual subscription is $30.

Chapter IX

ONE-DAY EXCURSIONS FROM DUBLIN

**South to Glendalough
North to Newgrange**

IF DISEMBARKING AT SHANNON gives you the freedom of the west coast, then basing yourself in Dublin gives you easy access to the wilds of the east. And wilds they are, although less tempestuous: moody glens, ancient monuments almost lost in history and upgrowing weeds, deep vales, and rushing rivers. From the center of Dublin, you are never more than 20 minutes from the mountains or sea. From the jet strip at Dublin Airport, you are less than 20 miles from the seat of the prehistoric High Kings of Ireland.

First rent a car, for one day or two. Then decide on direction—north or south? We'd suggest two days and both tours, for each offers its own intrigues. The southern tour provides more dramatic attractions; the northern, contemplative ones. Both are best done in good weather, so wait if need be for some shining morning and go on the spur of the moment. The Irish sky shedding its silver rays to halo the jagged ruins of Norman castles and monastic retreats is a scene you must not miss.

A note here on what we think is a marvelous way to supplement this guidebook and any other "homework" material you will have gathered in preparation for your Irish wanderings. There are three excellent **Auto-Tape Tours of Ireland** offered by Comprehensive Communications, Inc. (CCI), a U.S. firm which specializes in well-planned itineraries and a running commentary that covers everything from history and geography to folklore. The Irish tapes are done by both an American and an Irish guide, and even include snatches of appropriate music. They're timed to coordinate with local speed limits and come complete with a map and explicit voice instructions on when and where to turn (or turn off the taped itinerary for rambles on your own). Used together, the three tapes provide a circular tour of the country, beginning and ending at Shannon (Tape 2 includes Dublin and the day trips outlined below, along with a wealth of background information). You can order only one or two, but a better idea is to buy all three, then devote an evening at home before your departure to listening—a good way to reinforce the enthusiasm we hope you've caught from this book, as well as further help you pick and choose if your time in Ireland is limited. Tape 1 covers Shannon to Sligo, via Limerick, the Cliff of Moher, Galway, Yeats country, and dozens of prehistoric sites; Tape 2 takes you from Sligo to Cork, cross country to Dublin, then south through Wicklow, Wexford, and Waterford; Tape 3 returns you from Cork to Shannon past tiny coastal villages, majestic mountains, those not-to-be missed lakes of Killarney, and Tralee (of the roses). If your travel luggage includes a cassette player (or can stretch to accommodate one), any or all the tapes will add immeasurably to your Irish odyssey. Each costs $10.95 (plus $1 postage and handling per tape), and you can order them from CCI, P.O. Box 385, Scarsdale, NY 10583 (tel. 914/472-5133).

South to Glendalough

We're off, then, shaking the Dublin dust from our Wellingtons, hung over and more than ready to plunge into the soft-shadowed glens, the wild and weathered reaches of the Irish countryside. Start out early in the morning and make a leisurely day of this trip, because between Dublin and Arklow lie the Wicklow Mountains, as subtly contoured and laced with lush foliage as befits the area known as "the garden of Ireland." We once met an old Dublin man in a Galway restaurant who was taking his first trip to the west coast. He told us that he didn't know why he had bothered to spend the cash. "Everything I've seen in Ireland I could have found in County Wicklow." Wicklow fans feel that way. (Kerry, Connemara, and Donegal people don't.) And you may be equally captivated—once you've rambled through the rounded hills, stood beside the swirling waters of Avoca, and surrendered yourself to the moody timelessness of the tiny, ruined monastic city at Glendalough.

The route recommended in the following tour has been clocked at precisely 129 miles, leaving from and returning to O'Connell Bridge. Count on 4½ hours easy driving time, in good weather, and spread out the rest of your day among the sights you want to explore. Remember that summer nights are long—dark seldom descends before 9:30 p.m.

FROM DUBLIN TO SANDYCOVE: To leave Dublin, cross O'Connell Bridge heading south and turn left into Nassau Street. Follow this broad thoroughfare (it changes names by the block) out through Ballsbridge toward the coast. The first part of this road isn't terribly interesting; it's made up of small seaside suburbs and constitutes Dublin's back dormitory. **Dun Laoghaire,** seven miles south, is Ireland's major port-of-entry; the mail boats from Holyhead, across the Irish Sea, dock here daily. The harbor is en-

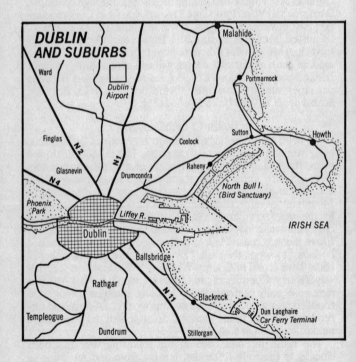

DUBLIN
AND SUBURBS

Ward

Dublin
Airport

Malahide

Portmarnock

Finglas

N2

N1

Coolock

Sutton

Howth

Glasnevin

N4

Drumcondra

Raheny

North Bull I.
(Bird Sanctuary)

Phoenix
Park

Liffey R.

Dublin

IRISH SEA

Ballsbridge

Rathgar

N 11

Blackrock

Dun Laoghaire
Car Ferry Terminal

Templeogue

Dundrum

Stillorgan

closed by two long stone piers which provide the perfect parade grounds for city dwellers in need of the sharp, fresh sea air. On Sunday afternoons and on the radiant summer nights the east pier streams with enthusiastic inhalers, and so ardent are the greetings and cryptic the verbal observations that one Dubliner has dubbed it "Ireland's Champs-Élysées." Just a little to the southeast, now, and you come to **Sandycove,** where, on a rocky cliff looking out on Dublin Bay, stands an early 19th-century martello tower—built originally to withstand a possible Napoleonic invasion, but known today more for its literary than military connections.

James Joyce Museum (County Dublin)

James Joyce lived in the tower with Oliver St. John Gogarty for a short time in 1904 when they were both very young men, and Stephen Dedalus lives there with Buck Mulligan on page 1 of *Ulysses.* Now the tower has become a museum and a must on the itinerary of every Joycean pilgrim to Ireland. The exhibition area on the ground floor contains personal mementos: letters and manuscripts, various editions of Joyce's books, including a 1922 first edition of *Ulysses,* a 1935 edition illustrated by Henri Matisse (donated by Cyril Cusack), Joyce's waistcoat (donated by Samuel Beckett), tie, walking-stick, cigar case, and his piano. A rare death mask of Joyce is also on display. From the top of the tower —the parapet where Mulligan props his shaving mirror and the gun rest where Stephen morosely surveys the sea—the view is fine and far-reaching. The museum is open weekdays May through September from 10 a.m. to 1 p.m. and 2 to 5 p.m., from 2:30 to 6 p.m. on Sunday. The rest of the year the museum may be visited by special arrangement with the Dublin and Eastern Tourism Organization (tel. 808571). Admission is 80p ($1.20) for adults, 60p (90¢) for students, 40p (60¢) for children.

BRAY AND ENNISKERRY: Continue down the coast eight miles to Bray, which is the most popular seaside resort on Ireland's east coast and has a mile-long beach and esplanade from which the sea views are quietly inspiring. Especially worthwhile is the view from **Bray Head,** an 800-foot cliff rising up from the sea on the southern end of the esplanade; cliff paths take you to the top.

At Bray, turn inland and drive two miles to **Enniskerry.** Postcard-picturesque, the village of Enniskerry straddles the Cookstown River and is delightfully representative of the many pretty mountain villages you'll find folded more deeply into the

Wicklow hills. Just south of the village is the entrance to Powerscourt Estate.

POWERSCOURT (County Wicklow): The granite-hewn and palatial 18th-century mansion that once served as the residence of the aristocratic Powerscourt family was extensively damaged by fire a few years back—a sad loss to the nation. But its exceptionally lovely Italian and Japanese gardens are being beautifully maintained and kept open to visitors. As well, you can visit the 14,000-acre demesne that contains the highest waterfall in Britain and Ireland (400 feet). Spend a refreshing hour or two driving through the Deer Park, strolling about the gardens, possibly plan to picnic beside the waterfall about four miles from the gardens or stretch full-length on the grass in view of Great Sugarloaf mountain. When you reach the demesne, park in the lot and follow the signs that lead you through the gardens. You'll come upon gold-leafed gates, marble statues and urns, a Pet's Cemetery where headstones read "Doodles Chow," "Busky," "Mrs. Mare," and a fortified tower flanked by cannon dating from the Spanish Armada. In the mansion's outbuildings, you can pause for afternoon tea and purchase a surprisingly inexpensive Aran sweater in the gift shop. The grounds are open daily from Easter to October, from 10:30 a.m. to 5:30 p.m. Admission to the gardens and demesne costs £1.60 ($2.40) per adult, 80p ($1.20) per child (5 to 16 years), with an additional 75p ($1.13) for adults, 35p (53¢) for children, to enter the waterfall area. (Children under 5 are free throughout.) But, while the waterfall is charming, it is also humble to the North American eye and more to be recommended as a picnic site than an outstanding attraction. By bus, take the no. 44 from College Street.

GLENCREE TO LARAGH: From Powerscourt you head due west on an unclassified road to **Glencree,** where you will meet an undulating mountain passageway that wends its way through some of the most enchanting scenery in Ireland. Originally cut after the Rebellion of 1798 to give the redcoats access to Dublin, it is known as the Military Road, and will take you up and over **Sally Gap** (1,631 feet), through the steep-sided valley of **Glenmacnass** and into the village of **Laragh,** near which lies famed Glendalough—second only to the Blarney Stone on most American lists of Irish "must sees."

GLENDALOUGH (County Wicklow): Literally translated from the Irish, Glendalough means "valley of two lakes." For sheer natural beauty, the lakes—smooth and silent in their deep mountain bowls, backed by the granite hills and forests of straight-limbed fir trees—are much to be admired. But natural beauty alone does not account for the enchantment, the perceptible aura of mysticism, the timelessness and haunting sense of sanctity that pervades the valley. In the 6th century, the hermit St. Kevin entered this valley and founded in it a monastic city that was to gain international fame as a center of learning. In the 9th and 10th centuries, the city was plundered by the Danes and in 1398 desecrated with more finality by the English, although various of the buildings were repaired and still in use when the monasteries were suppressed in the 16th century. It is before the placid ruins of those days—the stone beehive hut that once sheltered the saintly recluse, the little barrel-vaulted oratory in which he worshipped, the stone crosses, inscribed slabs, and almost perfect 110-foot round tower now over 1,000 years old—that time does a hushed and respectful obeisance.

The ruins are extensive and well worth exploring; you'll find them clustered about both the Upper and the Lower Lakes, with the principal group just east of the Lower Lake. Here, as everywhere else in Ireland, the antiquities are designated by small green road signs. The best thing you can do is to stop at the Tourist Information Office at Bray or Arklow and request the pamphlet dealing with County Wicklow, which gives a list, complete with locations, of antiquities to look for. Be sure to drive or hike up to the Upper Lake, which is far more impressive in its setting than the Lower Lake. Carved out of a cliff on the southern bank of the Upper Lake is a cave known as St. Kevin's Bed—supposed to have once been a prehistoric tomb. St. Kevin secreted himself in this shallow cave for long periods of retreat. It used to be possible to take a boat trip to the southern shore and climb the 30 feet up to the cave, but after they lost a tourist in the ascent one year, the tours were discontinued.

Backtrack to Laragh and drive southeast along the Avonmore River and through the wooded density of the Vale of Clara to **Rathdrum.** At Rathdrum, detour one mile east to—

AVONDALE (County Wicklow): Birthplace of the great Irish patriot, Charles Stewart Parnell (1846–1891), Avondale has been partially restored and opened to the public. Three of the rooms now look much as they did in Parnell's day—the square, high-ceilinged hallway; the sitting room with its Bossi mantelpiece, and the Mirror or Blue Room, the most impressive of the three, with mirrors set into blue panels and surrounded by ornamental plasterwork. One room is also open as a museum, with many mementos of Parnell, his family, and his times. The beautifully forested estate, now used as a Forestry Extension School (fitting tribute to the co-founder of the Land League), is open year round. Admission to car park: cars, £1 ($1.50), buses, £4 ($6). Admission to Avondale House: free.

Return to Rathdrum and drive south to **Woodenbridge,** an eight-mile stretch of exquisite mountain beauty that encompasses the deep and lovely Vale of Avoca and Tom Moore's immortalized "Meeting of the Waters."

MEETING OF THE WATERS: Thomas Moore was Ireland's national poet in 1807, when he sat himself on a stumpy tree beside the junction of the Avonmore and Avonbeg Rivers and composed his lyric tribute to the beauty of the scene:

> *There is not in the wide world a valley so sweet*
> *As the vale in whose bosom the bright waters meet.*

The "meeting" of which he wrote is about four miles south of Rathdrum; you can park your car on the road above the riverbanks and follow a flagstone path down to the waterside. **Moore's Tree,** where the poet composed his lines, is commemorated by a plaque. In a clearing by the shore stands a bust of Thomas Moore, eyes fixed in eternal concentration on the ever-flowing, ever-meeting waters.

In **Avoca,** allow time for a leisurely visit to Ireland's oldest hand-weaving mill, **Avoca Handweavers** (tel. 0402-5105). The shop is filled with woven goods of every description at prices which are competitive with other outlets. You'll find bedspreads, hooded cloaks, jackets, stoles, scarves, caps, sweaters, capes, and lovely cushion and pillow covers in a rainbow of colors and tweeds made on the premises. But the most memorable experience to carry away is a visit to the mill itself, down a little path, across a short bridge, and up a slight hillside. There, going happily about their work, are weavers who have learned their trade from parents and grandparents, and it is a joy to watch them at the looms. If you're lucky enough to run into Jim Barry—and if he's not too busy at the time—you'll learn from him firsthand some of the fascinating history of the old mill, which has gone through lean and prosperous times, but has continued turning out the world-famous woolens. Look for Dorothy Newman in the shop. In Avoca, the "finishing" and tailoring of goods is done outside the mill, in homes, as Jim told me, "from Wexford to Mayo." There's another shop, however, in Kilmacanogue (on the dual carriageway from Dublin, just outside Bray) where the tweed is converted into clothing right on the premises, and visitors are welcome there, as well, to wander about the mill and workshops, or to have clothing made to order from the cloth of their choice. You will also find a shop in Bunratty, County Clare.

The rivers meet for a second time at **Woodenbridge,** four miles farther south, and there are many people who consider the second meeting even more idyllic than the first—none of them, however, national poets. From Woodenbridge, the road works coastward again, passing through the Vale of Arklow and alongside the Avoca River till it reaches, in five miles—

ARKLOW (County Wicklow): Beautifully situated overlooking the sea, Arklow is a seaside resort town, a fishing village, and the site of **Arklow Pottery,** South Quay, Arklow, County Wicklow (tel. 0402-32401), makers of fine earthenware, tea sets, dinner sets, combination sets, and giftware, incorporating both modern and traditional designs. The retail shop attached to the factory carries a great selection of shapes and patterns, and is open from 10 a.m. to 5 p.m. daily. You can arrange a tour of the factory during the months of June, July, and August to watch the craftspeople at their trade.

Now head due north up to **Rathnew.** Turn left to **Ashford** and stop for a late afternoon visit at—

MOUNT USHER (County Wicklow): Surely this privately owned garden must rank among the loveliest works of horticulture in the country—20 acres of flowers, trees, shrubs, and lawns lying in the sheltered valley of the gentle Vartry River. Although this is not a botanical garden, it harbors plants from many parts of the globe: spindle trees from China, North American sweet gum and swamp cypress, the New Zealand ti tree, African broom, Burmese Juniper, and scores of other transplants. But the labels don't matter. It is the harmony of color, the magnificent setting, the superbly dream-like landscaping that make this spot a showpiece.

It is open daily from April to September 30 on weekdays from 10:30 a.m. to 6 p.m., on Sunday from 2 p.m. to 6 p.m. Admission is £1.50 ($2.25) for adults, 80p ($1.20) for children. There's a tearoom at the entrance serving morning coffee, sandwiches, snacks, and afternoon tea, as well as a small antique shop.

North to Newgrange

This is a tour not only into lovely countryside but back into the origins of a race. It is mainly concerned with quiet places, with mysterious mounds, anonymous artworks, sites hallowed by the presence of saints and kings. It is a day to feed fantasy and wonder, to set your mind to imaginings of other times and people. It is a day to gently roam.

This route has been clocked at 94 miles, from O'Connell Bridge and back, giving you four hours for driving and many others for discovery.

Although the places you will be seeing date back over 4,000 years, the area you are traversing has much meaning for today. Newgrange, nestled into the Boyne Valley, was built by people whose origins we don't even know. The River Boyne that flows through the valley where King William defeated King James in 1690 is the source of something we all know too well—the division of the Irish people that is only now working toward its final, agonized reconciliation.

From O'Connell Bridge, drive northeast through **Phoenix Park.** In 24 miles you reach the Hill of Tara.

TARA (County Meath): This is the most hallowed historical site in Ireland, although no one has really been able to separate history from legend. At the dawn of Irish history this low hillside was the center of pagan worship on the island, the seat of native priest-kings known as "Kings of Tara"—even though their actual realms lay miles away.

You'll be disappointed if you come to Tara seeking remnants of regality. Only earthworks remain—low earthen walls that once formed an Iron Age fortification; burial mounds that date back 4,000 years; a rock which was supposed to have roared when a king of Ireland was accepted—these are not spectacular. But they are permeated with the misty beginnings of the Irish people.

Years ago some religious fanatics half wrecked the place while searching for the Ark of the Covenant they believed was buried here. Their information came from a secondhand bookshop in London's Charing Cross Road, and their frantic digging was in vain. But this is a sample of the magical image still projected by the mysterious site of Tara.

From Tara, continue southeast along an unclassified road

through **Kilmessan** and drive four miles farther into the town of Trim.

TRIM CASTLE (County Meath): Trim is not only one of the prettiest little towns in Ireland but also the site of her largest Norman castle. Built in the first half of the 13th century, the castle dominates the town just as it did then. The tall, grimly gray central tower rises from the massive walls, built to withstand time as well as human enemies. Prince Hal of England—later to become King Henry V of Agincourt fame—once stayed in the drawbridge gate tower. Excavations have unearthed the headless skeletons of a large number of men who had been buried in the castle grounds. They were presumably soldiers who had helped to defend the stronghold against Cromwell's troops. Looking across the river from the castle you can see the remains of the 14th-century town wall and the so-called Yellow Steeple, once part of an abbey containing the miracle-working statue of the Virgin, venerated as the Idol of Trim.

North, now, through **Navan** to **Slane.** Drive 3½ miles more, turn right, and drive 1½ miles to Newgrange.

NEWGRANGE (County Meath): This is a fascinatingly mysterious burial mound, built about 4,500 years ago. We don't know who built it, but assume it was done by people who had come to Ireland from what is Brittany today. We know that they were remarkably sophisticated builders, but the symbolic meaning of their ornaments and structures is still lost in the gray shadow world of prehistory.

You enter the mound through a 62-foot-long passage that leads to the burial chamber itself. Who lies buried there? Again a shrug. Kings, priests, chieftains . . . in any case, people important enough to warrant this impressive monument. The corbeled roof above it has kept the chamber perfectly dry for over 40 centuries. The stone in front of the entrance is one of the finest examples of prehistoric European craftsmanship, ornamented with spirals, lozenges, and other shapes, whose meaning still baffles archeologists. An aperture above the doorway was so ingeniously placed that it allowed the sun to penetrate the burial chamber for exactly 17 minutes on December 21, the shortest day of the year. Was it done to bring a touch of sunlight to those buried in the darkness inside? Maybe future researchers will find the key.

The mound is open 10 a.m. to 7 p.m. from mid-June to mid-September. Hours vary throughout the rest of the year. Admission is 85p ($1.28) for adults, 25p (38¢) for students and children.

Return via **Dowth,** turn right, drive half a mile, and at King William's Glen turn left and drive through the glen until two left turns bring you to Mellifont Abbey.

MELLIFONT (County Louth): On the banks of the River Mattock, Mellifont was the first Cistercian monastery in Ireland, founded in 1142. Only the foundations remain of the original church. Most of the standing structures date from the renewal of the church in the 13th century—which is still pretty ancient. You can visit the tall Chapter House and see the remains of the cloister, including the graceful lavabo in which the monks washed their hands before and after meals. A wonderful air of calm and serenity hangs over the entire place, probably the reason those ancient monks chose it for their lifelong retreat. It is open all year, free.

Drive in the direction of **Collon** for a little over a mile. Turn right and drive two miles to—

MONASTERBOICE (County Louth): Only a small, cross-dappled churchyard and a round tower are left of what was once a great monastic foundation. But here rises **Muiredach's Cross,** the finest of Ireland's high crosses. These crosses were expressions of Christian sculpture in the eighth and ninth centuries. Muiredach's Cross stands 17 feet high. Cut from a single stone and set on a massive base, it is covered with an amazing profusion of carved ornaments and figures—perhaps half a lifetime's work for its unknown artist. Also unknown is the man after whom the cross is named. The Irish inscription on the shaft simply asks for prayers for one Muiredach, who had the cross made. Who he was and who created his monument are two of the unsolved riddles surrounding the cross. Much closer to our own times are the numerous dents left in the base of the cross. They were made by hundreds of Irish emigrants who wanted to take a chip of Muiredach's Cross with them to give them comfort and a feeling of home in the New World.

Next drive south through the town of Drogheda, situated on the River Boyne. This is the main road back to Dublin, and in 21 miles, you will reach Swords. Turn left and drive three miles to Malahide, site of one of Ireland's oldest and most historical castles.

MALAHIDE CASTLE (County Dublin): Founded about 1180 by Richard, Lord Talbot de Malahide, this fine castellated mansion was occupied by his descendants until 1976, when it became the property of the Dublin County Council. Situated in a 268-acre demesne which includes elegant formal gardens, the castle holds one of the country's best collections of Irish period furniture, as well as a marvelous collection of Irish historical oil portraits, among them some of Lord Talbot's descendants who lived here for 750 years. Architecture is post-medieval, for the most part, and there are a few traces of the old moat. Beside the castle are the ruins of the 15th-century Abbey of Malahide.

The castle is open Monday through Friday from 10 a.m. to 12:45 p.m. and 2 p.m. to 5 p.m. There are varying hours on weekends and holidays. Adults pay £1.90 ($2.85); students and senior citizens, £1.30 ($1.95); and children, £1 ($1.50).

AND BACK TO DUBLIN: It's time now to start thinking about dinner and the evening. There are several outstanding eateries on the north side of the city. Best to read up on them in Chapters IV and V and book ahead. In Malahide you can dine at **Johnnys.** Continue along the harbor and you can feast on seafood at the **King Sitric** in Howth or the new upstairs restaurant at the **Abbey Tavern.**

But wherever you dine, you are still excellently situated to end up a day spent among the silences of ancient Ireland in a contemporary and far more boisterous "abbey"—among the rollicking song and clink of glasses at Howth's Abbey Tavern!

Chapter X

BEYOND THE PALE

The Highlights of Ireland

BACK IN MEDIEVAL DAYS, when England controlled Ireland, the overlords protected themselves against raiding Irish tribes by ringing Dublin and the surrounding territory with trenches and manned watchtowers. The area within was known as "The Pale," while the Ireland of the Irish lay "beyond."

In many ways the dichotomy still exists; Dublin under Irish rule is still the seat of power and influence, the center of culture and art. See only Dublin and your image of Ireland will be sadly distorted. Set out into the glorious countryside, sip a pint with the locals in a riverside pub, hear the ancient Gaelic tongue in daily use on the western seaboard, talk farming to a man who ekes his living from the rocky soil of Connemara, talk breeding with the owners of the magnificent horses that thrive on the rich grasses of the midlands. Ireland's first industry is agriculture, and the "Ireland of the Irish" has little to do with the business concerns back in Dublin's "Big Smoke." City and country, in Ireland, are separate sides of one well-worn coin. Be sure to see both. One can't ring true without the other.

Getting around Ireland is simplicity itself. Renting a car and driving is the most flexible way to do it. The roads are well paved, if narrow (small cars are best), and not overly well signposted. One sign of the times, however, is the road building going on all over the country, and asking all those directions can lead to some marvelous personal experiences. CIE operates an all-encompassing network of buses and trains, quite capable of taking you comfortably to almost any pocket you might wish to visit. If you are traveling by public transport, it would be best to equip yourself with a **Rambler** ticket, giving you the freedom of the system. An eight-day rail-and-road ticket costs £70 ($105) for adults,

£35 ($52.50) for children. For 15 days, the price is £101 ($151.50) for adults, £50.50 ($75.75) for children. Rail-only tickets are less expensive, and there are discounts for families and groups. Contact CIE in Dublin at 59 Upper O'Connell St. for information. Tickets can be purchased at any CIE terminal. (Eurailpass and Eurail Youthpass are both now honored in Ireland.) CIE also operates sightseeing day tours out of all major centers. These take in just about every sight a visitor might want to see. Pick up the **Day Trip** folders from CIE offices or Tourist Offices around the country for prices, itineraries, and times.

Here, then, are the major attractions of Ireland that beckon you "beyond," with cross-references to the following chapters, where you'll find suggestions on where to stop for the night, have a meal, or indulge in a few "jars." To help in your planning, we've included a mileage chart.

The John F. Kennedy Park
(County Wexford)

The Irish loved—and mourned—JFK as one of their own. Just east of the Kennedy family's ancestral home, on the lower slopes of the hill of Slieve Coillte, they built a living memorial to "their" president. The lush, rolling parkland named after him, while primarily a scientific collection of trees and shrubs, is a place of fun and recreation as well as remembrance. There are picnic sites, trails for hiking, a 310-acre arboretum, and a viewing point commanding the entire countryside—all so breathtakingly green and serene that it catches you in the throat, especially after reading the plaque dedicating the area "to the memory of John Fitzgerald Kennedy." The picnic area has a café and souvenir store.

The park lies eight miles south of New Ross, County Wexford, 96 miles from Dublin. The actual Kennedy homestead, once the farm of JFK's great-grandfather, still stands in **Dunganstown**, five miles away, although the original straw-thatched farmhouse has been replaced by a sturdier and more comfortable dwelling. It now belongs to the Ryans (Mrs. Ryan's maiden name was Kennedy), but they have grown rather weary of shaking tourists' hands and prefer that you pass by without knocking.

Admission to the park is free, except for a £1 ($1.50) parking fee. The park is open from 10 a.m. to 8 p.m. May to August, 10 a.m. to 6:30 p.m. in September and April, 10 a.m. to 5 p.m. from October through March.

The **New Ross Galley,** a cruising restaurant, leaves from nearby New Ross quay. See Chapter XIII for details.

Mileage Between Major Irish Tourist Centers

	Athlone	Cork	Donegal	Dublin	Dundalk	Galway	Kilkenny	Killarney	Limerick	Roscommon	Rosslare Harbour	Shannon Airport	Sligo	Waterford	Wexford
Cork	136														
Donegal	114	250													
Dublin	78	160	138												
Dundalk	90	202	98	53											
Galway	58	130	127	136	148										
Kilkenny	78	92	192	73	123	107									
Killarney	144	54	253	192	219	120	123								
Limerick	75	65	184	123	150	65	70	69							
Roscommon	20	156	94	91	94	51	98	164	94						
Rosslare	130	129	243	101	153	170	62	171	131	150					
Shannon	83	80	176	138	165	57	85	84	15	96	146				
Sligo	73	209	41	135	104	86	152	213	144	53	203	136			
Waterford	108	78	222	98	151	137	30	120	80	129	51	95	182		
Wexford	117	116	231	88	141	157	50	158	118	138	12	133	191	39	

Kilkenny City
(County Kilkenny)

There's a look of graciousness and dignity about this ancient little Tudor town 73 miles southwest of Dublin. The streets have old English names like Pennyfeather Lane, and many of the houses bear the imprint of the solidly respectable wealthy Tudor merchant class. Kilkenny has always attracted skilled craftsmen and business folks and still does.

But that doesn't mean the place has a commercial look. Kilkenny is dominated by the turrets of **Kilkenny Castle;** it has a cathedral, a 14th-century **Bishop's Palace,** 10th-century **Round Tower,** and a gate from the original medieval city wall. The mingling strains of Norman and Gaelic culture have blended harmoniously here.

ROTHE HOUSE: What you might call the soul of the place is Rothe House. This was the town house of the family of John Rothe Fitzpiers, built in 1594. The original owners were driven out by Cromwell's soldiers. For years the mansion was used as a school; later it became the headquarters of the Gaelic League, which fired Ireland's literary renaissance. Today it's a museum and library and offers an intriguing insight into how the Tudor businessman lived after he'd made it (very handsomely). Summer admission times are 10:30 a.m. to 12:30 p.m. and 3 to 5 p.m. weekdays, 3 to 5 p.m. only on Sunday. Admission is 75p ($1.13) for adults, 50p (75¢) for students, and 30p (45¢) for children.

KILKENNY DESIGN CENTER: A piece of Ireland in a historical setting, the center is located in what were once the stables of 18th-century Kilkenny Castle. The horseshoe archways and carriage-wheel windows form a quaint contrast to the highly contemporary display inside.

The workshops represent a government-sponsored effort to inspire and produce modern Irish designs for the world market. The goods created here are selling well in England, Europe, and America, and even a brief glance at them will tell you why. They are an inspiring blend of traditional craftsmanship and modern patterning and have a flavor uniquely their own: a kind of deep, quiet pride of creation that denotes intense individuality.

There's a dazzling display of textiles, furniture, jewelry, ceramics, glassware, metals, and graphics. Items aren't exactly cheap, but it is possible to catch some bargains by watching for markdowns on discontinued lines. The shop is open Monday through Saturday from 9 a.m. to 6 p.m., and there's a Kilkenny shop in Nassau Street, Dublin, with the same stock and same hours.

KYTELER'S INN: If you've never had drinks in a genuine witch's home, do so now, at Kyteler's Inn, on Kieran St. (tel. 21888). Even the alley where it stands looks vaguely haunted. Back in the 1320s, this was the home of Dame Alice Kyteler, a beautiful and dangerous lady who outlived four husbands and was sentenced to burn at the stake for witchcraft. She vanished without a trace before her execution.

Today, Kyteler's functions as a normal, though unusually charming, pub and a good à la carte restaurant. You can have a few drinks and/or contemplate what might have happened to the disappearing dame. (Her witching companions, incidentally, were less fortunate. They all met a fiery death.)

The Rock of Cashel
(County Tipperary)

Three hundred feet high, with a two-acre summit, the Rock of Cashel in County Tipperary has been the site of kings' palaces and a worshipping place for men as far back into Gaelic antiquity as historians can probe. But for modern Ireland, its importance stems from one day in A.D. 450. On that day, Angus, the Irish king of Munster, was in residence when St. Patrick arrived at the rock on his evangelistic mission through Ireland. Angus welcomed St. Patrick, and royally. He and his family were converted and baptized. And on this rock, the Roman Catholic church in southern Ireland was securely founded. It was here, also, that St. Patrick likened the Trinity to the three leaves of a shamrock.

In 1101, the chiefs of Ireland presented "Cashel of the Kings" to the church for all time, and shortly after, Cormac MacCarthy built the perfect little chapel that bears his name and is considered the most beautiful ancient church extant in Ireland. In 1169 work began on the cathedral, work that continued into the 15th century. The cathedral remained Catholic through burnings and wars, persecutions and bloody massacres, until 1729, when the first Protestant service was held within. Twenty years later, the beautiful building was unroofed and abandoned by Protestant Archbishop Price, because, so the Irish tell it, he couldn't drive his coach-and-four up the rock's steep sides.

What you find today at the Rock of Cashel is a carefully tended set of fascinating ruins under the care of the commissioners of public works. There's a good deal to explore, and to help you do it, you might pick up the excellent booklet *The Rock of Cashel* at the souvenir desk just inside the entrance. Also, there are free guided tours given every hour on the hour during summer. Admission charge to the ruins is £1.50 ($2.25) for adults, 75p ($1.13) for children. In the nave of the cathedral you'll find a floor plan on a pedestal that outlines and dates the various sections. Not counting the remains of an undated palace, the oldest building on the rock is a tenth-century round tower. Don't miss Cormac's Chapel, which is beautifully preserved. In the cathedral, you can climb through the walls to the top of the central tower for wide views of the surrounding country. Look for the stone Cross of Cashel, which is one of the oldest crosses in Ireland. Its base is thought to be a pre-Christian sacrificial altar, with some spiral carvings still evident. On the cross, there's an image of Christ on one side and a figure of a bishop, who is difficult to discern but may be St. Patrick, on the other. Hours are 10 a.m. to 7 p.m. daily, June through September; the rest of the year, Tuesday through Saturday 10 a.m. to 1 p.m. and 2 to 5 p.m. (on Sunday, 2 to 5 p.m.; closed Monday).

Cashel is located 100 miles southwest of Dublin, 51 miles southeast of Shannon, and can be neatly fitted into a day's drive across country, with Kilkenny as a first or second stop, depending on driving direction. But the antiquity-studded and lushly rural area of Cashel is worthy of a lengthier pause. You can overnight near Cashel in an elegant yet intimate Georgian country home five miles away. (See Longueville House in the following chapters for details.)

The Blarney Stone
(County Cork)

This is undoubtedly the most famous piece of rock in the world and—for thousands of tourists—virtually the only reason for visiting Ireland. The curious word "blarney," incidentally, was coined by the formidable Queen Elizabeth I. When the lord of Blarney Castle, MacCarthy, kept stalling her royal commands with a glorious line of soft soap, she finally exploded: "This is all just Blarney. That man never means what he says!"

We don't know how and when the fable arose that you can imbibe MacCarthy's special talent by kissing a certain stone in his battlement. But the stone forms part of the remnants of Blarney Castle, a square tower, 83 feet high, rising five miles northwest of Cork City. You'll have to climb 127 steps to the top of the tower, a pretty breathless undertaking. Then you lie down on your back, with a guard clutching your ankles, bend backward between the battlements, and kiss the illustrious block of limestone—4'11" long, 1'1" wide. Quite a number of people perform these gymnastics in vain—they end up kissing the wrong stone, the one above it. So make sure your aim is true.

Anyway, you're lucky. You have guard rails to hang on to. In the old days, there was nothing between the kissers and the 90-foot drop. Nevertheless, some very famous people came to kiss, among them Sir Walter Scott in 1825, whom a friend held by his trousers while an escorting artist immortalized the scene.

At the foot of the keep a lady will sell you a certificate testifying that you've kissed the stone—whether you have or not. And that's *her* line of blarney. Admission to the grounds is £1.50 ($2.25) for adults, 75p ($1.13) for children. It's open Monday to Saturday from 9 a.m. to 8:30 p.m. in June and July, till 7:30 in August, 7 p.m. in May, 6:30 in September, and sundown from October to April. Sunday hours are 9:30 a.m. to 5:30 p.m. in summer, 9:30 a.m. to sundown in winter. (For accommodations and meals in the Cork City area, See Chapters XII and XIII.)

Kinsale
(County Cork)

Lying 18 miles south of Cork, this little picturesque fishing town is actually one of the oldest cities in Ireland. Its charter dates back to 1333, although it certainly doesn't look like what you might call a "city." Some wonderful ancient ruins invite exploration: the **Carmelite Friary,** built in 1314; the crumbled walls of **King James's Fort,** briefly occupied by the Spaniards in 1601; and **Charles Fort,** a military stronghold from 1677 till the 1920s, now used chiefly as a picnic ground and site for pretty lively beer parties. Some wonderfully atmospheric restaurants invite equally enthusiastic attention (consult Chapter XIV.)

But Kinsale's main attraction is deep-sea fishing. The shoals offshore have always been superb fishing grounds. Back in 1563, the Spaniards agreed to pay Queen Elizabeth the regal sum of £1,000 a year to operate a fishing fleet there. That right, however, expired together with the Spanish Armada.

During the summer the town is thronged with young tourists from every part of the globe, and the local pub life is hectic enough to make this "fun city" (see Chapter XIV). Crowds of youngsters, in fact, never get any farther in Ireland than the nearby hostel and caravan campgrounds. They get a taste of Kinsale and promptly settle down for the remainder of their holidays.

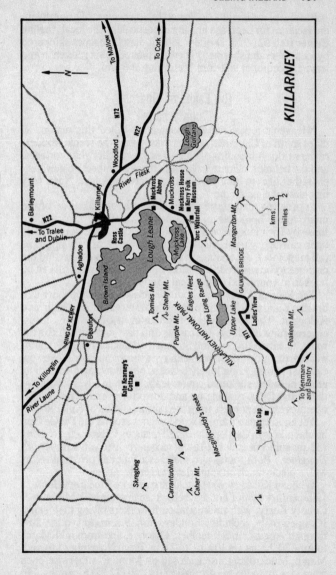

KILLARNEY

To Mallow

To Cork

N72

N22

Woodford

Barleymount

River Flesk

Lough Guitane

N22

Killarney

To Tralee
and Dublin

Muckross
Abbey

Muckross

Muckross House
Kerry Folk
Museum

Torc Waterfall

Mangerton Mt.

kms.   3
miles 2
0   2

Aghadoe

Ross
Castle

Brown Island

Lough Leane

Muckross Lake

GALWAY'S BRIDGE

RING OF KERRY

Beaufort

Tomies Mt.

Shehy Mt.

Purple Mt.

Eagles Nest

The Long Range

KILLARNEY NATIONAL PARK

Upper Lake

Ladies' View

N71

Peakeen Mt.

To Killorglin

River Laune

Kate Kearney's
Cottage

Macgillycuddy's Reeks

Moll's Gap

To Kenmare
and Bantry

Skregbeg

Carrantuohill

Caher Mt.

But the place is still a dedicated fishing center, offering splendid facilities for deep-sea angling in particular. The local **Angling Center** (tel. 021-72611) offers 36-foot diesel launches skippered by local veteran fishermen. They are limited to six rods each and leave the center at 9:30 a.m., returning at 6 p.m.

The Lakes of Killarney
(County Kerry)

"Heaven's reflex" is what somebody called this region, 69 miles south of Limerick, which ranks among the scenic wonders of the world. A blending of blue lakes, green hills, white cottages, and the balmiest climate in Ireland, it has an impact on newcomers rather like, to lift a phrase from Brendan Behan, "their very first glass of champagne."

In order to really taste the area you should take one of the many tours, bookable in Killarney Town. Some favorites are those by Irish jaunting car (which isn't a car, but a horse-drawn open carriage with blarney-dispensing driver), at varying prices (all moderate), depending on the number of passengers and the distance to be covered. Bus tours of the Killarney region can be booked at your hotel or the local Tourist Office.

The **Ring of Kerry** is a winding circle of magical beauty embracing Killarney, Kenmare, Sneem, Waterville, Glenbeigh, and Killorglin. The road hugs the water most of the way, moss-covered ruins of abbeys and castles drift past your eyes, and in the warm air carried by the Gulf Stream that touches Ireland's southwest corner grow Mediterranean-type shrubs and trees, even occasional palms. Long lonely beaches of yellow sand, incredibly green hillsides, sheltered coves, leaping fish in silvery waters—that is the Ring, running up and down for over 140 miles. CIE operates excellent tours from the railway station of Killarney.

Yet another panoramic excursion goes around the **Dingle Peninsula,** taking in Castlemaine and Tralee, by CIE coach, covering 132 magnificent miles. (You'll recognize it if you saw *Ryan's Daughter.*) Both routes also make excellent day drives, possibly with a picnic lunch on some deserted crescent beach.

While in Killarney you should also explore **Muckross House,** a 19th-century manor house where you can see a Folk Museum of County Kerry, with traditional craft workers plying their skills. It's open daily, including Sunday, from 9 a.m. to 9 p.m., July through August. In September, October, and from mid-March to June 30, hours are 10 a.m. to 7 p.m. From November 1 to mid-March, Muckross House is closed on Monday, otherwise open from 11 a.m. to 5 p.m. Admission is £1.50 ($2.25) for adults, 75p

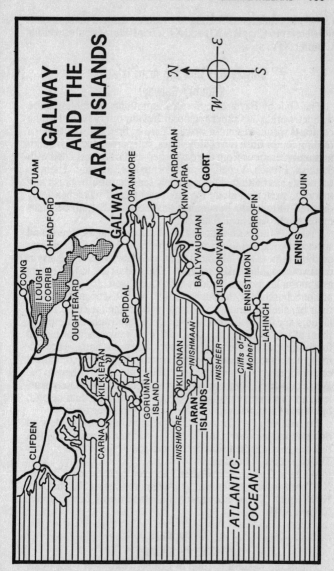

($1.13) for children. For Killarney restaurants and accommodations, refer to Chapters XII and XIII. For Killarney pubs, consult Chapter XIV.

Galway Bay and the Aran Islands
(County Galway)

The Galway Bay area embraces something resembling three distinct worlds. No other region in Ireland offers such startling contrasts within so small a space. There is, first, **Galway Town,** a trading center since the Middle Ages, still permeated with buildings and memories from the days when its harbor was filled with Spanish, French, Venetian, and Portuguese shipping. Then, to the west, lies **Salthill.** This is a lively seaside suburb, brash and modern, stretching along the bay beaches and wholeheartedly devoted to tourism. In summer the accent of Salthill becomes more Anglo-American than Irish.

Finally, 30 miles off the coast, are the **Aran Islands:** three small specks of rock and sandy soil, steeped in the Celtic twilight, incredibly remote and inhabited by fisherfolk who brave the seas in craft you wouldn't take on a river. The islands are as fascinating as a moon landscape, studded with round watchtowers and tiny ancient churches, with thatched-roof inns that keep no bottles on their bar shelves, and with stone forts guarding the cliffs. The islanders speak Gaelic as a workaday tongue (although most of them also know English), clip, spin, and weave their own wool for the famous sweaters and costumes they wear, and live according to a year-round pattern of toil, rituals, feasts, and communal celebrations you wouldn't believe still continues anywhere in the Western world. They are courteous, dignified, absolutely fearless, and arch-conservative. You'll find them polite and helpful, but it takes about a decade before you get to *know* them.

You can visit the islands by CIE steamer, but crossings depend on tides and weather (tel. 091-62141). Or **Aer Arann** will fly you there in twin-engined Islander aircraft (tel. 091-65119 or 65110). The trip takes 20 minutes.

While in Galway, try to attend an evening at **Seoda** (Chapter XIV) or the banquet in nearby **Dunguaire Castle** (Chapter XI). For County Galway accommodations and meals, see Chapters XII and XIII.

Connemara
(County Galway)

This is the western portion of County Galway, a wild, thinly peopled, incredibly enchanting stretch of land between Lough

Corrib and the Atlantic Ocean. Connemara is more than scenery; it's feeling, almost a state of soul. People may ooh! and ah! at other beauty spots—in Connemara they fall silent. There are certain delights that exclamations can only spoil. This is one of them.

As you follow the coastline from Galway to Sligo town, you drive through a region that seems empty of people, a countryside filled with a majestic silence that accentuates every rustle of wind, every gull scream. The narrow winding roads glow red with fuchsia, the rocks shimmer green with Connemara marble. The shoreline is deeply penetrated by fingers of ocean, lapping blue and white against the little fields huddling between low, lacy walls of loosely fitted stones. In the background stretches the mountain range known as the **Twelve Bens,** which you can never count completely because drifts of dappled clouds keep veiling and revealing them in a constantly changing pattern.

Now and again—always unexpectedly—you meet the horses, the picture-book-pretty little steeds called Connemara ponies, the only native breed of horse in Ireland. They graze and frolic along the ocean as if they were marine animals, ready to dive back into their home element. And south of Clifden rises the proud, lonely monument to **Alcock and Brown,** who landed here after completing the first transatlantic flight in 1919, *before* Lindbergh.

If Connemara is comparatively empty of people, it is well populated with rustic summer inns for superb overnight stays, lunches, and dinners. Consult Chapters XII and XIII for recommendations and Chapter XV for some of the best shops in Ireland, also located in the area.

The Yeats Country
(County Sligo)

Although the poet William Butler Yeats was actually born in Dublin, the "Yeats Country" is Sligo and surrounding territory. Yeats spent most of his boyhood summers there and set it to words as a composer might set it to music. The trouble is that now you can't really describe it without quoting him. He lies buried in **Drumcliff** churchyard five miles from town, under a stone that bears his own epitaph ending with the immortally chilling lines: "Cast a cold eye—On life, on death—Horseman, pass by!"

Another pilgrimage point for Yeats admirers is the tower at **Thoor Ballylee,** 3½ miles northeast of Gort, County Galway. The poet wrote in it and about it for a dozen summers, and visitors can tour the tower house with a rented sound

Based on the Ordnance Survey by permission of the Government of Ireland (Permit No. 2107)

KEY TO THE NUMBERED REFERENCES ON OUR MAP OF SLIGO:
1—Railway Station; 2—Gen. Post Office; 3—Town Hall; 4—Technical School; 5—Garda Station; 6—Courthouse and Co. Council Offices; 7—Sligo Abbey; 8—Catholic Cathedral; 9—Church of Ireland Cathedral; 10—Calvary Church and Grammar School; 11—Presbyterian Church; 12—Dominican Church; 13—Methodist Church; 14—Tourist Office, Co. Library and Museum; 15—Swimming Pool.

guide, including the thatched cottage alongside that was once Yeats's kitchen. It is open from 10 a.m. to 6 p.m. daily, June through September, at £1.50 ($2.25) for adults, 50p (75¢) for children.

Sligo Town is a serene and quiet place, surrounded by picture-postcard hills and set on beautiful Lough Gill. While Yeats is not quite the patron saint of this friendly little town, he is certainly the magnet that draws most of the tourists. You can take a tour by yourself or follow one of the immensely knowledgeable (and gratis) guides supplied by the Tourist Office at 11 a.m. daily in July and August. The one-hour-and-15-minute walk covers all points of historical and cultural interest. (*Note:* Consider tipping the student guides at least 50p per person in your party.) On Stephen Street stands the **Sligo County Museum,** of which part has been turned into the **Yeats Memorial Museum,** containing a large collection of the poet's manuscripts, letters, and printed editions, which is open 3 to 5 p.m. Tuesday and Friday.

For dedicated students, there is the **Yeats International Summer School,** Yeats Memorial Building, Douglas Hyde Bridge, featuring a brilliant lecture program annually two weeks in August.

While in Sligo during July and August, stop at **Dolly's Cottage** in Strandhill, the last thatched cottage in town, built in 1800 and now preserved and maintained by members of the Irish Countrywoman's Association. These good ladies display and sell their home crafts at the cottage and offer visitors a warm Irish welcome daily from 3 to 5 p.m.

As Donegal lies just north of Sligo, consider overnighting in that area. The **Sand House,** just an hour away, is our recommendation (see Chapter XII).

The Highlands of Donegal
(County Donegal)

This is the wild northwest of Ireland, a place where time seems to have stood still—but only *seems*. Donegal is *different*, not only from the rest of the country but from any other country anywhere. The highlands are big, the seascapes are spectacular, and the people few. Nature rules supreme, and there's a solitary splendor about the landscape that makes the lone whitewashed cottages among the hills almost unnoticeable. Yet there is a strange softness about the scenery, a gentle stillness as the wind sways the honeysuckle and heather, the mist rolls over the valleys, and from the edge of every lake sounds the plaintive song of the sandpipers.

Donegal town, situated at the head of Donegal Bay, is an excellent center for touring and filled with interesting attractions itself. The imposing ruin of Donegal Castle, which dates from 1505, was the stronghold of the O'Donnells and is remarkably preserved, with a fine Jacobean wing on the south and a massive gabled tower sporting two bartizan turrets. In the Diamond (where most towns have a square, Donegal has a "diamond"), notice the **Four Masters Memorial,** a 25-foot obelisk bearing the names of the Four Masters who wrote the monumental literary work *The Annals of the Four Masters* in 1632–1636. Just west of Donegal town, visit **Mountcharles,** built up a steep hill, from whose summit there are sweeping views of Donegal Bay. Stop in at **Gillespie Brothers** and **Kathleen's** for fine shopping (see Chapter XV). Visit the lonely **Lough Derg,** due east of Donegal town, where St. Patrick spent 40 days of prayer and fasting on an island and where present-day pilgrims spend three days of penance. Try to reach **Killybegs** in time to see the arrival of its fishing fleet in the fine natural harbor amid a swarm of seagulls. Take in the lovely **Glencolumbkille,** with some of the most splendid mountain and coastal scenery in this part of Ireland, and plan to stop at the remarkable folk village, where four cottages are furnished to represent different centuries of Irish life (guided tours are given hourly at no cost, and there's a craft shop with locally made products on sale). In **Ardara,** shop for handsome Donegal homespun tweeds for which the town is famous. North of Ardara, the headlands of **The Rosses** is a treasure trove of unspoiled mountains, rivers, lakes, and beaches, and at **Burtonport** it is possible to take a boat out to **Arranmore Island,** some three miles offshore, with its striking cliff scenery and marine caves. Not far away is **Cruit Island,** connected now to the mainland by a bridge and site of the holiday-cottages described in Chapter XVII.

Other Donegal highlights include the peninsula between Gweedore and Falcarragh which ends in the headland of **Bloody Foreland,** whose rocks glow blood red in the rays of the setting sun; Gweedore, where traditional Irish music springs spontaneously to life in Gallagher's Pub; Horn Head and the picturesque villages of Dunfanaghy, Port-na-Blagh and Marble Hill; the Fanad peninsular, from whose lofty cliffs there are sweeping sea views; **Rathmullan,** from whence the Flight of the Earls began in 1607 and the **Grianan of Aileach,** near Burnfoot, a perfectly preserved circular stone fort atop Greenan Mountain which dates from about 1700 B.C.

You'll find several excellent accommodation recommendations at various locations around County Donegal in Chapter XII.

The Midlands (County Cavan)

County Cavan is part of the vast plains that stretch across the middle of Ireland en route from Sligo or Donegal to Dublin. In the little town of **Butlersbridge,** just four miles north of Cavan town, you'll find one of the oldest inns in the country, the Derragarra Inn (see Chapter XIII for a description of its award-winning food service).

Stately Homes and Gardens

Whatever else may be said about the proudly aloof Anglo-Irish aristocracy, no one has ever denied their talent for gracious living. These hard-riding, hard-drinking, fox-hunting gentry built and inhabited some of the most exquisite castles and mansions on earth. A few—a mere handful—still dwell in their ancestral homes and offer you an opportunity to see a choice selection of them from the inside. The small admission fees charged help to maintain the buildings; their upkeep is staggering in these days of soaring costs. And after you've viewed a few of them you'll probably agree that it would be a virtual crime to allow these gems to crumble into ruins and eventually give way to cigar-box motels and parking lots. Some are even older than the Anglo-Irish era and go back to the royal Irish Gaelic aristocracy. A mixture of cultures, histories, and traditions lives within historic walls such as these throughout Ireland.

There is **Castletown** in County Kildare, headquarters of the Irish Georgian Society, with its curved colonnades embracing the geometrical shrubs and hedges of the garden in front; **Bunratty Castle** in County Clare, restored to its 15th-century grandeur; **Powerscourt Demesne** in County Wicklow, with a breathtaking Italian garden laid out with terraces, statues, and fountains; **Clonalis House,** County Roscommon, a Victorian mansion filled with original Irish manuscripts, state documents, and priceless books; **Knappogue Castle** in County Clare, built in 1467 and a fantastic blend of original Norman and added Georgian and Regency architecture. Then there are gardens like **Mount Usher** in County Wicklow, a planted naturalistic wonderland of rare plants and shrubs snaked through by the Vartry River.

Luckily, Ireland has produced several organizations dedicated to preserving these beauty spots against the onslaught of real-estate speculators, highway fanatics, and rocketing maintenance costs alike.

HITHA (Historic Irish Tourist Houses and Gardens Association) has brought out a free illustrated leaflet available from the Irish Tourist Board or local Tourist Offices. For further information contact Mr. Fred Martin, Secretary, HITHA, 3-A Castle St., Dalkey, County Dublin (tel. 01-859323). A leaflet description with admission charges and hours is available free from the Irish Tourist Board or local Tourist Offices. Admission charges range from £1.50 ($2.25) to £3 ($4.50).

The Open Forests

More pockets of beauty, thankfully being preserved for the people, are Ireland's **state forests.** Of the 230 sprinkled throughout the country, few are large or developed, but all are very special areas of unspoiled woodland provided with trails, picnic tables, a car park—and peace. Ask at the Tourist Office for **The Open Forest** booklet, which lists all parks administered by the Forest and Wildlife Service. Tuck it into the glove compartment, and plan a few forests into your driving itinerary for picnics, afternoon strolls, moments of blissful rest. The only charge would be an occasional small parking fee at the more sophisticated spots.

Some parks are simply roadside stops with magnificent views. Some, such as the **John F. Kennedy Park** described earlier, are worth a special trip. Another park with its own restaurant, shop, and tourist amenities is the **Lough Key Forest Park,** a gloriously planted lakeshore demesne, seven miles from Carrick-on-Shannon in County Roscommon. During summer, Shannon cruisers pull up at the picturesque harbor below the restaurant windows and bonhomie reigns.

Although each park is special, some are more special than others. Among our favorites, which we almost hesitate to share, are:

Gougane Barra, at Pass of Keimaneigh, County Cork, where a marked motor trail leads you through a great cliff-fringed, glacially formed amphitheater dominated by the peak of Maolach from which eagles once soared.

Ards Forest Park, on Sheephaven Bay, two miles north of Creeslough, County Donegal, where a white crescent beach banked with shell-scattered stones is augmented by rolling fields of grass and straight stands of pine.

Coole Demesne, 1½ miles north of Gort, County Galway, once the site of Lady Gregory's home, where W. B. Yeats and other literary luminaries gathered and carved their names for posterity on the "autograph tree." The tree, fenced against vandals, still stands and you picnic within the ivy-hung walls and among the mature foliage of the original garden.

Dooney Rock, four miles from Sligo, County Sligo. Follow a leafleted nature walk along the heavily wooded lakeside to the rock where Yeats's "Fiddler of Dooney" played.

Gortavoher, four miles from Tipperary on the Lisvernane road, County Tipperary, which offers many-angled views into the shadowed verdancy of the Glen of Aherlow.

Glendalough, one mile from Laragh, County Wicklow, possibly the most haunting spot in Ireland, with its ruined monastery, its perfect conical tower, the lake where St. Kevin bedded in an inhospitable cave.

As ever, the code of the country applies: take only photographs, leave only footprints. Ireland trusts you.

Chapter XI

LIFE IN THE CASTLES

Castle Hotels
Castle Banquets

BANQUETING IN A CASTLE is only a—literal—taste of the luxury available to you in Ireland. Here you can actually *live* in a castle as a pampered guest—stroll your private demesne, fish in your personal lake, sip cocktails in a dungeon, sleep in a canopy bed, and stand watch on the battlements for any attackers bringing 20th-century tensions, even rent your own private castle (see Chapter XVII). Take your pick from the following—

Castle Hotels

Dromoland Castle, Newmarket-on-Fergus, Co. Clare (tel. 061-71144)

To every man (or woman), his (or her) home is a castle, right? But when is a castle a *home*? When it's Dromoland Castle, *that's* when—probably because Dromoland *was* home to the royal O'Brien clan, later declared Barons of Inchiquin by King Henry VIII, from the 1570s right up to 1962, when the 16th Baron of Inchiquin sold it to an American financier who thought he was buying a summer home for himself. Instead, Bernard McDonough decided to completely rebuild and redecorate the interior as a luxury hotel—in so doing, he never lost sight of its feeling of "home" and went to great pains and expense to see that it was retained.

Today, when you enter the grounds through impressive tower gates, wind your way through a velvet-smooth golf course, then pass beneath the dignified old gray castle's turrets through massive carved doors, you may be totally unprepared for the warmth and total charm which greet you in such a baronial setting. Royal it most certainly is, but from the informal friendliness of its staff to the country coziness of its pretty guestrooms, Dromoland exudes the spirit of a luxury home-away-from-home.

From the high, dark-green walls of a wide central hall, huge gold-framed paintings of O'Briens and their royal friends gaze down on thick carpets, wonderfully comfortable armchairs arranged in intimate groupings, and a large fireplace with its welcoming wood-and-turf fire. You'll sign in with a goose-quill pen, then luxuriate behind picture windows that frame magnificent views of the exquisitely groomed 1,500-acre estate. There's a natural lake for boating, a winding river for fishing, an old-fashioned garden to explore, and wooded walks beneath ancient trees. There's an 18-hole golf course (par 71), a putting green, a tennis court, and facilities for horseback riding and duck shooting.

Indoors, the sumptuous scarlet-and-gold dining room serves up one of the best Irish breakfasts in the country as well as a continental dinner cuisine featuring the freshest in native seafoods, lamb, and beef. The small paneled bar (once the Baron's library) has entertainment most nights, and Dromoland's gift shop is outstanding in both selection and value. Bedrooms are beautifully decorated in bright colors and flowery prints, have private bath, telephones, commodious closets, and those wonderful views.

Just eight miles from Shannon Airport, Dromoland makes an ideal base for sightseeing, medieval banqueting, and touring a great deal of the west of Ireland. Singles start at £75 ($112.50), doubles at £95 ($142.50), and vary according to size and location. Rates include VAT and there's no service charge; a one-third deduction for children. Open April through October.

Ashford Castle, Cong, County Mayo (tel. 094-71444)

In 1984, Ashford added President Reagan's name to its list of illustrious guests. One reason this blue-gray fairytale fortress appeals so to the world's celebrities is that it's part pleasure palace, part military relic. The relic portion dates back to 1228, when the original Castle of Cong was built by the Anglo-Norman de Burgos family. In the 19th-century, Sir Benjamin Lee Guinness added two large extensions in the French château style. You can still see the division where the mighty old keep ends and the Victorian luxury villa begins. Yet somehow the two have fused into a wonderfully harmonious one, rising amid green lawns and cascading fountains, chimneyed, curlicued, and turreted like a transatlantic version of Oz.

Ashford stands on the northern shore of Lough Corrib, Ireland's second-largest lake, at Cong, half an hour's drive north-

west of Galway City. The reception hall greets you—figuratively
—with a fanfare blast. Suits of armor along the walls, coats-of-
arms above. The most magnificent carpeted staircase you've seen
outside a movie set leads into the higher regions. Immense oil
paintings in gilded frames gaze down upon you.

But immediately beyond this the castle gets cozier, more
intimate—more hotel-like. The guest lounge, although equipped
with a baronial oak-carved fireplace, is thickly carpeted and lazily
comfortable. Down below there's a smart little cocktail bar fitted
out as a dungeon. The building has central heating and—
amazingly—an elevator. And all around lies the most serenely
green landscape on earth, so gentle and soothing that it's hard to
believe how many battles were fought on it.

The Ashford estate has artfully ornamental gardens, tangled
woodlands, walks running along the edge of the lake, and a nine-
hole golf course overlooking the castle. Lough Corrib is renowned for its trout and salmon, and during the winter the
pheasant, snipe, and duck attract hunting parties from Europe
and overseas.

The 56 standard rooms, 20 super-deluxe rooms, and 6 suites
(all with private baths) have either lake or river views. Color
schemes and fittings are contemporary, the bathrooms carpeted
and equipped with tubs as well as showers. Bedside panels contain radio buttons and light switches. Each room has a telephone.
If anything, they're a bit *too* comfortably modern—it detracts
from the castle atmosphere. But unless you happen to be a medieval purist, you probably won't mind.

Seasonal rates begin at £60 ($90) for singles, £100 ($150) for
doubles. Full Irish breakfasts cost £8 ($12). The castle is closed
during February and March. Weekly rates are available. For information on the dining room, see Chapter XIII.

Kilkea Castle, Castledermot, County Kildare (tel. 0503-45156)

This is allegedly the oldest inhabited castle in all of Ireland, although today's occupants consist mainly of tourists with a yen for
historical romance. Rising in gray, turreted magnificence from
the surrounding gardens, Kilkea was built in 1180 as a stronghold
for the area's military governor, Hugh de Lacy. He happened to
be left-handed, and the castle was designed for the convenience
of a left-handed warrior. Thus one staircase spirals in the
"wrong" direction to enable him to swing his sword without hit-
ting the wall.

Inside, however, the grimly beautiful fortress walls enclose a
completely modernized hostelry: central heating throughout,

piped music in the public rooms, and dial telephones in every bedroom. No elevators, though, so be prepared for a bit of climbing.

"Baronial" is the only word to describe the dining room and the vaulted cellar bar. Scarlet carpets are on the floor, gleaming crystal and white linen above. Not a trace of Norman starkness remains, despite the battle-scene prints that decorate the walls. The bedrooms have the same rather startling streamlining. Carpeted wall to wall, featuring ample wardrobes and golden-brown wallpaper, intimate lighting, and excellent bathrooms, they certainly provide more comfort than any medieval baron ever dreamed of.

The room most in demand is in the top tower, built into one of the turrets. The bathroom is perfectly round—the tub in the center—with slit apertures, originally meant to shoot arrows through, now offering views in all directions to anyone soaking in the bath.

The rates are £30 ($45) for single rooms, £50 ($75) for doubles. There is a 12½% service charge and a one-third reduction for children.

Castle Banquets

Nobody who comes to Ireland should pass up a chance to banquet in a castle. *Which* castle you choose is a matter of taste, for each of the three evenings has its own personality (there's no rule, however, that restricts you to *one*). Bunratty is boisterous, Knappogue moving, Dunguaire romantic—match your mood. All are identically priced at £25.75 ($38.63), which includes your meal, entertainment, wine, service, and taxes. All can be booked through the same office: **Shannon Castle Tours,** Shannon Airport, County Clare, Ireland (tel. 061-61788). Make reservations well in advance for any of the three during summer months. Travel agents abroad and tourist offices in Ireland will handle bookings for you.

The Shannon Ceili can also be arranged through Shannon Castle Tours. But as a barn hardly qualifies as a castle, consult "Irish Nights" in Chapter XIV for details.

BUNRATTY CASTLE: Standing six miles from Limerick on the road to Shannon Airport, this 15th-century stronghold of the Earls of Thomond has achieved contemporary fame for its medieval banquets. The castle itself, rising square and massive from the banks of the Shannon River, has been restored fairly accurately as the seat of a feudal baron of four centuries ago. The banquet is an immensely entertaining blend of medieval usage and tourist trappings, with just enough feudal flavor to make it one of the highlights of your trip.

Guests are received with a cup of mulled wine presented by court damsels richly arrayed in velvet gowns. Welcoming speeches flow in Old English, then you're ushered into the "Main Guard" for dinner. The velvety lasses tuck bibs around the guests' necks, which you need because the only eating utensils supplied are knives. You use your fingers throughout, drinking soup from the bowls exactly like the original inhabitants of the castle, although presumably with less noise. The ladies entertain you with songs, music, and recitations. One of the guests is appointed temporary "Earl of Thomond" to rule over the banquet, and—in due course—confines someone to the dungeon.

The meal is served in "removes," usually consisting of broth, spareribs, capon, brown bread, salads, vegetables, and rich sweetmeats. Your cup is kept filled with mead—a very heady brew of fermented apples and honey—and the atmosphere gets livelier the more the mead mugs get emptied. Banquets are held twice nightly, at 6 and 9 p.m., all year. The inclusive cost is £25.75 ($38.63).

KNAPPOGUE CASTLE: Ten miles from Shannon Airport and 15 miles from Limerick City, this massive gray stronghold was built in 1467 to keep out the Norman conquerors. Today it is the scene of one of the most moving and impressive "entertainments" ever witnessed. Poetic pageant with music would be a better term, but even that does not quite convey the dramatic impact of the show. The magnificent drawing room that forms its background, the lighting, the dialogue, the varying strains of love ballads, folk tunes, and immensely stirring battle songs that link together the spoken words, all blend into an experience that will haunt you long after you've left the castle walls.

First, however, comes the banquet—modified medieval, insofar as each guest gets his or her own drinking cup instead of using a communal beaker, as was common practice even among the feudal lords of the Dark Ages. The menu is written in the old usage, so let us tell you that "samoun fumme" means smoked salmon and that the other courses consist of chekyn supreme, a hearty soup, dessert, and a grand selection of cheeses.

The entertainment that follows is really a cavalcade of Irish history—triumphs, tragedies, passion, hatred, loyalty, and treason, and, above all, songs. We defy anyone to listen unmoved to

Dunguaire Castle

The smallest of Ireland's "banquet castles" and, in our opinion, the most charming is a gray square-towered stone gem set in the Atlantic coast at the village of Kinvara, 17 miles south of Galway. The present structure dates from about 1520, and changed owners time and again as first one warring faction, then another, took it by siege or by storm. But in 1924 it fell—peacefully—into the hands of poet, author, and wit Oliver St. John Gogarty. And you might say that his urbanely polished ghost haunts the entertainment you'll enjoy here today.

It's a unique combination of medieval banquet and literary presentation—but the "literary" portion is as delightfully frothy and tart as vintage champagne. Foods first: Every guest is greeted with claret. The meal that follows consists of lobster cream soup, smoked salmon, "chekyn supreme," wheaten bread, salad greens, and candied cream. Having thus been "duly sweetened," you sit back and enjoy the fun.

The costumed waiters and waitresses turn into highly polished performers. And they present a witty, sentimental, gently ribald, and sometimes amazingly irreverent medley of Irish legendry, poetry, song, and literature, linked together by running dialogue and mutual banter. You'll hear snatches of W. B. Yeats, Sean O'Casey, J. M. Synge, and—of course—St. John Gogarty, laced with anecdotes about them and their contemporaries. Just enough to whet your appetite for more. Also the kind of Irish folk poems you *don't* usually hear as a tourist. So forget about the "literary" part of the title. It's great, sometimes superlative entertainment, delivered with wonderfully contagious verve and gusto.

Banquets are held twice nightly, at 6 and 9 p.m., from May 15 to September 30. The inclusive charge is £25.75 ($38.63).

the ballad of the 1916 Easter Rising: "No pipes did hum nor battle drum did sound its dread tattoo, But the Angelus bell o'er the Liffey swell rang out in the foggy dew. . . ."

The banquet/pageant takes place twice nightly, at 6 and 9 p.m., from May 1 to October 31. The inclusive price is £25.75 ($38.63).

Chapter XII

HOTELS OUTSIDE DUBLIN

Fine Havens of Hospitality

THIS IS A SECTION to read and savor. It is a careful collection of what may be the most interesting and delightful hostelries in Ireland, each one a true find in its category. Not that every fine place in Ireland has found its way into these pages—there simply aren't enough pages available for that. It's just that each place picked has something special to offer, something of atmosphere or quality that—whatever your taste—will contribute to your tour and confirm that much-vaunted Irish hospitality.

Some of the following are spots to stop over when viewing a particular sight, others for claiming as your Irish base. Note that all price ranges pertain to 1987: off-season will be lower, all 1988 prices will be higher. Many country hotels close down completely during winter.

Hotels are listed in this section, not by price, but by county, to help you plan your itinerary by the sights you want to see. Counties are listed alphabetically.

County Cork

Arbutus Lodge, Montenotte, Cork, County Cork (tel. 021-501237)

This elegant 1802 townhouse overlooking Cork City is surrounded by gardens, features a surprising and excellent collection of the works of modern Irish artists, and holds only 20 guest rooms, each of which is beautifully and individually decorated and furnished. Owner/Manager Declan Ryan personally oversees the comfort of his guests, and a stay at Arbutus is much like a visit in a private home. Guest rooms overlook either the garden or the city (the cityscape is stunning!). Rates, which include breakfast, are £35 ($52.50) per person, single or double.

IRELAND: PROVINCES
AND COUNTIES

Based on the Ordnance Survey by permission of the Government of Ireland (Permit No. 2107)

Ard-na-Greine, Schull, County Cork, (tel. 028-28181)

One of the most delightful places in West Cork, Ard-na-Greine is guaranteed to furnish accommodations that will pamper you, sending you on your way rested and refreshed, both in body and spirit. Its name means "Height of the Sun," and that seems quite appropriate when you drive about a mile west of Schull and find it perched on a broad, high hill where it catches every ray of sunshine all day long. The 200-year-old, modernized inn is owned and run by Frank and Rhona O'Sullivan with an eye to maximum comfort in surroundings that blend antiquity with sophistication. The 14 rooms are reached via hallways painted a soft rose hue and all can vie with many deluxe hotels in furnishings (including facilities for making tea or coffee). There's a Resident's Bar with a stone fireplace, whitewashed walls and beamed ceiling, and the flagstone-floored Grouse Bar, which is open to the public. Nonresidents can—and do, in droves—also have dinner in the lovely dining room, with its beamed ceiling and a fireplace at either end. Meals, cooked by Rhona, are so good they've won listings in the best food guides. Everything is fresh, and while seafood is featured, a delicate smoked turkey or chicken entrée runs a close second. The wine cellar is truly exceptional. It's a bit out of the way to include in our "Restaurants Outside Dublin" chapter, but the food here is a definite plus for the overnight guest. Rates for bed-and-breakfast start at £25 ($37.50) single, £22 ($33) per person sharing, and that gorgeous dinner is £16 ($24). If you manage to arrive here on a weekend during the low season, there's an all-inclusive weekend rate of about £65 ($97.50) from Friday dinner to Sunday lunch.

Ballymaloe House, Shanagarry (Midleton), County Cork (tel. 021-652531)

A curious, bewildering, and totally enchanting cross between a 14th-century castle and a country estate, with some of the finest cuisine in Ireland thrown in for good measure. Ballymaloe lies in the middle of a 400-acre farm (grazing sheep keep the lawns cropped), 20 miles east of Cork City on the Ballycotton road (two miles outside Cloyne). It takes a bit of finding, but, believe us, it's worth the effort.

The house itself has 30 rooms, all with private bath or shower. But the real highlight is the double bedroom inside the 16th-century gatehouse, which you should consider only if you can tackle a steep wooden stairway leading from the bathroom below to the bedchamber above.

Most of the rooms are not numbered but "colored"—the White Room, Gray Room, Blue Room, etc., named after their decor. Interiors vary from room to room, no two of them alike. Individual styling is the keynote of the place; Mrs. Myrtle Allen, your hostess, won't tolerate a lamp that doesn't blend with the character of the house, with the result that some of the lighting fixtures are more decorative than illuminating.

The downstairs dining room is a charmer with huge Georgian windows overlooking the unspoiled rural countryside sprinkled with ambling sheep. The food served is based on the produce of the district (see Chapter XIII); the jams and honey make for memorable breakfasts. There are direct-dial telephones in every room and a library for guests.

Rates average £29 ($43.50) per person for bed and continental breakfast. A full Irish breakfast costs £5 ($7.50). Add 10% for service charge.

Longueville House, Longueville, Mallow, County Cork (tel. 022-27176)

Three miles west of Mallow on the main Rosslare–Killarney road, the lovely Georgian mansion of Longueville overlooks 500 peaceful wooded acres and the Blackwater River in the valley below. Built in 1720 by the Longfields, who acquired the property from Cromwell, the house consists of a three-story main block flanked by a couple of two-story wings. A charmingly ornate, curved white ironwork conservatory added in 1866 provides extra dining space in summer.

All 20 bedrooms have private bath. These are mainly on the second floor—spacious rooms, nicely papered, with elegant furnishings including heavy square writing tables and comfortable seating areas. Baths have showers, tubs, and shaver points. The large windows looking toward the front frame views of the river, the ruins of the 16th-century Dromaneen Castle on the steep escarpment opposite, and rows of oak trees planted in the formation of the English and French battle lines at Waterloo.

The present owners of Longueville are Michael and Jane O'Callaghan. Michael's father, who served 30 years in the Irish Senate until his death a few years ago, purchased the property in 1938—and thereby hangs a unique Irish tale. For the man who originally forfeited these lands to Cromwell after the collapse of the 1641 Rebellion was Donough O'Callaghan, a direct ancestor. Which is why, as Michael puts it: "In most Big Houses in Ireland you won't see portraits of Irish patriots hanging. You do here."

You certainly do. In the handsome entrance hall floored with Portland stone ("mined by Irish Fenian prisoners"), the portraits of the O'Callaghans Senior gaze out from under the light of a golden eagle lamp. Off the hallway is one of the loveliest lounges of any house in Ireland—soft gold, with plush armchairs in a semicircle around the carved wood fireplace and a beautifully stuccoed ceiling. Parnell has a place of honor there. Politics doesn't enter the wine-red Victorian lounge bar, except verbally, but the dining room, described in Chapter XIII, is called the President's Room and features portraits of all presidents to serve since the Republic was declared.

Staying at Longueville gives you access to free golf three miles away, fishing on the estate and along the Blackwater, hunting in season, horses from a nearby farm, billiards, TV, and reading in the well-stocked library. Children are not encouraged. Longueville is an adult retreat.

Rates are £30 ($45) to £60 ($90) per person, with private bath and breakfast. Weekly rates are available. The estate is open from Easter to late October.

Assolas Country House, Kanturk, County Cork (tel. 029-50015)

You're only about an hour's drive (through scenic and historic countryside) from Killarney to the west and Cork to the east when you stop here. The 17th-century Queen Anne–style house is set in 100 acres of parkland, and its flower gardens have won more than one award. Towering old trees and green lawns lead down to the edge of the Blackwater River (where guests fish free). Inside the wide front doors, there are spacious public rooms with a traditional country-house decor and open fires and a large rumpus room with stone fireplace, and the 10 upstairs guest rooms come in a variety of sizes and shapes, all done up in country fabrics and colors. There's a comfortable, relaxed air about the place that is the direct result of Eleanor and Hugh Bourke's gracious hospitality. Dining is superb (the restaurant is recognized internationally—see below), and in addition to fishing, guests have access to tennis, boating, and croquet. Rates for bed-and-breakfast range from £23 ($34.50) to £28 ($42), with a 25% reduction for children and a 10% service charge. Open from mid-April through September.

Ashbourne House Hotel, Glounthaune, County Cork (tel. 021-353319)

This lovely hotel, overlooking the River Lee and just ten minutes from Cork City (on the Waterford road), has the old-world charm of a country home, which indeed is how it began life. Surrounded by gardens which include trees and shrubs from Kew Gardens and magnolias, flame trees, eucalyptus, and camellias from around the world, Ashbourne was originally known as Harmony Lodge because of the songfests conducted daily by vast numbers of wild birds attracted to the botanical setting.

Inside, the residents' lounge and public bar are paneled in glowing walnut and feature open fires on cool days. The Fisherman's Kitchen restaurant is a light, airy garden room replete with colorful furnishings and masses of flowers. Bedrooms are brightly decorated in a country style and come with bath/shower, direct-dial telephone, television, and video. There's a heated swimming pool, sauna, two tennis courts, and nearby facilities for golf, fishing, riding, and croquet. During summer months, there's entertainment (in 1986 it was a guitarist on Wednesday night and jazz on Thursday night) in the bar or lounge.

Its location makes Ashbourne an ideal touring base for day trips from which you can return in the evenings to beautiful, relaxed accommodations in an idyllic setting. Rates begin at £32 ($48) single, £50 ($75) double; dinner is £15 ($22.50). There's a 50% reduction for children and a 10% service charge.

County Donegal

The Sand House Hotel, Rossnowlagh, County Donegal (tel. 072-61777)

Base yourself in Rossnowlagh, 30 miles north of Sligo, and you have the perfect launching point for explorations of the Yeats County to the south, the drama of the Donegal Highlands to the north. Stay at the Sand House and you are also perched over one of the most marvelous strands in Ireland.

The Sand House is a modern, first-class hotel under the dynamic management of Mary Britton and her son, Conor. Straight-lined and sand-colored, the three-story hotel rises above a faultless, two-mile crescent beach embracing the sea. All 40 spotless rooms have private bath. Many of the twin rooms and some private suites face the sea at the front of the hotel—a view worth requesting when making reservations. Back rooms look out on the nine-hole golf course and a miniature golf range.

Rooms are tastefully decorated in warm shades of beige, brown, rust, and green, with prettily fringed bedspreads. Window walls face the sea side. On the rambling main floor, all four resident lounges are carpeted in Celtic patterns and warm shades. As the Brittons' hobby is haunting auctions, antique furnishings are scattered through the hallways; shelves of bedwarmers and copper utensils are on display in the pub.

The pub, reflecting the theme of the sea with fishnets and a 19th-century steamboat wheel, is the center of much activity in the area. With its own surf club, the Sand House attracts local surfing enthusiasts as well as tourists, and the pub is often filled at night with attractive athletic types who join in lustily at the weekend ballad sings. For a quieter drink, there is an exceptionally pleasant lounge, with one wall of stained glass and beaten copper etched in Irish scenes.

The dining room at the Sand House features fresh seafood daily, as well as a selection of continental and Irish dishes. Breakfasts are hearty—especially appreciated after a morning stroll along Donegal Bay. The bay is known for its ideal surfing conditions and guests can obtain surfboards from the hotel at no extra charge. Golf is also free to guests and canoes can be rented. Pony trekking is available.

Rates range from £32 ($48) to £38 ($57) for singles, £52 ($78) to £62 ($93) double. Children receive a one-third reduction in July and August, 50% in May, June, and September. Service charge is 10%. The hotel is closed from October through Easter.

Rathmullan House, Rathmullan, County Donegal (tel. 1074-58188)

For more than 20 years, Robin and Bob Wheeler have welcomed guests to this gracious old country home, built in the early 1800s. Lovingly restored by the Wheelers after years of neglect, the house has spacious public rooms to which warmth has been added by tasteful furnishings, many of them antiques, and log or turf fires which burn brightly on cool evenings. Mindful of the need to preserve the tranquility so sought after by many of their guests, the owners have thoughtfully relegated the telly to its own separate room, so that reading, chatting, or enjoying an after-dinner drink in the drawing room or library is free from distraction. Bedrooms are available in two categories: the best rooms, large and beautifully furnished, overlook Lough Swilly or the award-winning gardens; smaller rooms (some, however, large enough to accommodate families) are plainly, but comfortably, furnished and go for lower rates. Most rooms, regardless of category, have private bath or shower. The dining room, whose cuisine features the freshest of seafood and locally grown lamb, beef, and vegetables, is a glass-enclosed pavilion that looks out onto the garden. There's a cellar bar for conviviality before or after meals. Both the cooking and the wine list excel.

Rates at this Grade A hostelry range from £20 ($30) to £35 ($52.50) per person. Daily and weekly half-board rates are available. Rathmullan House is open from Easter to early October, and accepts American Express, VISA, Diners, and Access credit cards.

Hyland Central Hotel, The Diamond, Donegal Town, County Donegal (tel. 073-21027)

Located right in the heart of Donegal town, the Hyland has been a family-run hotel since the early '40s, and over all those years has been characterized by the sort of personal care and attention every guest receives today. The 60 rooms are modern, yet homey, with color schemes of cool blues, greens, and golds combined with pristine white. Rooms are especially spacious and some overlook Donegal Bay (those are on the back of the hotel). All have private bath, color TV, and direct-dial telephone. The attractive dining room has cream walls with lots of dark wood trim, gilt-framed paintings, and large windows along one side. The Hyland has long been noted for its high standard of food and wine, and a traveler's bonus is the lunch special consisting of a hot entrée and vegetables for about £3 ($4.50). There's a mini-dinner menu at £8 ($12), and full dinners at £12 ($18). Rates run from £21 ($31.50) to £26 ($39) for singles, £32 ($48) to £40 ($60) for doubles, depending on season.

See Chapter XVII for details of Donegal holiday accommodations on Cruit Island.

County Galway

Cashel House Hotel, Cashel Bay, County Galway (tel. 094-21252 or 31001)

The first thing you usually hear about this establishment is that General and Madame de Gaulle stayed there during their Irish visit in 1969. Since they were a most exacting pair of visitors, you can expect a high standard of hospitality at this gracious old home at the head of Cashel Bay, 97 miles from Shannon Airport. It is, in fact, one of the loveliest buildings in Connemara.

The house, with 30 bedrooms, is stylish rather than showy. But there's an air of self-assured quality about the unfrilled residents' lounge with its antique furniture and the extended dining room with the beautiful garden view. The guest rooms have a Victorian flavor; all have a large recess for clothing, light wall-to-wall carpets, and private baths. Some of the bathrooms are large enough to put a couple of extra beds in. The towel racks are heated, the tubs spacious. Although the entire house is centrally heated, traditional crackling peat fires lend the right atmosphere to the lounges.

Cashel's owners, Dermot and Kay McEvilly, will arrange for salmon and trout fishing, horseback riding, and picnic itineraries. There are acres of heather-clad mountains, fish-swarming streams, and little lakes here—and a well-known dinery (see Chapter XIII).

Bed-and-breakfast costs £28 ($42) to £32 ($48), depending on the season. Service charge is 12½%.

Sweeneys Oughterard House Hotel, Oughterard, County Galway (tel. 091-82207 or 82142)

The enchanting little village of Oughterard lies in the region of Connemara, one of the most unforgettably beautiful areas in Ireland. It's only 74 miles north of Shannon Airport, but seems half a world away. Oughterard House blends into the village: a white, blue-roofed, ivy-covered country mansion, nestling in 14 green acres, built nearly 200 years ago. The place still seems more like a country home than a hotel, and that's the way the Higginses—who own it—want it. The four floppy house dogs adopt each guest at the moment of arrival. Two will take you walking, two go shooting, and their roles are not interchangeable.

The guest lounge is a *family* room, the dining room—with beamed ceiling, gleaming parquet floor, and carved wooden tables—cozy enough to belong in a weekend cottage. The house has an extension, and the 33 bedrooms vary according to which wing they're in. The furnishings are fairly simple, but absolutely comfortable, with wall-to-wall carpets, central heating, and telephones above the beds. The bathrooms have ventilators that come on the moment you work the fluorescent light, also wonderfully large mirrors along one entire wall.

The downstairs bar is surprisingly large and streamlined, the decor a restful nut brown, the windows overlooking flowers, shrubs, and velvety lawns. Just across the road, the Owneriff River whirls crazily through a steep, rocky gorge—leaping with salmon when they ascend the falls. A nine-hole golf course is close by.

Rooms with private bath start at £32 ($48).

Rock Glen Country House, Clifden, Connemara, County Galway (tel. 095-21035)

This former shooting lodge is beautifully situated about 1½

miles out the Roundstone/Ballyconneely road from Clifden. Its low, rambling profile belies the spaciousness inside, where a large, lovely drawing room sets a gracious and informal tone. There's also a cozy bar and a dining room that features excellent meals prepared by the friendly owner/manager, John Roche. All 31 bedrooms have private baths, and 15 of them are on the ground floor (a boon to the handicapped and those of us who tote around tons of luggage!). Rates, which include a hearty Irish breakfast, range from £26 ($39) to £28 ($42) per person, with a one-third reduction for children and a 12½% service charge.

Rosleague Manor Country House, Letterfrack, County Galway (tel. 095/41101)

Right in the middle of the ruggedly beautiful Connemara region, Rosleague Manor Country House overlooks Ballinakill Bay. The fine old Georgian mansion has the high ceilings, tall windows, and spacious rooms typical of this style, and its furnishings include many fine period pieces and works of art. Open turf fires complement the central heating. Anne and Patrick Foyle are the friendly owners, who run the small hotel with special regard for guests' comfort and enjoyment of the area, giving it a distinctly "family" flavor. Bedrooms all have private baths and are nicely decorated and furnished. Rates range from £22 ($33) to £28 ($42) per person, with a 20% reduction for children, plus a 10% service charge. Open from Easter through October.

Curravagh House, Oughterard, County Galway (tel. 091-82313)

Guests often feel as if they're visiting in a private home, as indeed they are, for this is the family home of the present owner, Harry Hodgson, who manages the small inn with his lovely wife, June. The mid-19th-century country house sits in 150 wooded acres on the shores of Lough Corrib, and the Hodgsons provide boats and ghillies (guides), if you wish, for some of the best trout fishing in the country. There's a tennis court on the grounds, golf and horseback riding close by. Furnishings and decor carry out the relaxed informality of the place, and spacious guest rooms look out to splendid views. Rates, including breakfast, are £22 ($39) per person, plus a 10% service charge. A marvelous country dinner will run about £13.75 ($20.63). Open Easter to early October.

County Kerry

Hotel Dunloe Castle, Killarney, County Kerry (tel. 064-44111)

This is no castle—or even a faint replica of one—but a beautiful modern hotel. The white-walled exterior, red awnings, and palm trees give it an exotic Mediterranean appearance, forming an intriguing contrast to the neo-medieval public rooms inside. The Dunloe Castle has more sumptuous trappings, including a sauna and a stone-tiled, magnificently carpeted lobby.

The 150 bedrooms, each with private bath and direct-dial telephone, radio, and color TV, look out on the award-winning gardens belonging to the hotel. The gourmet restaurant, serving French, German, and Irish choices, has a terrace surrounded by subtropical plants. There's a huge ballroom that features nightly summer entertainment, a riding stable, tennis courts, and an indoor swimming pool. The hotel even bakes its own bread and serves it up oven fresh. While somewhat lacking in local color, the Dunloe is everything a luxury resort spot should be and—like most such establishments—aims at offering guests complete holiday recreation without ever having to step beyond its grounds, which include a putting green, driving range—and the most cosmopolitan clientele in Killarney.

Singles go for £35 ($52.50) to £48 ($72); doubles range from £57 ($85.50) to £77 ($112.50); the higher price in each category is for rooms with a view of the world-famous Dunloe Gap. Rates include service charges and Irish breakfasts.

Great Southern Hotel, Killarney, County Kerry (tel. 064-31611)

Great is the only suitable term for this grande dame among Irish country hostelries. Actually, it's two hotels in one. The old portion, built in 1854, is the epitome of curlicued Victorian splendor and spaciousness. The new wing, added in the 1960s, is streamlined and up to the minute, including an oval indoor swimming pool with two saunas tucked beneath. Pick your period.

Located directly opposite the railroad station (it's named after one of the great Irish rail companies), the Great Southern has a reception lobby as large as a terminal, ornately pillared, with plush niches and intimate salons adjoining. There are two bars, a riding school on the hotel grounds (with resident instructor), and a ballroom. The dining room, viewing the expanses of velvety lawns outside the window, seats 200 guests beneath glittering chandeliers.

Among the hotel's special attractions is the hall steward,

Denis, a veteran of more than 30 years' service who reputedly never forgets a guest's face. After a stay of one day you may reappear a decade later, only to be greeted by name by Denis as if you had departed the evening before.

From mid-May to mid-October, the hotel presents "When Irish Eyes Are Smiling," an evening of Irish dancing, music, and song beginning at 9 p.m.

The hotel's 180 rooms, all with bath, telephone, central heating, and hand showers, range from vintage (but very comfortable) Victoriana to brand-spanking modern.

The bathrooms have heated towel racks, and radios and lights are worked from bedside control panels, and some boast the very latest one-piece telephones. Small balconies overlook the garden, and the decor—regardless of the room's period—comes in expertly matched and soothing color shades.

Singles begin at £38 ($57), doubles at £53 ($79.50). Service charge is 12½%.

Hotel Ard-na-Sidhe, Caragh Lake, Killorglin, County Kerry (tel. 066-69105)

You won't believe it when you see this grand red sandstone Victorian mansion, but it was built more than a century-and-a-half ago by one Lady O'Connell as a *private guesthouse*! And the Lady certainly knew how to accommodate guests, a tradition which has not eroded over the years that have seen the magnificent structure perched above the shores of Caragh Lake evolve into a *professional* guesthouse that combines traditional elegance with all the amenities of a modern luxury hotel.

It should be pointed out that the hotel's location is a bit isolated, and I can only echo what the management itself tries to impress on prospective guests: Ard-na-Sidhe (which means "height of the fairies") is strictly for those who enjoy a *quiet* holiday—wooded walks, fishing (boats and guides are available), and reading or other such pursuits are the main activities here. Personally, I can't think of a more beautiful spot for a retreat with loved ones—or better yet, for a honeymoon! However, I should also add that Killarney is only 17 miles away for those whose tastes are a bit more lively. Also, golf links are only three miles away, and the sporting facilities of Hotel Dunloe Castle and Hotel Europe (under the same ownership) are free to all guests here.

Spacious public rooms are decorated in soft tones of blues and browns and beige, furnished with antiques and feature open fireplaces. The dining room is an intimate and restful setting for fine dining.

As for the bedrooms, they're a far cry from your standard hotel room—no two are the same size or shape; there are some without bath; and views are either of the lake or the beautifully landscaped gardens. A short distance from the main house, there's a modern block where rooms and suites are more uniform and of a different character than in the older building.

Per-room rates range from £21 ($31.50) for a single room without bath to £38 ($57) for a single with bath (garden view; lake view costs more) to £35 ($52.50) for a double without bath to £50 ($75) for a double with garden view. Rates include a full Irish breakfast, all taxes and service charges. Open May to September.

Dun an Oir Hotel, Ballyferriter, Dingle Peninsula, County Kerry (tel. 066-56133)

Right at the tip of the Dingle Peninsula between the villages of Ballyferriter and Ferriters Cove and nestled into some of Ireland's most dramatic scenery, a cluster of sparkling white cottages surrounds this equally sparkling hotel. All blend into the landscape, looking for all the world like another of the charming fishing villages which populate this unique part of the country.

Surprisingly, the Dun an Oir offers all the amenities of a modern luxury hotel without intruding on either the native environment or culture. And whether you come, complete with family, to settle happily into one of the cottages (see Chapter XVII) or opt to stay in the hotel itself, you'll soon feel very much a part of this Gaeltacht (Irish-speaking) district, even if you find it utterly impossible to get your tongue around the musical, but difficult language. That this is so is due largely to personable manager Matt Britton, who welcomes locals in the hotel's bar, lounge, and restaurant. In this isolated location, Dingle's residents flock to such a center of friendly conviviality. "Our guests love to hear the language spoken around them," Matt says, "and you'd be surprised how many are ordering drinks or meals in Irish by the time they leave."

In addition to their soft language, however, the natives bring along their music, and although the hotel provides traditional music and entertainment, it's not at all unusual to see a fiddle or tin whistle appear in the hands of someone just in to while away the evening. That makes for the kind of spontaneous good times that outshine any you might plan, and the stuffiest shirt is likely to find itself lustily joining in a singsong of old Irish ballads. One of Dun an Oir's superb seafood dinners (need I say everything is fresh?) and an evening in such company is the perfect ending for a day of rambling through the unbelievable beauty nature has concentrated on the peninsula.

The hotel's public areas are warm and attractively decorated with native motifs, and guest rooms all have private baths, telephones, TV, and windows looking out to that gorgeous scenery. There's a 9-hole golf course, heated swimming pool, and hardsurface tennis court on the premises, as well as a lovely sandy beach in front of the hotel. Rates begin at £24 ($36) single, £38 ($57) double; children under 10 stay free in parents' rooms; and there's a 12½% service charge. Open May through September.

County Leitrim

Drumlease Glebe House, Bromahair, County Leitrim (tel. 071-64141)

Only about 12 miles outside Sligo Town, Drumlease Glebe House is situated near the River Bonet amid green lawns and wooded grounds. The Georgian house, presided over by an American couple, Barbara and Andrew Greenstein, has all the elegance of a bygone era, but adds a rather surprising modern touch—a 40-foot outdoor swimming pool. Fishing on Lough Melvin can be on your own, or in the care of ghillies (guides) provided by the Greensteins, who also supply boats and tackle. Although the house has central heating, cheerful log fires create another kind of warmth, and you'll find this a truly relaxing atmosphere. Guest rooms are beautifully appointed, and dinners are by candlelight, accompanied by good wines and ended with a selection of Irish cheeses. Rates for bed-and-breakfast start at £25 ($37.50), with a 12½% service charge. No children under 16. Open mid-March to mid-October.

County Limerick

Dunraven Arms Hotel, Adare, County Limerick (tel. 061-94209)

On the edge of what has been called Ireland's prettiest village, Dunraven Arms Hotel is a two-story, traditional-style, goldcolored hotel that has the look of an old-time inn. Indeed, that small inn–type hospitality greets you at the door and never diminishes throughout your stay. There's the pleasant glow of being a welcomed guest in a comfortable, country-style hostelry where friendliness and courtesy are outstanding. The spacious lounge bar overlooks pretty gardens and offers excellent bar lunches at inexpensive rates, and the dining room features French cuisine, using fresh ingredients from local farms. Comfortable, traditional furnishings add a homey touch. Both public rooms and guest rooms are attractively done up in country prints, and all guest rooms have private baths and telephones. This is where Princess Grace and Prince Rainier stayed during their 1963 visit. Not only is this a great sightseeing base—only 10 miles from Limerick, 16 from Bunratty Castle, 25 from Shannon Airport, 61 from Killarney, and 60 from Cork—but fishing, horseback riding, and golf are close at hand. Rates, which include breakfast, start at £32 ($48) single, £46 ($69) double. There's a 50% discount for children and a 12½% service charge.

County Louth

Ballymascanlon House Hotel, Dundalk, County Louth (tel. 042-71124)
Set in 130 wooded acres and surrounded by green lawns, Ballymascanlon House has twice won awards for its lovely gardens. The peaked-gabled old country mansion has high ceilings and spacious rooms in the original house, and there's a modern extension with more standardized guest rooms. A sports center that includes a heated indoor swimming pool, sauna, solarium, gym, children's playground, and squash and tennis courts makes it an all-round, self-contained resort, with golf and the seaside nearby. All 36 guest rooms have telephones and private baths and are attractively decorated. Its location just about at midpoint on the main Dublin/Belfast road makes this a convenient stopping point. Seasonal rates range from £26 ($39) to £28 ($42).

County Mayo

Breaffy House Hotel, Castlebar, County Mayo (tel. 094-22033)
Two miles from Castlebar on the main road to Claremorris and Dublin stands the absolutely beautiful gray stone building, looking like a cross between a stately country home and an exceptionally jolly cloister. Surrounded by 60 acres of parkland, blue-roofed and gabled, Breaffy House is so completely in character with the Mayo landscape that it seems to have grown naturally out of the soil.

There's a nine-hole pitch-and-putt course on the lawn just outside, tree-lined walks in the grounds, lake fishing, pony trekking, and shooting (in season) in the immediate vicinity. The establishment is run with an even mixture of charm and efficiency. Special touches are particularly noticeable in the 43 bedrooms, which have precisely those little extra points designed to comfort weary wayfarers—like tea- and coffee-making facilities; little mending kits to sew on that missing button; hot-water bottles; enough hooks to hang dressing gowns, bathrobes, negligees, and what-have-you so they're within reach when you need them; and excellent lighting, fluorescent over the beds and writing desks where you need illumination. The rooms are elegantly modern without being motel uniform—wood paneled, with soft carpets, pastel-colored decor, and views of the lawns outside. All have private bathrooms, small and compact, with instantaneous hot water.

Two lounges are downstairs, one equipped with a television set, big armchairs, and fireplace; and two bars fitted in different period styles: one tobacco hued and cocktailish; the other Tudor, with hanging lanterns, wooden rafters, pewter dishes, and a Falstaffian air.

The rates here include breakfast—and wait till you see it! Grilled kippers, black pudding, sausages or bacon, home-baked brown bread, and outstanding coffee. Plus genuine *doughnuts* to dunk into it. And you probably won't need another meal till dinner. For other dining details, consult Chapter XIII.

Bed-and-breakfast costs £23 ($34.50) per person sharing, with a supplement for singles of £4.70 ($7.05). There's no service charge, and a one-third reduction for children sharing their parents' room.

County Monaghan

Nuremore Hotel, Carnickmacross, County Monaghan (tel. 042-61438)

The family-owned and -operated Nuremore Hotel is only about 50 miles from Dublin, and its 100 acres of surrounding woodlands, green lawns, gardens, and smooth golf course provide a restful country setting for sightseeing in either the Midlands or the Eastern Regions. There's also an indoor heated swimming pool, a spa pool, snooker room, sauna, and squash court, as well as good fishing in the hotel's own lakes. The thoroughly modern guest rooms all have private bath, TV, video, and telephone, and there's an excellent restaurant. Rates, which include breakfast, range from £30 ($45) to £34 ($51) for single, £47 ($70.50) to £52 ($78) double, with a 25% reduction for children.

County Tipperary

Dundrum House Hotel, Dundrum, Cashel, County Tipperary (tel. 062-71116 and 71409)

When sightseeing takes you to Cashel and its famous Rock, you couldn't do better than to book into the Dundrum House Hotel. This magnificent Georgian mansion dates from the 18th century and sits on over 100 acres of scenic countryside. There are some 30 handsome guest rooms, and Mary and Austin Crowe are proud of the fact that they have installed an elevator to upper floors and otherwise cater to handicapped or disabled travelers. All guest rooms have private baths and telephones. There's also an excellent dining room with superb cuisine and a good wine list. Rates, including breakfast, are £24.50 ($36.75) to £28.50 ($42.75) single, £39 ($58.50) to £49 ($73.50) double, with a one-third reduction for children and a 10% service charge.

County Waterford

Granville Hotel, The Quay, Waterford, County Waterford (tel. 051-55111)

The Granville has figured in Waterford's history since it was built during the reign of George III as a gracious residence for the Quan family. A daughter of that family gave birth to Thomas Francis Meagher in 1823 in this house. He grew up to become a close friend of Daniel O'Connell; be sentenced to death for his part in the Young Ireland rising of 1848; be banished by transportation for life when the death sentence was commuted; escape to America in 1852; form the famous "Fighting 69th" Irish Brigade during America's Civil War; and become Acting Governor of Montana. During its years as Commins' Hotel, Parnell always stayed here when in Waterford and delivered one of his last speeches from the hotel windows.

In 1980, Ann and Liam Cusack bought the old hotel and set about transforming it into the Grade A hostelry that today attracts visitors drawn by its luxury accommodations, gracious decor, and central location, as well as its friendly and efficient staff. Public rooms reflect the gleam of polished wood, warm red carpets, and crystal chandeliers. The bar is a favorite Waterford meeting place and lunch spot; the Bianconi Room offers an extensive menu; and the Tapestry Room serves up elegance with fine cuisine. As for guest rooms, they're all attractively decorated, and all have bath/shower, direct-dial telephone, color TV, and radio. Family rooms even include baby-listening devices.

Rates begin at £30 ($45) single, £58 ($87) double. All service charges and VAT are included; special weekend rates available.

Tower Hotel, The Mall, Waterford, County Waterford (tel. 051-75801)

The Tower (just across from the 11th-century Reginald's Tower) has been a mainstay of Waterford hotels for years. Recent renovations, however, have made it even more desirable as a Waterford base. It combines the best of the old (Waterford glass chandeliers in the lobby and dining room) with the best of modern conveniences, and all in a convenient location for shopping and sightseeing, with more-than-adequate parking facilities (an important factor in Waterford!).

The bar has dark-green upholstery and carpeting, lots of mahogany, opaque globe lighting, and inviting "snug" seating areas. The dining room is done in shades of pink, and the Grill Room offers a moderately priced menu and comfortable fittings. Guest rooms are brightly decorated and comfortably furnished. All this goes into a mix that makes this one of the city's most popular places to stay. It is a particular favorite of tour groups, and yet you're just as likely to find a local wedding party (as I did recently) as busloads of visiting tourists.

Rates range from £26 ($39) to £28 ($42) single, £40 ($60) to £44 ($66) double, depending on the season.

Dooley's Hotel, The Quay, Waterford, County Waterford (tel. 051-73531)

It says something nice about Dooley's that the grandniece of the original Dooley family owners still books into this descendant of a leading 19th-century coaching inn to enjoy its homelike atmosphere. For the past 42 years the hotel has been owned and operated by Mrs. June Darrer and her family, and longevity pervades the staff: Chris Cleary, Manageress, confesses to being a "newcomer" after some 16 years of service, and Co-Manageress Lucy Collins has spent the last 24 years at Dooley's. The owner's aunt, Mrs. Halpin, is Executive Housekeeper and keeps a keen personal eye on all the little details that distinguish a really good hotel from those which fall into mediocrity. In short, Dooley's is that rare combination of comfort, efficiency, and friendliness.

The lobby and lounge bar welcome you into a setting of deep, rich reds and greens, stained-glass hanging lamps, oil paintings, prints, and leather circular booths. There's a pub grub available in the pretty lounge, low-cost Tourist Menu meals in the restaurant from May to October (for which they won the 1983 Bord Failte Award for special value), and full à la carte and table d'hôte offerings at both lunch and dinner year round. Both lounge and restaurant are favorites with Waterford residents.

Upstairs, guest rooms are reached via a network of hallways leading off in all directions. In the oldest section of the hotel, you may mount a step or two to enter your room, and once there you're more than likely to find it an odd shape and size, with all the character of bygone days. Some are small and cozy, others large and full of interesting nooks and crannies. Furnishings in all are attractive and comfortable, and even those rooms in the newer wing have traditional furniture and Donegal tweed spreads in keeping with the place. Most have private baths, and all have radio, color TV, and telephone.

Rates start at £27.50 ($41.25) single, £37.40 ($56.10) double, and vary according to size, location, and season. There's a 10% service charge; children under 10 stay free in their parents' room.

Ballyrafter House, Lismore, County Waterford (tel. 058-54002)

Situated on top of a hill that overlooks some spectacular scenery, Ballyrafter House is a hotel in the country-house tradition. Its graciousness is reflected in the spacious entry hall with its antiques, the wood-paneled lounge where comfortable sofas and padded booths invite relaxed conversation over drinks from the attractive bar, and especially in the lovely dining room with its antique furnishings, sparkling linens, and charming bay window overlooking the garden. As for the views, there are the gardens, woodlands, and wide open spaces (thoroughbred horses graze on the sloping pastureland out front) right in the hotel's own grounds. But lift your eyes a bit and you'll see Lismore Castle, seat of the Duke of Devonshire and one of the loveliest castles in Ireland. It's one of the few that has been in continuous use as a residence since its construction by King John in 1185—Sir Walter Raleigh owned it at one time, but the Devonshire dukes have been here since 1763. The charming town of Lismore is a half mile away, across a pretty stone bridge over the Blackwater River. And a short drive takes you to the famous Vee road which crosses the Knockmealdown Mountains.

James and Nancy Willoughby run Ballyrafter House as you'd expect hosts to care for guests in their home, with concern for your comfort that is extraordinary even in Ireland, where hospitality is never "ordinary."

There are only 14 rooms, all with hot and cold water, some with private bath. Decor is simple, but attractive, and although single rooms tend to be a bit small, doubles are quite spacious. Bed-and-breakfast rates are £18 ($24) single, £33 ($49.50) double, with private bath. Dinners are quite good and cost about £12 ($18). Advance booking is advisable for all accommodations at Ballyrafter House because of its wide popularity. It's open from Easter until September 30.

County Wexford

Marlfield House, Gorey, County Wexford (tel. 055-21124 and 21572)

Surrounded by some 35 acres of wooded countryside and landscaped gardens, this stately Regency house is filled with antiques, gilt-framed mirrors, and crystal chandeliers. Log fires in the public rooms add a gracious note of warmth, and a lovely curved staircase sweeps up to elegantly decorated and furnished guest rooms. Wallpapers, draperies, and bedspreads are all coordinated, antiques are used lavishly, and all 11 rooms have private baths. Mary and Ray Bowe, the charming owners who have brought the old home back to its former glory, go out of their way to see that guests are catered to. There's an excellent restaurant (see below). Rates, which include a full Irish breakfast, are £42 ($63) to £47 ($70.50), and only children over the age of six are accepted.

Ferrycarrig Hotel, Ferrycarrig Bridge, P.O. Box 11, Wexford (tel. 053-22999)

One reviewer described the Ferrycarrig as "a modern lump of concrete," and I'd have to go along with that description except for several things that make it quite exceptional (as, indeed, that reviewer went on to do).

First of all, it is situated just across the Ferrycarrig Bridge on the Enniscorthy side of the Slaney Estuary, and although it is very close to a main thoroughfare, it is nestled right down on the riverbank, out of sight and sound of traffic, with green lawns that give it a true country setting. Then, there's that terrific view of the river and the scores of boats (sail and fishing) that ply up and down in pursuit of pleasure or profit. Not only that, but every single room faces the river with broad picture windows to take advantage of those river views. And best of all, I'd have to count personable Paddy and Mary Hatton, who run the hotel (Mary's in charge of the kitchen and dining room) with the sort of hospitality you expect in Ireland, but not in a modern hotel. Add to all those reasons for staying at the Ferrycarrig the fact that Wexford is just two miles away, and they make this an ideal touring base for the Wexford area.

Actually, an outstanding sightseeing attraction is almost at the doorstep of the hotel. A wooded river walk from the hotel grounds leads (in about three minutes) to the ruined tower perched atop a craggy cliff at the northern edge of the bridge which crosses the Slaney. Some historians claim this is all that remains of the first Anglo-Norman castle erected in Ireland, although others dispute that. No matter, it's certainly ancient (all agree it dates at least to the 15th century), and the short climb up to the tower rewards you with unbounded admiration for its builders as well as a superb overview of the Slaney rushing through a narrow gorge below. There's also a unique Wexford Heritage Park under construction on the south side of the river, although at this writing it is impossible to say when that will be completed.

As for the hotel, bedrooms are all attractively furnished, with comfortable chairs arranged to add living-room comfort. All have private bath. There's a cozy bar, and the Sandpiper Restaurant (a favorite with locals as well as guests) specializes in the freshest of local seafood, meats, and vegetables. A conservatory offers comfortable viewing of the river.

Rates for bed-and-breakfast start at £26 ($39) single, rising to a high of £40 ($60) double (high rates apply during Wexford Festival as well as July and August). Special weekend and package rates are available. Children under 10 sharing a room with parents stay free. Send a £20 ($30) deposit to confirm all bookings. Open Easter to Christmas.

County Wicklow

Woodenbridge Hotel, Vale of Avoca, Arklow, County Wicklow (tel. 0402-5146 or 5219)

Just two miles from the village of Avoca, in what is sometimes called the "Garden of Ireland," you'll find the Woodenbridge Hotel, one of the oldest inns in the country. It was built in 1608 and has been in continuous operation ever since.

The two-story wooden structure sits on a hill overlooking some of Wicklow's loveliest scenery, and its interior gives a hint, but doesn't reek, of its antiquity. The bar/lounge comes closest, perhaps, to the "olde tymes" look you might expect, but even with its stucco walls, overhead beams, huge stone fireplace, and tankards hanging over the corner bar, the effect is one of comfort and conviviality rather than carefully preserved history. Owners Jim and Bridget Hogan project that same air, moving among their guests with complete ease to be sure that every need is met. Across the hall from the lounge is the pretty, simply decorated dining room, with a long, glassed-in sun porch along one side where meals are sometimes served to take advantage of the great view out front (green rolling hills and mountains). Upstairs, the 12 bedrooms vary in size and shape, most have private baths, and all are comfortably furnished in a rather plain style. It was here, in one of the large front bedrooms, that Eamon de Valera spent his honeymoon. Step inside the Woodenbridge and you'll feel you've entered an old, assured, country residence where serenity enlivened with an Irish twinkle reigns supreme.

Close enough to the meeting of the waters, Avoca's pottery works, Glendalough, and many other attractions to offer glorious days of sightseeing, the Woodenbridge can also arrange free fishing in its own river, riding and pony trekking at nearby stables, golf on one of the most scenic courses in Ireland (just 200 yards from the hotel), and rough shooting. Evening entertainment is often scheduled in the large function room that has been added (so skillfully you'll think it's part of the original building) back of the lounge. As for meals, they're mouthwatering, from the full Irish breakfast to the high tea to dinners featuring all fresh produce and specialties like grilled rainbow trout and roast stuffed chicken with Wexford ham. Light lunches are available in the lounge, where our personal favorite is boiled Wexford bacon with a delicate parsley sauce.

High-season bed-and-breakfast rates begin at £18 ($27) single, £36 ($54) double. Those lovely dinners go for £12 ($18) including everything from starters to desserts.

Hunter's Hotel, Rathnew, County Wicklow (tel. 0404-4106)

This lovely old coaching inn is situated on the banks of the River Vartry. Its beautifully landscaped gardens have won awards, and they're the perfect place to relax in the late afternoon or early evening. In fine weather, pre-lunch and pre-dinner drinks, as well as afternoon tea, are served in these serene outdoor surroundings. The restaurant is superb (see below) and much patronized by locals and Dubliners. Mrs. Maureen Gelletlie is the fifth generation of her family to own and manage

Hunter's, and she takes great pride in seeing to the personal comfort of all guests. There are only 17 guest rooms, all charmingly decorated in country-house style, and some come with private baths. Rates (which include breakfast) are £17 ($25.50) per person, single or double, with a 25% reduction for children and a 10% service charge.

Chapter XIII

RESTAURANTS OUTSIDE DUBLIN

Fresh from the Farmlands

COUNTRY CUISINE IN IRELAND can consist of some of the finest ingredients in the world, direct from the rich farmlands, the unpolluted streams, and the sea. The following restaurants are not grouped by price—although all price levels are represented—but by counties in alphabetical order, as were the hotels, to help you locate them while on tour. Many of the restaurants mentioned here are actually the dining rooms of hotels featured in Chapter XII. You need not stay at a hotel to dine there. But in all cases in Ireland, if you wish to dine in a specific place, it is best to book several hours in advance.

One happy item you'll note, should you see the country after Dublin: the farther you get from the expense-account echelons, the lower meal prices go. And in almost every locality at least one restaurant will offer the special Food Fare, three-course meals at £4.65 ($6.98) and £6.40 ($9.60). The directory is available from the Tourist Offices.

County Cavan

The Robin Hill, Loch Gowna, County Cavan (tel. Loch Gowna 21)
In a region not noted for exemplary cuisine, this tiny, 12-seater is an exquisite find. Use it when driving through the Midlands toward Sligo and Donegal. But reserve a minimum of one day in advance. Twelve chairs take that many minutes to fill up.

Robin Hill is a former rectory, built in the 1830s and standing in a lovely garden. It is just ten yards west of the crossroads in the center of the sleepy hamlet of Lough Gowna (whose original, less inviting name—Scrabby—was changed by a bill in the Dail). Taking the main road from Dublin to Sligo, you would turn off at Edgeworthstown, drive north to Granard, and follow signposts from there. The detour totals 19 miles.

Mrs. Stephenson, the owner-manager of this combination guesthouse and restaurant, is a local lady who specializes in "Traditional and Creative Cuisine." You might have a choice of Hungarian goulash, chicken provençal, and sweet-and-sour pork. It's a grab bag, but a delightful one. There is no menu. You come into the small, homey dining room with a bay window facing the garden, and are given the night's choices. There is always a fresh starter, your choice of two homemade soups, three main courses accompanied by fresh vegetables, and such mouthwatering sweets as a waffle topped with homemade raspberry jam, ice cream, and fresh cream. Coffee is ground and brewed by the individual cup—so warn them if you want a pot. Mrs. Stephenson is very competent at all sorts of dietary requirements, especially vegetarian, and will provide special meals on request. So personal is the attention at Robin Hill that a dossier of menus enjoyed by regulars is kept on file.

Dinners are served from 7 to 9 p.m. at a price of £10.50 ($15.75). Closed Monday. Book at least one day ahead. Wine license only.

Derragarra Inn, Butlersbridge, County Cavan (tel. 049-31003 or 31205)

Four miles outside Cavan town (to the north), the Derragarra Inn sits on the banks of the River Annalee. There are no fancy dinners here, just bar food that is so exemplary it's won no fewer than *seven* national awards. John Clancy has raised the excellence of his food to meet that of its setting, one of the oldest inns in Ireland. Salad plates of chicken and ham, roast beef and other combinations (£4.50 or $6.75) come to table so beautifully arranged you know a treat is in store—and you're right. The fisherman's platter that appeared before us on a recent visit looked too good to eat, but proved to be even better than it looked, and held more food than is sometimes found on much more expensive dinner plates (£7, or $10.50, for four kinds of fish, vegetables, and french fries). Clancy has even won an award for his pub cheese snacks!

County Cork

Arbutus Lodge, Cork City, County Cork (tel. 021-501237)

Up on a midtown hill called Montenotte stands a stylish little hostelry that is both literally and figuratively the culinary high spot of Cork. There's no use describing how to get there—just ask for the Arbutus; it's a local institution.

The building looks like an aristocratic townhouse—which it once was. The dining procedure is quite elaborate. You are handed a menu at the reception desk or in the bar, order your meal, then wait in the bar overlooking the city. When your meal is ready, you're ushered into the actual dining room, which looks as private as the entire building: Georgian pillars, modern prints on the walls, large windows overlooking the city below. The atmosphere is quiet, slightly formal; the service, silent and wonderfully attentive. Here you don't just eat—you *dine*.

Recommended is the table d'hôte lunch for £12.50 ($18.75), with perhaps potage à la Crécy, then a rich and tangy mushroom omelet (the mushrooms came from a nearby forest, not a can), finishing with apple tart. The Arbutus also serves excellent coffee. If you prefer something stronger, try the Gaelic coffee (pungent with whisky, smothered in cream).

Also recommended are the chicken Hibernia (a house specialty served with nutmeggy spinach and sautéed potatoes), wild duck (with a sauce of enriched pan juices), and escalope of salmon with sorrel sauce. And don't miss their outstanding cheese board, served with walnut bread. The dinner is priced at £18.50 ($27.75), and an à la carte menu is also available. The Arbutus is open for lunch from 1 to 2 p.m., dinner from 7 to 9:30 p.m., six days a week. Closed on Sunday.

Ballymaloe House, Shanagarry, Midleton, County Cork (tel. 021-62531)

Ballymaloe House has already been described as a hotel. But its restaurant is considerably more famous and deserves a special mention.

One of the chief reasons for the restaurant's excellence is that its cuisine rests on the products of Ballymaloe farm. Chickens, geese, sheep, pigs, mushrooms, and vegetables come to the table straight from soil and pasture. Their taste makes almost anything you get in American dineries seem stale by comparison. And you can grow an awful lot of edibles on 400 lush acres. In fact, the restaurant is very nearly self-sufficient. In addition, Ballymaloe's

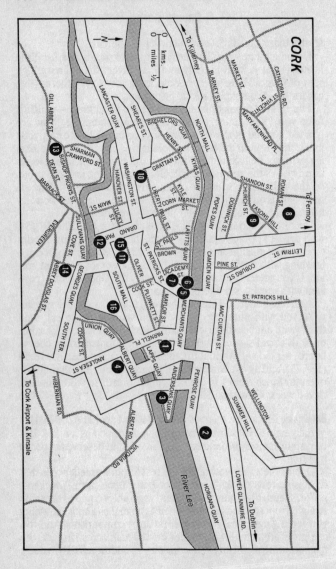

gourmet cooking school is internationally known for training chefs in the art of fine cooking.

KEY TO NUMBERED REFERENCES: 1—Bus Station; 2—Kent Train Station; 3—Custom House; 4—City Hall; 5—Fr. Matthew Statue; 6—Opera House; 7—Art Gallery; 8—Shandon Church; 9—St. Mary's Cathedral; 10—Courthouse; 11—Irish Tourist Office; 12—National Monument; 13—St. Finbarr's Cathedral; 14—Red Abbey Tower; 15—Iverria Theatre; 16—Everyman Playhouse.

The nightly menu is quite small, but quality looms immense. The simplest dishes have the flavor you'd never expect to find outside the little auberges of rural France, and for much the same reason: home-grown ingredients and the culinary craftsmanship of the cook, in this case Mrs. Allen. There's no predicting what exactly will be on the evening you dine there. But we know that every meal offers a choice of three soups, three or four fish dishes, six main courses, and at least four desserts. We can only hope that Mrs. Allen's superb pâté is on the menu. Followed, perhaps, by watercress soup, the escalopes of stuffed baby beef, and the savarin au rhum. The meal comes to £18.25 ($27.38); lunch is less. There's a 10% service charge.

Dinner is served from 7 to 9:30 p.m.

The Vintage, Main Street, Kinsale, County Cork (tel. 021-772502)

The Vintage is a small restaurant, very cozy, very romantic, and totally delicious. There is an open fire in the dining room, which is decorated with two-hundred-year-old beams and the original masts from sailing ships that came into Kinsale. Every evening, in a kitchen that is minuscule by restaurant standards, master chef Michael Riese, who was formerly head chef at the Four Seasons Hotel in his native Hamburg, conjures up a menu remarkable for its freshness of ingredients and approach. As much as possible Michael uses local foodstuffs—organically grown vegetables, free-range goose, duckling, and rabbits, eggs from free-range chickens, and seafood caught just offshore. His Kinsale hot smoked salmon steak and his sole Véronique (filets sauced with white wine, cream, and grapes) are superb. There's an excellent wine list and the Vintage is a member of the Kinsale Good Food Circle. Main courses average about £11 ($16.50).

Hours are 7 to 10:30 p.m., closed Sundays except holiday weekends. All credit cards are honored.

Moran's Oyster Cottage, The Weir, Kilcolgan, County Galway

Watch out for this eatery—it's easy to miss and a great pity that would be. As you're driving from Dungaire Castle, Kinvara, to Galway town, you'll pass through the village of Kilcolgan. Look for a small sign on the road to your left, saying Moran's. Turn in and you'll come to a totally unpretentious country pub that boasts a glorious claim to fame—it serves possibly the finest oysters in all Ireland.

The Moran family gets them from oyster beds lying right beside the rocks their mussels come from, another house specialty, when in season. Moran's pub dates back some 200 years and the family has been innkeeping for five generations. Their house is a little white thatched cottage, furnished with the barest dining necessities. But the oysters and other saltwater goodies they provide are of a quality unmatched in any haute-cuisine palace.

Try a full dozen of the fresh Galway oysters for £5.50 ($8.25), together with some of Mrs. Moran's home-baked brown bread and fresh butter, moistened with a tall black Guinness. It's a lunch you'll be talking about when you're back eating the frozen substitutes that pass for seafood at home. Or, in case you don't like oysters, try a plate of the smoked salmon for £4.35 ($7.28) or crabmeat at the same price. Food is served throughout pub hours.

Assolas Country House, Kanturk, County Cork (tel. 029-56015)

A 17th-century house lying in 100 acres of private land about three miles outside Kanturk and containing one of the finest restaurants in the country, the house—or rather mansion—is an ivy-covered gem, the dining room filled with furnishings of the Queen Anne period. Dresden china plates decorate the walls, the tables are mahogany, and there's an adjoining salon in which you sip drinks until dinner is ready.

The set menu costs £16 ($24), plus a 10% service charge. You can start with the pâté maison (it really *is* maison, that is, home-made). Follow with chilled cucumber soup. Then, perhaps, the oven-poached Blackwater salmon from the local river, creamed garden spinach, baked potatoes, savory tomatoes, and the freshest of garden salads. Finish off with Irish coffee mousse and raspberries with cream. There's an extensive array of wines, and a bottle will cost £7.50 ($11.25) to £14 ($21).

The whole meal has the ambience of a Queen Anne manor house dinner, the kind of leisured, painstaking air that is almost impossible to duplicate in large city restaurants. Book before noon on the day you plan to eat there. Dinner is served from 7:30 p.m. six nights a week. Closed Sunday.

Assolas Country House is also a charming country guesthouse (see description above).

Longueville House, Mallow, County Cork (tel. 022-27156)

Three miles from Mallow and 22 from Killarney, the handsome Georgian mansion of Longueville House, described under hotels in the previous chapter, provides excellent dining to those touring the southwest. Casual guests are served only by reservation, but it's worth planning ahead for this stop.

Meals are served in the President's Room, hung with portraits of Presidents Hyde, O'Kelly, De Valera, and Childers. The ornate plaster ceiling was delicately painted by an Italian artist over a century ago. The copal wood floor and wooden tables and chairs were built by owner Michael O'Callaghan from wood cut by his own sawmill. Extending from the formal Georgian dining room is the most glorious fantasy piece of a white ironwork Victorian conservatory, dotted with several magnificent plants and surrounded by gardens. In summer, this glassed-in conservatory is a prime choice for dining.

The food at Longueville is highly rated by *Michelin Guide*, and well it should be. The O'Callaghans catch their own fish, grow their own vegetables, even butcher their own lamb (lamb is a specialty), and planted the first commercial vineyard in Ireland, which is providing their own wine. During the season, mallard and venison are on the menu.

Dinner would come to about £20 ($30), and Longueville House is fully licensed to diners. Dinner is served 7 to 9 p.m. from Easter to mid-October, but not on Sunday or Monday to nonresidents. Reservations are required.

County Galway

Raftery's Rest, Kilcolgan, County Galway (tel. 091-96175)

This delightful old-style bar and restaurant is named for a blind poet who was born in Mayo but frequently traveled this countryside and was finally laid to rest not far away. It is located some 12 miles south of Galway City on the Limerick road (one mile from Clarenbridge), and is well worth the drive.

You enter through a country pub, with wooden booths and tables and a big stone fireplace. Indeed, you may never get beyond this informal, warm space, especially if you happen in when there's Irish music (as there almost always is on weekends). And if it's Bohemian you're feeling at the time, you can dine on very good pub grub in those surroundings. But if you're in the mood for something a little more elegant, linger in the pub for drinks, then make your way to the more formal, candlelit dining room, where the menu offers a frequently changed range of specialties like filet de sole Kilcolgan (poached and served on a bed of spinach with a classic fish sauce) or tournedos Rossini (filet steak on toast, covered with pâté and madeira sauce). If you're a devotee of duck (and if it's listed when you visit), don't miss their canard rôti au jus—roasted naturally in its own juices, duck never tasted so good. Vegetables are all fresh and delicious; there's a wide range of very good desserts, and a Stilton cheese.

There's a table d'hôte lunch at £4 ($6), and dinner is à la carte, with entrées ranging from £6.95 ($10.43) to £9.95 ($14.93). Hours are 10:30 a.m. to 11:30 p.m. every day except Good Friday and Christmas.

Cashel House, Cashel Bay, Connemara, County Galway (tel. 095-21252 or 31001)

Don't get this place mixed up with the Cashel Palace Hotel in County Tipperary. The Galway one is also a hotel (see hotel section) but operates a first-class restaurant as well. General de Gaulle ate here during his entire stay in Ireland, and His Excellency had a most discriminating palate.

The food is honest, fresh country fare with a minimum of frills, but lovingly prepared and well served. The dining room has a wonderful garden view and a very cheerful, relaxing atmosphere. A typical dinner, costing about £17 ($25.50), might consist of chicken-liver pâté, tomato soup, a tangy Irish seafood salad, and stuffed shoulder of lamb. In conclusion, try the poached pears in red wine—a delicious combination of sweet and tart flavors. If it should be on when you're eating there, try the boiled bacon and cabbage. The locally caught and smoked salmon is famed throughout the country.

The hotel is open only from March 1 to October 31. Lunch, served from 1 to 2 p.m., is à la carte; dinner is at 7:30 p.m. Book ahead.

Currarevagh House, Oughterard, County Galway (tel. 091-82313)

You'd be hard put to locate a more established eatery anywhere on earth. The Hodgson family, proprietors, are the sixth
generation living in this beautifully mellow country home dating
from 1830. Surrounded by 160 acres of wooded grounds on the
banks of Lough Corrib, hung with impressively gold-framed oils,
Currarevagh offers the kind of private-mansion atmosphere that
makes you—almost—forget that it is also a distinguished hotel
and restaurant. Dinner here is a house party, but one under the
auspices of an unusually talented chef. And there is just enough
formality and service ritual to give the affair a delightful dash of
old-world style.

The dining room, overlooking the garden, seats 30 guests. The
dinner menu is set at £13.75 ($20.63), plus 10% service charge. A
typical repast would consist of homemade mulligatawny, mushroom omelet, filets of turbot with french beans and mashed potatoes, and in conclusion lemon soufflé, biscuits, and cheese. The
bread at the table is homemade, as are the cakes, and the cream
comes fresh from the Hodgsons' own dairy. The wine list is not
extensive, but choice.

Dinner is served at 8 p.m. seven days a week from Easter to
early October. Reserve a table one day in advance.

Currarevagh House is primarily a Grade A guesthouse and an
excellent base for touring County Galway. Bed-and-breakfast
rates start at £26 ($39) plus a 10% service charge.

County Kerry

Linden House, New Road, Killarney, County Kerry (tel. 064-31379)

Proprietor and chef Franz Knoblauch, a German who married
an Irish girl, now operates a restaurant remarkable for both quality and budget prices. Housed in a small villa-style hotel in a quiet
Killarney street, his establishment has a local reputation that
makes advance booking (and arriving on time) a *must* if you want
to enjoy dinner there.

The dining room has a distinctly Bavarian flavor: low ceiling,
wooden peasant chairs, and a scattering of German ornaments.
But the cooking is strictly Herr Knoblauch's own. It follows no
distinct ethnic direction—the chef takes the best of Irish ingredients and imprints his personal touch on them. Recently, we dined
for £10 ($15) starting with seafood hors d'oeuvres (outstanding),
continuing with cream Milanese soup, climaxing with a succulent
roast prime rib of beef. The dressed Brussels sprouts that formed

the main vegetables were more than just good—they were memorable. Our Irish neighbor swore by the virtue of the beef Stroganoff, which costs extra. Herr Knoblauch's desserts carry a special fame in the region, so try and leave room for them; they come with the dinner price.

Linden House serves no lunches and is closed Monday to non-residents and from mid-November through mid-January. Otherwise, dinner is on from 6 to 8:30 p.m.

Foley's Steak & Seafood Restaurant, 23 High St., Killarney, County Kerry (tel. 064-31217)

Friends in Killarney put me on to Foley's, and it turned out to be a culinary delight—one of those Irish restaurants you dream about. Housed in what was once a coaching inn, the restaurant has a friendly, relaxing air, with a peat fire in the bar/lounge area up front, soft shades of green on walls and carpets, and chairs upholstered in rose. There's a resident pianist on Friday, Saturday, and Sunday nights during summer months.

This is a family-owned and -run eatery, with Carol Hartnett working her magic in the kitchen and husband Denis dealing with the front (as well as with searching the markets for meats and produce that meet their high standards). As you might expect, seafood is a specialty, but if you're the least bit steak-inclined, this is your chance to dine on some of the most succulent in Ireland. They cut their own, and whether you order filets, stuffed filets, T-bones, or peppered steaks, you won't be disappointed. The excellent rack of lamb also should not be overlooked—Denis buys only Kerry mountain lamb and uses only center-line cuts.

Foley's is a full-service restaurant, serving all three meals (a good place to breakfast if you're not going the B&B route) beginning at 8 a.m. There's bar food available right through to 7:30 p.m. (you can even order sirloin and T-bone steaks with chips or the fresh seafood platter—with six different kinds of fish!).

Lunch is priced from £7.50 ($11.25) and the dining room opens for dinner from 5 to 10:30 p.m., seven days a week, with an à la carte menu. Main courses range from £7.50 ($11.25) to £10.50 ($15.75), and the special Tourist Menu is available year round.

Nick's Restaurant, Lower Bridge Street, Killorglin, County Kerry (tel. 066-61233 or 61219)

Nick and Ann Foley have converted what was once a butcher shop into a charming multilevel steak and seafood restaurant with exposed-stone walls, lots of dark wood, open fires, oil paintings, a grand piano, and comfortable seating with plush upholstering in shades of red and green. The small private dining room upstairs (available for parties of 10 to 30) is furnished with antiques, overstuffed sofas and chairs, and its own bar.

As for the food, well, Nick is, himself, a master butcher who knows his meats and serves only the best. Prime beef comes in enormous steaks that actually earn the accolade "melt in your mouth." Lobsters, crawfish, and oysters reside in the restaurant's fish tank until they are to be cooked, and other fish dishes feature only same-day catches. The soups, be they beef and vegetable, mussel, or whatever, are thick and hearty with the unmistakable taste of "homemade." The menu is extensive, with ten starters and a choice from more than a dozen main courses, followed by a mouthwatering dessert trolley. But if you should have a yen for a special dish not listed—and if the makings are available—the Foleys are quite happy to prepare it for you. Lunch salads of ham, beef, or seafood, featured on the special pub menu from noon to 5 p.m. along with main-course meals, are very good. There's an extensive wine list and à la carte prices range upwards from £9 ($13.50) for main courses.

Nick's is open from noon to 10:30 p.m., seven days a week. Closed Christmas Eve to New Year's Day.

Doyle's Seafood Bar, John Street, Dingle, County Kerry (tel. 066-51174)

In the heart of Dingle where the sea scent hangs lightly in the air, this is a perfect stop-off for lunch or dinner. John and Stella Doyle have turned their atmospheric pub with flagstone floor, rock walls, and paneled ceiling, into a simple but excellent, fully licensed seafood restaurant. John tends the bar, Stella does most of the cooking. No menu exists—you come in and read off what's on the blackboard which always features the day's fresh catch. Oysters, lobster, salmon, and a selection of shellfish are usually on tap, all simply cooked and just lightly flavored with sauces, if at all. Accompanying your main dish are homemade soup, fresh-baked scones, salad with house mayonnaise, a baked potato (at dinner), a gâteau or apple tart. Items are few but each is perfectly prepared.

The restaurant can serve only 28 at a time, so no reservations are taken and you cool your heels hospitably at the bar if all the Sugan chairs are filled.

Main courses are priced according to the raw materials used that day, but average £6 ($9) to £8 ($12). Lunch is served from 12:30 to 2:15 p.m., dinner from 6 to 9 p.m. Closed Sunday. Open mid-March to mid-November.

The Half Door, John Street, Dingle, County Kerry (tel. 066-51600)

John and Celeste Slye can count more awards than we have space to list among their achievements at The Half Door, and the residents of Dingle are as fond of the place as visitors, always the sign of a good eatery. Just one meal in the bright, informal dining room or the skylighted arbor room out back will add you to their list of boosters. But before we get into the food, let me say something about the atmosphere here: It's as friendly, relaxed, and jovial a place as you'll find anywhere, which makes every lunch or dinner something of a special occasion.

But in the final analysis, it's the food that counts, and that's where all those awards come in. Celeste rules the kitchen, turning out mostly seafood dishes prepared with a marvelous simplicity that enhances their natural tastes. No need to worry about freshness—John has constructed huge tanks to hold several varieties until they're ready to pop into the pot, and others come right from Dingle's fishing fleet to the kitchen. I especially like, too, the fresh side salads that come with main courses. As for the wine list, it is extensive and of such excellence that it won the Woodford Bourne National Wine Award two years running.

The Half Door is open from 12:30 to 2 p.m. for lunch, 6 to 9 p.m. for dinner. À la carte prices begin at £9.50 ($14.25). Closed November to mid-March.

County Kildare

Curryhills House, Prosperous, Naas, County Kildare (tel. 045-68150)

Set in a Georgian-style country house, the dining room at Curryhills House is the pride and joy of owner/managers Bridie and Bill Travers. Decor is Tudor, and cuisine features gourmet dishes prepared from local, fresh ingredients. On Fridays, there's traditional Irish music, and on Saturdays you're invited to an old-fashioned singalong. Hours are 12:30 to 2 p.m. for lunch, 6:30 to 11 p.m. for dinner; lunch prices begin at £8 ($12), dinner prices at £15 ($22.50). Closed Sunday.

John Doyle's Schoolhouse Restaurant, Castledermot, County Kildare (tel. 0503-44282)

John Doyle's is a small, cozy place for a relaxed, beautifully prepared Big Splurge dinner. John is always on hand to see that both service and meals are perfection, and the menu strikes a nice balance, with offerings of seafood, beef, chicken, and seasonal specialties. All ingredients are of the highest standards. Dinner begins at 6:30 p.m. from April to October, at 7:30 p.m. other months; the restaurant is closed Sunday and Monday. There's a table d'hôte dinner at £18 ($27), and à la carte prices begin at £12 ($18). There's seating for only 30, so best book ahead.

County Mayo

Ashford Castle, Cong, County Mayo (tel. 094-22644)

You'll find this place listed among our castle hotels. The restaurant, too, is worthy of mention. Here's an episode that will illustrate why: Once at dinner there, the maître d' apologized to the guests about a delay before the next course. It seemed that a fisherman had just caught a magnificent salmon on Lough Corrib—and would they mind waiting until the fish had been prepared for the table? There was a rustle of applause all around. Then an air of reverent expectation while the salmon was sautéed on a little trolley before their eyes. Then the feast.

There aren't very many dineries in this day and age which would go to *that* kind of trouble on behalf of their patrons.

The dining room is downright palatial, supported by Doric pillars and gleaming with crystal chandeliers. The tall Gothic windows overlook the lake. It seats 200 guests without forcing them to rub elbows. It is not, as you may have gathered, a budget eatery, but prices are reasonable for the quality.

The set dinner costs £29 ($43.50). For starters you may get a choice of eggs Benedictine, hors d'oeuvres, smoken salmon, or Genoa salami. Then either a cold vichyssoise or two kinds of hot soup. In culmination, perhaps a splendid beef Stroganoff, poached turbot with hollandaise sauce, or escalope de veau Tipperary. Salads and mixed vegetables go along with these. As a finale, select from at least eight choices of dessert (the rum baba is outstanding) or a selection of cheeses. À la carte meals are also available.

Closed from the end of December to April 1. Booking is essential.

Breaffy House, Castlebar, County Mayo (tel. 094-22033)

This too in our hotel section, Breaffy House also operates a restaurant of renown. The dining room is both modern and cozy, a fairly rare combination. The royal-blue carpet matches the chairs, there's an exceptionally handsome batik on the wall, the lighting is soft amber, and there's an air of unhurried pride—all dishes are freshly made and take approximately 20 minutes.

The menu is lengthy and offers a vast array of regional specialties sprinkled with some cosmopolitan surprises. In among the native Irish seafood, pork, lamb, and beef, you'll find an amazing Madras curried prawn dish, American chicken Maryland, French pork Bergère, and mousse Chantilly.

The set dinner costs from £12 ($18) up. An à la carte menu is also available. On one particular night, the menu offered a choice of four entrées, including barbecued spareribs and lasagne, then either consommé or vegetable soup. Following that a crisply baked Aylesbury duckling with orange sauce, cauliflower, creamed spinach, and Parisienne potatoes. Finally the pineapple spongeburgers—a ghastly name for an exceptional dessert.

Dinner is served from 7 to 9 p.m. daily. Reserve ahead.

County Waterford

Seanachie Restaurant, Pulla, Ring, Dungarvin (on Cork Road), County Waterford (tel. 058-46285)

Things have changed considerably at the Seanachie (the name means storyteller, the source of Irish entertainment before TV) since there was first a public house here in 1847. At that time, the Great Famine was raging throughout the land, and a pitiful reminder is just next to the present carpark—a mass famine graveyard. Nowadays, however, there's food aplenty, and what food it is. Fresh prawns, turbot, lobster, and salmon from nearby Helvick Head, and vegetables straight from surrounding farms. So good is the cuisine, in fact, that it has won several national awards for excellence.

The Seanachie, as you might expect from its name, is in the traditional style and is actually a complex of restored farmyard outbuildings, one of which houses the restaurant. In the bar, pub food is available, and during the summer months, you're likely to encounter some of the area's best traditional musicians entertaining guests.

Prices are in the moderate range, with lunch in the bar from £3 ($4.50) and dinner (complete) from £14 ($21). There's also an à la carte menu. Hours are 11 a.m. to 11:30 p.m., with continuous food service in the bar, 6:30 to 9:30 p.m. in the dining room. Closed Sunday and holidays.

County Wexford

The Oak Tavern, Ferrycarrig, Wexford, County Wexford (tel. 053-22138)

I remember the Oak Tavern from the days of the old bridge, when it was a "must" stop for its genuine tavern atmosphere and the genuine fishermen and local characters who always seemed to be in residence. With the building of the present bridge, I feared the worst—that it would be demolished or be refurbished right out of its natural character. I needn't have worried: John and Barbara Igoe have treated this century-and-a-half-old building with all the respect and affection it deserves and installed an outstanding restaurant, to boot!

The original two front rooms have been retained as the Locals Bar, just as I remember them (with, however, a lot less dirt and grime!). There's an open fire and piano and the same local faces I remember. Out back, they've added an intimate and utterly charming Ferry Restaurant, with windows looking out onto the Slaney, tapestry-upholstered seating, and an open fire. A bonus that came with the new bridge is the large land portion of the old

---

New Ross Galley, New Ross, County Wexford (tel. 051-21723)

Ireland's only cruising restaurant, this trim little river craft departs several times daily from the main quay in New Ross. The course is up or downstream on the Nore or Barrow River, depending on the tide. There is no disturbing commentary, no background music, just the tranquil peace of the river, the lush scenery along the banks, and excellent food. Skipper-cum-host Dick Fletcher knows as much about good eating as he knows about navigation. Which is plenty.

The menu depends on which cruise you take. Lunch is often a buffet affair (all-you-can-eat), with huge tureens of homemade soup, hot and cold meat plates, cold chicken, hamburgers, and four kinds of salad. The entire meal costs £10 ($15). Afternoon tea is Irish afternoon tea: heaped plates of scones and cakes at £4 ($6). The dinner cruise is the most lavish—four courses at £14 ($21) or six courses at £18 ($27). And as you eat, the landscape glides by, the river sparkles, the waves lap softly. . . .

The Galley is fully licensed, but drinks, of course, cost extra. Otherwise all prices include service charge and tax. The Galley operates from April to November. From June through August the cruises go daily. The rest of the time it usually remains docked on Monday and Tuesday. The lunch cruise lasts from 12:30 to 2:30 p.m., the afternoon tea cruise from 3 to 5 p.m., the dinner cruise from 7 to 10 p.m. (6 to 9 p.m. in September). June through August there are special lunch cruises to Waterford, which combine with a local cruise for afternoon tea, high tea, or dinner, bringing you back to New Ross in the evening.

Since the boat holds only 70 guests, you should book a place in advance. Phone 051-21723 between 10 a.m. and 7 p.m.

which stands at the river's edge and in summer months becomes a delightful outdoor eatery, with food served from 12:30 p.m. right up to 9:30 p.m.

John considers the well-hung steak cooked over charcoal to be the star of his menu, but in my opinion the river trout poached in a fresh tomato provençale concasse deserves star billing as well. Nor could one put in second place the huge (10-ounce) grilled salmon steak with parsley butter. Black or Dover sole comes on or off the bone, and the chicken tavern-style is sautéed with vegetables and herbs and finished in wine and cream. All main courses include baked potato with sour-cream dressing, and portions go beyond "ample." Prices range from £6.50 ($9.75) to £13 ($19.50) at dinner, and bar lunches of soup, sandwiches, seafood snacks and pâté are under £6 ($9), or about £2 ($3) if you settle for soup and sandwiches.

Just two miles from Wexford, the Oak Tavern is open every day except Monday, and the Ferry Restaurant serves dinner from 7 to 10 p.m.

County Wicklow

Old Rectory Country House, Wicklow Town, County Wicklow (tel. 0404-2048)

This is an 1870s Georgian-style rectory that has blossomed as one of County Wicklow's premier eateries under the loving guidance of Paul and Linda Saunders. Set in its own gardens on the edge of town, the house exudes tranquil elegance, with spacious public rooms, high ceilings, and cheerful log fires. Dinner is served by candlelight, with Linda in the kitchen and Paul attending to the very personal service in the lovely dining room. Fresh seafoods and local produce and meats are the basis of the gourmet menu, and there's a good wine list. There's a table d'hôte dinner for £19 ($28.50), and an à la carte menu with selections from £15 ($22.50) to £25 ($37.50). From Sunday to Thursday, there's only one seating, at 7:30 p.m.; on Friday and Saturday, hours are 7:30 to 9 p.m.; and advance booking is absolutely essential. Accommodations are also available in bright, attractive guestrooms with private bath and telephone, at rates of £28 ($42) per person for bed-and-breakfast.

Hunter's Hotel, Rathnew, County Wicklow (tel. 0404-4106)

This popular dining room serves lunch from 1 to 3 p.m., dinner from 7:30 to 9:30 p.m., and afternoon tea in between. Vegetables come straight from the hotel's own garden, seafood is freshly caught, and roasts, steaks, and other meats come from local sources. Service is the pampering kind. Lunch runs about £8 ($12), afternoon tea is £4 ($6), and dinner will cost about £16 ($24), and there's a 10% service charge. Be sure to book ahead.

Chapter XIV

ENTERTAINMENT AND PUBS OUTSIDE DUBLIN

Drinks and Do's

SEEING THE SIGHTS, eating, and sleeping well are by no means the full extent of your experience in Ireland. We can almost guarantee that, once back at home and retelling your trip to friends, you will seldom dwell on the charming room or delicious meal you had here or there but will be filled with stories that start: "And then the man said to me. . . ." People are what Ireland is all about, and far more so in the country—where time has little meaning—than in the city where time gets captured too often between nine and five. And where best to meet the country people? Where they meet each other—in the pubs and at country *ceilis*.

Special Irish Nights

A *ceili* is a dance, a *hoolie* is a party—whatever the term, a relaxed night with the Irish, dancing, singing, listening to tales, is great fun. And not to be missed. Make a point of catching at least one of the following evenings while on tour, if at all possible.

SHANNON CEILI: The meal and entertainment provided in a large barn in **Bunratty Folk Park** (behind the castle), nine miles from Shannon Airport, is no banquet. And the performers are no minstrels. Yet a great many visitors actually prefer this offering to the more stylish fare in the castle. The event has the intimacy, the shirtsleeved nonchalance, the spontaneous good humor of an Irish folk event; the entertainment as well as the food seems to spring directly from the Irish earth.

You get, first of all, a traditional Irish feast: Irish stew and vegetables, spotted dick, apple tart and cream. The only alien note at the table is the wine served. There's an open turf fire, and after the meal you draw around and watch the performers.

Pretty girls in whirling dresses go through intricate jigs and step dances. Fiddlers and pipers and accordionists stroke and blow and squeeze Irish airs. A *seaneachai*—a village storyteller—spins one of those long rollicking tales that have made the rurals chortle for a couple of hundred years. And the remarkable thing about these stories is that they don't sound nearly so funny when you retell them afterward. Because *you* don't have the voice and the brogue and the mimicry that are essential to their effect.

When the evening is over you'll leave with the warm feeling of having come close to the very stuff basic happiness is made of, and the warmth keeps lingering for a long time afterward.

The Shannon Ceili is on twice nightly, at 6 and 9 p.m., from June 15 to September 30. The inclusive cost is £22 ($33). Make reservations through Shannon Airport Tours Manager (tel. 061-61788).

SIAMSA: The word means "merrymaking" in Gaelic, but that doesn't really describe this amazing mixture of traditional music, song, dance, ballet, and mime. Performed every Monday, Tuesday, Thursday, and Friday, from mid-June to mid-September, at the **Siamsa Tire Theatre in Tralee** (20 miles northwest of Killarney), this is a pageant set to music about Irish farm life. Around a thatched cottage on stage gather the familiar characters of rurality. They go—or rather dance and sing—through their daily chores and pleasures. Thatching a roof, churning butter, milking cows, hunting a fox—all are acted out in dance rhythms accompanied by wonderfully evocative tunes on fiddle, harp, flute, and pipes. The language sung and spoken is Gaelic, but that doesn't matter to the listeners. You feel you understand every word, since the words merely underscore the actions on stage. And the tunes and dances are terrific in any language. Bookings can be made at the Siamsa Tire Theatre in Tralee (tel. 066-23055).

SEODA: This is a Gaelic evening such as you're not likely to see anywhere else—not even in Ireland. For the **Taibhdhearc Theater** (tel. 091-62024) in Middle Street, Galway, is a unique institution, a showplace devoted to Gaelic theatrical art, imbued with a fire, dedication, and sheer artistic talent that leaves you breathless with admiration. The internationally acclaimed actress Siobhan McKenna began her career here. And Brendan Behan's classic, *The Hostage*, was performed here in its *original* Irish version. (It had to be *re*-translated for the purpose.) Now it is the home base of the Taibhdhearc dancers, perhaps the most exciting troupe Ireland has to offer.

The entire show runs for about two hours. Only part of it consists of a stage play, which may be virtually anything in Gaelic—a tongue so magically melodious that it makes listening a joy even when you don't understand the lines. (You'll get a complete commentary in English nonetheless.) The major part of the program is made up of native Irish music and Irish dancing—the real thing, undiluted, such as is rarely performed these days. The movements are all in the feet; body, arms, and face don't join in. But the footwork has an almost incredible speed and grace, and eye-blurring tempo that can only be compared to the climactic moments of an Andalusian heel-stomping dance. Watching the beautiful young dancers go through their ethnic paces is an experience that stays with you for weeks.

Seoda is performed regularly during July and August (except during Race Week from July 29 to August 2). Check with the Tourist Office or the theater for exact days of the week and admission charges.

SEISIUN: A "good session" is Irish for a fun night. Seisiun is the Gaelic version of the word. Originally it meant a home entertainment: singing, playing, and wonderfully uninhibited ceili dancing, with the tables and chairs pushed aside and everybody joining in. Now a group of traditional musicians perform their seisiun around the country for eight weeks in summer. It's still a come-all, join-all affair, but the driving force now comes from a band of tremendously talented young men and women who pipe, blow, fiddle, squeeze, and step in a way that makes you forget you ever had troubles.

The only trouble is catching them. You can get information concerning your area from the local Tourist Office. Performances are held in hotels, cottages, even King John's Castle in Limerick —but usually only on one particular night a week. And these sessions are too good to miss.

Admission averages £2 ($3)—a very minor fee for a very major evening of fun.

Unique Country Pubs

A pub crawl across rural Ireland is quite a different experience from a similar excursion through metropolitan Dublin. Country pubs are not so much drinking establishments as meeting places. The locals visit them several times during an average day: between shopping, before dinner, after dinner. The main purpose of these visits is not the pint, but the opportunity to chat kindly with each other and less kindly about those who don't happen to be present. The casual visitor is welcome—he's a new face, a fascinating foreigner, a fresh conversation topic.

As you proceed along your way, you'll learn to distinguish the various species of public houses. By and large they fall into four categories:

There's the **singing pub,** where local talent holds forth nightly and talk takes second place to tone.

The **river pub**—particularly along the Shannon—is frequented by boatmen and anglers and devoted to their special interests.

The **seashore pub** is where fishermen and yachtsmen gather to exchange fish stories and sailing yarns, turning the air blue and purple with technicolor lies.

And finally there's the **common street pub**—which in Ireland is hardly ever "common," but a subtle mixture of Masonic lodge, courthouse square, neighborhood bar, and political club.

Frequently these definitions overlap and become heavily laced with visiting foreigners to produce a new and quite indefinable breed of drinkery—the kind of place where you're as likely to meet a millionaire yachtsman from Boston Bay as a farm laborer from Ballyduff.

In the following pages you'll find a few outstanding examples of each species. And now, *Slainte!*

O'Connor's Pub, Doolin, Country Clare

The permanent joke about this delightful spot is that it isn't in Doolin at all. It couldn't be, because "Doolin" is actually an area of ocean a mile off the coast. O'Connor's stands in Fisher Street, half a mile from the coast. You can't miss it—the road there leads to the sea and nowhere else.

A large rustic pub, lit by miniature lobster pots, this is a mecca for Irish fiddlers, singers, and talkers, and that embraces just about everybody in the area. On weekends the place overflows with the locals, plus whatever musicians happen to be visiting the district. Dropping in at O'Connor's is a *must* with them—and that naturally means playing a number or two or five or ten.

On Sunday, weather permitting, the Aran Islanders drop in.

Durty Nelly's, Bunratty, County Clare

To call this place a mere pub would be an insult, although it certainly is a pub. But it's also an international crossroads, an institution, a social club, a piece of history, and, for many tourists, their most nostalgic Irish memory. Squatting on the arched bridge that leads to Bunratty Castle, the inn is almost like an extension of the fortress. It did, in fact, act as canteen for the castle soldiers when it was built in 1620, and a right grubby lot they were too—hence (probably) the name.

Today Durty Nelly's attracts roughly equal numbers of locals and visitors. The tourists swarm in on their way to or from the Castle Banquets. The local farmers come to bend elbows with the fascinating foreigners. Together they produce an atmosphere that's a combination of permanent party and permanent riot, with a couple of song fests thrown in for good measure.

The white-walled, thatched-roofed pub is furnished farmhouse style, with crackling peat fires and wooden benches. Only the original "durty" part has been eliminated. The noisier action goes on downstairs, where the crowd gets so thick and convivial that groups frequently spill out into the yard, pint jars in their hands, songs on their lips, brotherhood in their souls.

Upstairs, in the loft softly lit by lanterns, things are a little quieter. You can actually hear yourself talk or listen to the Irish balladeer who sings in Gaelic, and so expressively that you imagine you understand the lyrics. Whatever else you may miss in Ireland—don't miss Durty Nelly's. The auld girl would never forgive you.

They come over the water in their self-built, deceptively fragile-looking curraghs, and they come 40 or so at a time in a fleet of seven or eight of these canoes. This is one of the best opportunities for meeting these fascinating islanders, who wear traditional dress and speak Gaelic. There's barfood (featuring fresh seafood) on offer all day, as well as a full-service restaurant, The Pipers Chair.

Don't forget, though, that this is a social spot for the locals, not a tourist hangout. The customers are very friendly, but tend to be cautious (not shy) at first. Give them a little time to warm up. Your patience will be rewarded by some of the best Irish yarns anyone has ever taken back Stateside. And genuine, for a change. Should you wish to stay over, Gus's daughter, Susan Daly, offers bed-and-breakfast in her home just behind the pub.

The Merriman Tavern, Scarriff, County Clare (tel. 0619-21011)

Situated in the center of this Shannonside town, the Merriman Tavern—built into an action brick warehouse off a stone courtyard—looks like a perfect highwayman's rendezvous. What it is is the most famous ballad club in the west and the perfect rendezvous for cruising folk singers, balladeers, lovers of good music and talk.

The pub is named after Brian Merriman, late 18th-century County Clare poet, whose most famous poem, "The Midnight Court," caused quite a scandal among the clergy of the day (but not the populace who quoted it gleefully) and was fastidiously banned by the Irish government in the 20th. In the poem, written in ribald Gaelic, the poet is called to a fairy court where the prosecutor, a young Clare woman, charges him with the shortcomings of Clare men at love. What scandalized the clergy was the poet's condemnation of their chastity in the light of the needs of Clare women. A scene from the trial forms a mural on one wall.

The rock-walled pub is divided into several areas. The main pub has old barrel tables and turf fires in stone fireplaces. At the front is an intimate snug called the *síbin* (meaning illicit drinkery). The large ballad room, with cartwheel lamps hanging from the rafters, opens on Friday and Saturday nights (plus two other nights a week in summer), when the biggest names in Irish balladry—Stockton's Wing, Clannad, the Furys, Dubliners, Chieftains—might appear at £5 ($7.50) admission, or lesser known but equally lively local groups at £2.50 ($3.75). There is a beer garden at the rear of the pub where open-air concerts are held during the summer. The Merriman also serves morning coffee, lunch, and dinner at reasonable prices. If you're in the area —don't miss!

Shanachai Pub, Market Street, Kinsale, County Cork

Tucked away on a picture-postcard-pretty street in seaside Kinsale, the Shanachie (which also spells its name phonetically— Shanakee) is over 200 years old. Brothers Vincent and Gerard McCarthy, both musical, are genial hosts to resident locals who come in scores and warmly welcome all visitors in a manner that turns them into instant regulars. I'll warrant you won't be able to go along to the Shanachai just *once*—it's as habit-forming as peanuts!

In the two small front rooms, you'll find original old stone walls, open fires, and a marvelous painting of the legendary Irish storytellers for whom the pub is named. To those, the brothers

McCarthy have added a larger back room by means of opening up equally old adjacent buildings, retaining stone walls, and restoring ceiling beams and crumbling fireplaces. There's also a salad and seafood lunch bar.

During summer months, there's music seven days a week. And that means traditional Irish music as well as the beloved sing-a-long ballads which can seem a bit trite in other settings, but never in the Shanachai. Michael Buckley, the beloved All-Ireland accordion player, plays regularly, as do other local musicians who seem to enjoy the crack almost as much as the music. There's also dancing in the back room on weekends all through the summer, but absolutely *nothing* could draw yours truly from those front rooms where music and talk and the brown stuff flow easily until the "Time, gentlemen, please," call.

The Danny Mann, New Street, Killarney, County Kerry

Probably the world's only pub named after a murderer (you'll find the macabre background story on a plaque beside the door), the Danny Mann nevertheless manages to be a very jolly spot indeed. This is a singing pub; seven nights a week Irish balladeers perform, and a goodly portion of the patrons join in.

The Danny Mann is a fairly posh place, packed with tourists throughout the summer and drawing the reputedly prettiest lasses in Killarney and environs. Large, firelit, and wood paneled, this is a late starter as Irish inns go. It doesn't really get under way until around 9:30 p.m., but by 10 the bartenders and waitresses can hardly keep up with the orders. If you feel the night is still young when ballads end at 11:30 p.m., there's a new, even *more* posh nightclub appended where the action goes on till 1:30 a.m.

O'Flaherty's Pub, Dingle, County Kerry

The sign over the red-and-white pub in the old brick building on Bridge Street reads *UaFlaibeartaig,* augmented by various dots and accents marks—meaning O'Flaherty's to us who do not deal "in the medium," and O'Flaherty's pub is a landmark on the Dingle Peninsula. The father of the O'Flahertys, who sadly passed away in 1970, was one of the finest traditional musicians in the country and considered the best at the bodhran drum. He passed on his passion, playing talent, and pub to his children, and now Fergus holds forth on the instruments while sister Marie sings traditional tunes and adaptations in a beautifully clear voice. Mrs. O'Flaherty can be found tapping happily in one corner while the music plays on and another son might be tending the bar. The whole atmosphere is warm, friendly, and homey, aided by the hodgepodge decor of Christmas colors and lights, rough-wood walls papered with maps and posters, and marvelous pub mirrors speckled with age.

The singing sessions are casual, usually starting about 10 p.m., go on all year round, often involve many locals, and cost nothing on top of your drinks.

Austi Gillen's, Rosses Point, County Sligo

The traditions of Rosses Point, that wild stretch of beach five miles from Sligo town where Jack Yeats's midnight-blue horses romp on canvas, have always dealt with the sea. And this pub a few feet from the sea wall is almost a museum of marine lore.

The name over the door reads John Bruen, a larger-than-life character who traveled the seas, arriving in the Yukon for the gold rush, in San Francisco for the earthquake, making the guano run to South America, and engaging in intrigue in Shanghai.

Ship's lanterns, compasses, a model of the *Queen Elizabeth*, and the collected medals of sailors who lost their lives off Rosses Point, form only part of the decor. Surprisingly, the clientele is not made up of rough-hewn fishermen in caps and boots, but some of the most sophisticated and intellectual society County Sligo has to offer. When hunger pangs strike, there's the moderately priced Elsinore Restaurant right on the premises.

The Crown Bar, Monck Street, Wexford, County Wexford

Originally built as a stagecoach inn back in 1841, the Crown is today the country's oldest pub to be run by the same family. The owner is Mrs. Kelly and her establishment is a mixture of bar and private museum. Located just around the corner from White's Hotel in this historic little town, the Crown is a picturesque enough drinking spot in its own right. But its special claim to fame can be found in the two small rear lounges.

There, neatly racked and cased, stands the late Mr. Kelly's personal collection of ancient arms and armor (the reason, incidentally, why the locals have dubbed the place "The Armoury"). You'll find some of the lethal pikes used in the so-called Vinegar Hill rebellion, dueling pistols and flintlocks, and the kind of brass, wide-muzzled blunderbusses that were favored weapons for coachmen and highwaymen alike because they scattered so broadly that you were bound to hit *something*, even from a

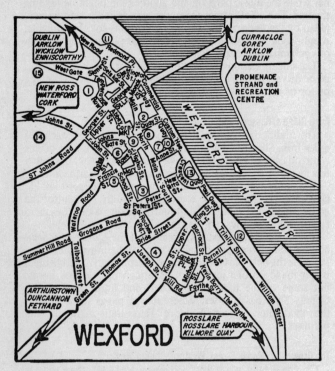

Based on the Ordnance Survey by permission of the Government of Ireland (Permit No. 906)

KEY TO THE NUMBERED REFERENCES ON OUR MAP OF WEX-FORD: 1—Westgate Tower, Selskar Church, and Ruined Abbey; 2—The Bull Ring; 3—St. Patrick's Church and Graveyard; 4—Church of the Assumption; 5—Franciscan Church; 6—Church of the Immaculate Conception; 7—Presbyterian Church; 8—St. Iberius Church; 9—Methodist Church; 10—General Post Office; 11—Wexford North Railway Station and Local Bus Terminus; 12—Wexford South Railway Station; 13—Barry Memorial; 14—Municipal Buildings; 15—County Hall.

bounding coach seat or horse's saddle. Also swords, curved sabers, and powder horns. So famous is the Crown that it has been the subject of no fewer than *six* television features and the Visitor's Books hold over 25,000 signatures.

The drinks come at normal pub prices. The museum is on the house.

Chapter XV

SHOPPING OUTSIDE DUBLIN

Bargains and Crafts

MANY FINE-QUALITY SHOPS selling Irish goods dot the countryside, and half the fun is discovering them for yourself. We'll just call your attention here to a selected few you would not want to miss should you be nearby.

Our motto when shopping in Ireland, especially for local crafts, is: buy what you like when you see it, for you may never see its like again. The following selections should stack the odds for happy discovery in your favor.

And should you be in Kilkenny, whatever you do, don't neglect a browse through that showcase of the finest in Irish production: the **Kilkenny Design Center** (see Chapter X).

County Clare

Bunratty Cottage International Fashion Shop, Bunratty, County Clare (tel. 061-74321)

A golden-walled, slate-roofed, century-old restored cottage situated directly across the road from Bunratty Castle, this two-level shop is an elegant little boutique vending the best quality in Irish creations of tweed, lace, wool, and linen. Pallas hand-crocheted linen outfits, shirtdresses and shirtwaists, John Hagarty's light tweed skirts, blouses, and long dresses—all top Irish designers at top prices. There are frequent fashion shows held right on the premises. The guiding spirit of the shop is owner Vonnie Reynolds, who designs her own highly original creations with great emphasis on velvets, handmade lace, lightweight wools, and tweeds.

The main floor concentrates on Irish goods; upstairs features carefully chosen continental fashions.

The shop is open May through October from 10 a.m. to 6 p.m. year round, and Vonnie Reynolds also has a boutique in Killarney's Hotel Europe as well as in Annapolis, Maryland, in the States.

Jim Connolly, Sculptor, Kilbaha, Kilrush, County Clare (tel. Carrigaholt 34)

To find one of Ireland's foremost contemporary sculptors, you must make the long drive out the northern shore of the River Shannon, almost to Loop Head, which marks its entrance to the sea. The drive alone would be a glorious travel experience as you pass through quaint little fishing villages, but it is at journey's end, in the settlement of Kilbaha, that an art lover's endurance will be rewarded. There, in a thatched cottage, Jim Connolly lives with his wife and three children and works in a studio from which emerge brilliant works in bronze. Most recent acclaim has come to Jim for his commissioned statue of Eamon de Valera which stands in the public square in Ennis. He has, however, done statues and plaques for many well-known figures and has held exhibitions in leading cities. He is glad to work on commission if you have a special subject in mind, or you can shop among the completed pieces in his studio, which run in price from £650 ($975) upward. If that's a little rich for your pocketbook, you can choose from ceramics priced in the £2.50 ($3.75) to £20 ($30) range while gazing your fill at the bronzes. One word of caution: It's best to call ahead, since Jim is sometimes away and the studio is not open.

Mike McGlynn Antiques, Bunratty, County Clare (tel. 061-62011)

Just beyond Fitzpatrick's Shannon Shamrock Hotel, this interesting collection of antiques is housed in an old-style thatched cottage. Mike and his brother have something to offer everyone from the dedicated antique hunter to those of us who would simply like to bring back home some of Ireland's antiquity. For me, it was an elegant teak walking stick which undoubtedly reached these shores by way of an Irish seafarer. For you, it might be a small bit of fine porcelain or some bit of ironwork. There are works of art, china, paintings, furniture, and a host of other larger items. They'll gladly insure and ship any purchases too large to tote home.

County Cork

West Cork Craft Centre, Leap, County Cork (tel. 028-33217)

West Cork is noted for beautiful scenery, superb restaurants, and some highly individualistic craftspeople. Much of their work has been gathered together by Mr. and Mrs. Thompson, who have turned one large room of their bluff-top house into a showcase and shop of local art.

The centre is located halfway between Rosscarbery and Skibbereen, on the right-hand side of the road opposite gleaming Glandore Harbour. You reach it up a flight of steps through a terraced garden. Claire Thompson is always on hand to greet you and she will explain the origins of the items on sale. Her own lovely crocheted collars and toys are also for purchase.

The stock consists of pottery, tweeds, copperware, glass animals and paperweights, woolens, paintings—anything that is both good quality, different, and Irish made.

The Centre is open daily from 9:30 a.m. to 7 p.m., except when the Thompsons go on yearly holiday, usually in January. If you should find the door locked, just ring the bell—Claire has only gone into the house and hasn't heard you drive up.

Raymond Klee, Artist, Ballylickey, County Cork (tel. 027-50157)

On the edge of the little town of Ballylickey, nestled in a curve of the road (on the side nearest the sea), if you look carefully you'll see an unpretentious sign reading "Artist's Studio, Paintings of Irish Scenes." That modest sign is little indication of the fine paintings you'll find inside Raymond Klee's studio that adjoins his home The Welsh-born artist has lived and worked all over the world and has won such coveted awards as those bestowed by the French Salon and the Fine Arts Guild (in England), but has chosen to settle in this beauty spot and devote his time and his art to depicting the very scenes that have won your own heart since you first put foot on Irish soil.

His landscape canvases are remarkable in that they capture the elusive colors and sweeping majesty of Irish skies as well as the earthbound beauties most often painted by other artists. Sunsets over a dune-rimmed strand, storm skies which have fishermen scurrying to bring curraghs to safety ashore, and graceful configurations of sun-touched clouds are there to perpetuate your memories of those same scenes. Stone-enclosed fishing harbors and mountain stretches are other subjects, and hanging on the walls of his studio are portraits of that craggy Irish farmer or fisherman you were talking to just last night over a friendly pint.

Surprisingly, the prices for such priceless souvenirs run from just under £60 ($90) to just under £100 ($150), and there are sizes small enough to wrap securely and take back home easily, as well as a larger canvas that might well become the focal point of a Stateside room. Whether you buy a painting or not, do stop by to see these marvelous works and chat with an interesting and talented artist.

County Donegal

Gillespie Brothers, Main Street, Mountcharles, County Donegal

In a small, white-and-red-front shop on Mountcharles' main street, the Gillespie family has long offered bargains in tweed, hand-knits, and other craft products which average about 10% lower in price than larger stores. In addition to tweed lengths, there are jackets and suits (no charge for alterations), blankets, lap rugs, tweed throws, long hand-crocheted capes, dresses, and tops, all at very good prices. From time to time, the Gillespies run special offers when prices are discounted even more. They'll also be happy to mail purchases.

Kathleen's, Main Street, Mountcharles, County Donegal (tel. 073-35108 or 21672)

A little beyond Gillespie's, in a row of terrace houses, Kathleen Alcock has a small shop packed with some of Ireland's best giftware at lower-than-usual prices. There are tweeds carefully selected by Kathleen personally, hand-knits, mohair, and Irish linen items, as well as a good selection of Belleek and Royal Tara china, Waterford and Cavan crystal, Connemara marble, and hand-crocheted separates. Kathleen, who spent several years in the U.S., cheerfully mails purchases and accepts American Express, VISA, and Access credit cards. She also makes VAT refunds on the spot, a decided bonus for overseas visitors. You'll find a second shop in Main Street in Donegal Town.

County Galway

Mairtin Standun, Spiddal, County Galway (tel. 091-83108)

If you're driving west from Galway City into Connemara, just before you get into Spiddal, you'll see a unique country store named Standun. Don't just drive past. You won't regret a closer inspection.

This is a kind of miniature supermarket for homemade Irish folk items. Standing in the heart of the tradition-bound, Irish-speaking district known as the **Gaeltacht,** its 5,000 square feet of floor space brims with the handcrafted products of the region. This is a family store, where the Standuns mount guard over the quality of whatever they carry. The slightest imperfection will banish an item to the back shelves reserved for markdowns—which is where you'll consequently find the bargains. It some-times takes a bit of looking—as we said, this is a supermarket, not a boutique.

But even on the perfect products you get a rare degree of quali-ty for fairly modest prices. The main accent is on hand-knitted *bainim,* the name of the natural wool used in making the world-famous Aran sweaters. These bulky knits are fantastically warm and water-resistant, as you'd expect from sweaters made for and by fishermen who wear them in icy ocean gales. Every Aran Is-land family knits its own pattern, which becomes its trademark, as clearly recognizable to them as tartans are to the Scottish clans. Choose the pattern you fancy, but remember that every hand-stitch that went in has some symbolic significance relating to the sea or earth. The color is the creamy hue of the raw wool. There's also an extensive range of hand-woven throws, blankets, and bedspreads.

Other items carried include crystal and Belleek, tweed jackets and kilts (almost indestructible), sheepskin and Foxford rugs, and a large selection of cashmere garments. Standun's produces a small brochure so that you can buy here or order from home. When feet are weary, rest at the coffee bar.

Padraic O'Maille, Dominic Street, Galway City, County Galway (tel. 091-62696)

Since 1938, "tweed" in Galway has meant Padraic O'Maille's shop in Dominic Street. The late Mr. O'Maille pioneered the commercial marketing of Aran hand-knitted sweaters and the hand-woven tweeds that have been made in local cottages for centuries, and today his widow and children carry on the tradi-tion he established. Among customers who regularly come in to choose tweed lengths from which to have O'Maille's fashion jackets, skirts, dresses, overcoats, etc., made are Maureen O'Hara, Peter Ustinov, and the late John Ford (John Wayne was also a longtime client). The family-run shop also features Irish linen, Connemara rugs, lambskin gloves (for both sexes), caps and hats, and a large selection of fine ties. There's a branch (small, but with a representative stock) in the Irish Tourist Board building, and you can pick up a mail-order catalog in case you have afterthoughts. VISA, MasterCard, and American Express cards are accepted. Both shops are open Monday through Saturday from 9 a.m. to 6 p.m.

Millar's Connemara Tweeds, Main Street, Clifden, Connemara, County Galway (tel. 095-21038)

A landmark on the main street of Clifden, Millar's is a long-term family concern that gives major employment to the weavers in the district. Millar's mills produce some of the finest pure wool fabrics in some of the most glowing shades in the country. But the shop is stocked with more than fabric lengths. There's a good selection of Waterford crystal and the best of Irish handcrafts. Up a spiral staircase an art gallery displays paintings on Connemara scenes, some quite superb, priced from £45 ($67.50) to £1,000 ($1,500). One wing of the shop, where Irish fashions are displayed, is stonewalled. Woven belts and ties are draped over an antique spinning wheel, and a turf fire glows on the stone hearth.

The shop carries just about everything that is handmade of wool in Ireland: tweed hats, caps, ties, floor rugs, table mats, bedspreads, curtains, belts, scarves, sweaters, tams, and blankets. Most unusual are the patchwork bedspreads (not always available) made from wool ends of factory tweed worked into cottage scenes, flowers, even a farm woman in colorful dress, each one different.

The shop is open from 9 a.m. to 6 p.m.; closed Sunday.

Connemara Handcrafts, Letterfrack, County Galway (tel. 095-41058)

If there is any shop in Ireland guaranteed to thrill the seeker after fine crafts, this is it. Located on an exquisite small harbor just outside of Letterfrack, the large, multi-room shop is jam-packed with excellent Irish crafts combed from the entire country, including many items seldom seen elsewhere.

The shop is owned and operated by the Pratt family, and their personal concern can be seen everywhere. Crafts are displayed individually, with a special room for knitwear, one for crystal, another for fine Irish linens, a section for Irish records and books, and one for hand-woven tweeds and clothing. The Exhibition Room sets out museum pieces: beautifully wrought jewelry, glassware, hand-painted pottery, and paintings. Scoop up a handful of feathered bird brooches for lightweight gifts. Or indulge in a collector's item, one of Aine Stack's beautifully detailed and witty character dolls. Prices, for the originality and quality of workmanship shown here, are reasonable indeed.

After wearing yourself out deciding on what to leave behind, have a restful cup of tea and homemade buttered brack (traditional fruitcake) or apple pie with cream in the bright, clean upstairs tearoom overlooking the garden. From Easter through the end of May the shop is open daily except Sunday from 9:30 a.m. to 6 p.m.; in June, July, and August, until 7 p.m. (and open on Sunday these months from 11 a.m. to 6 p.m.).

Maam Valley Pottery and Sweater Shop, Maam Village, County Galway (tel. 091-71109)

Located about halfway between Leenane and Maam Bridge, this shop is the love child of Ann and Dennis Kendrick, who left Dublin 11 years ago to set up shop in the unspoiled countryside of the west. All the items you see on display are manufactured in the Connemara area, most within a 20-mile radius of the pottery. You'll find Connemara marble, wool knitwear, Lough Mask rushwork, candles, jewelry, and hand-loomed ties, hats, scarves, shawls, blankets, and rugs. And, as the name implies, there's a working pottery right on the premises. In fact, you can visit the workroom and watch the potters throwing the very items on sale in the shop. You won't find better prices anywhere, or a more individualistic selection, or a more interested, attentive staff. What's more, they offer a mail-order service.

County Kerry

Dunquin Pottery, Dunquin, near Dingle, County Kerry

There are various small potteries scattered around the country, but this one—perched on a bluff overlooking the sea, on the road to Dunquin Village, just past Slea Head—is special. Operated by local people Mairin, Eiblín, and Séan Daly, the pottery produces only ovenproof stoneware, hand-thrown, glazed with Irish limestone and turf ashes, and fired to 1,280 degrees Centigrade. The result is a distinctive sandy color mottled with browns and blues—the tones of the Dingle Peninsula from which all ingredients come.

The motifs are equally subdued and in character. A plump-bellied vase bears three simple megalithic swirls; the popular "fish vase" stands on its nose with a triangle of scales reaching from snout to graceful, upwaving tail.

Prices are reasonable, from £2.75 ($4.13) for a ramekin to £44.50 ($66.75) for a complete coffee set. The six-inch fish vase costs only £4.58 ($6.87). Unfortunately, they do no shipping. But it's open from Easter through mid-November, 10 a.m. to 7 p.m. daily.

Shannon Airport Duty-Free Shopping Center

Back in 1947 Shannon Airport pioneered the "Buy As You Fly" concept of duty-free shopping for bona fide travelers. Since then similar centers have sprung up at airports around the globe, but Shannon remains the first and one of the finest. The original bargain corner has today grown into a department-store-size complex consisting of 18 mini-shops and employing a sales staff of 120. The merchandise displayed comes from every part of the world and includes celebrated brand names. Bargains abound because the retailers buy direct from the factory and sell free of import duties and taxes. Thus the 30,000 square feet of shopping space is crammed with choice goods that would cost you considerably more if purchased in ordinary stores anywhere.

Some bargains, of course, are better than others, so it pays to take a really close look around and to know something about the price range of a particular item at home. Generally speaking, the real snaps are electronic items, watches, perfumes, liquor (you can take back up to one liter free of U.S. Customs duty), Irish thick knits, and certain woolen lines.

There has always been one major problem with shopping at Shannon: Suppose you leave it for departure time and the very thing you have had your heart set on doesn't happen to be there! Well, now the Duty-Free Shopping Center has solved that problem rather brilliantly. You can now browse through the shopping area when you deplane in Ireland to see just what is available. If you make your purchase then, it will be set aside for your return trip or mailed home immediately (in which case, be sure it is addressed to friends who will be there to receive it). If you're looking for gifts and can't make up your mind, Shannon Shops has gift cheque books in $10 and $25 denominations which will be mailed along with their mail-order catalog.

Because some of those tax-free goodies just may carry Customs duty when you re-enter the U.S., it's a good idea to know the regulations before you shop. Two very useful—and free—publications to study before you leave home are: **Know Before**

You Go, which you can order from the U.S. Customs Service, Box 7407, Washington, D.C. 20044; and **Travelers' Tips,** which deals with foods and other agricultural products and may be ordered from the U.S. Department of Agriculture, Animal and Plant Health Inspection Service, 732 Federal Bldg., 6505, Belcrest Rd., Hyattsville, MD 20782.

Chapter XVI

THE SHANNON AREA

Eating and Sleeping in the West

DISEMBARK AT SHANNON after a full night's flight, and you will want to do nothing more than sleep—or at least take it easy. Don't plan very strenuous activities for your first day in Ireland. The west coast has weathered many a century and it can await your afternoon nap.

In the airport, you can change your money, pick up a rental car, book a castle banquet or an extended CIE tour, or dine moderately at the grill. Shannon also handles bookings for the Rent-An-Irish-Cottage scheme and many special-interest holidays.

The Shannon area is replete with attractions. Many are clustered around Bunratty, nine miles from the airport on the Limerick road, where the famed Medieval Banquet takes place nightly at the castle, where you can study Ireland Past in the showcase cottages at the folk park, where you can indulge with Ireland Present in libations at Durty Nelly's at the foot of the castle keep. The old walls of Limerick and King John's Castle lie 15 miles to the west of the airport and the Shannon River courses close by. An easy drive will take you to a reconstruction of a fourth-century crannog at Craggaunowen on the grounds of a 16th-century castle, and not far away is Knappoge Castle, open for sightseeing and/or banqueting. There's much to do in the Shannon area. Stick around.

Accommodations

Several good-value hotels are easily accessible to the airport. One of the most luxurious (and expensive) castle hotels in Ireland —Dromoland—is but eight miles away (see Chapter XI). Drive toward Limerick on the Ennis road and you will find an entire line-up of bed-and-breakfast houses where summer prices seldom top £10 ($15) per person for humble yet homey accommodations. The airport area is well-supplied with resting spots, whatever your preferred price range.

Fitzpatrick's Shannon Shamrock Hotel, Bunratty, County Clare (tel. 061-61177)

You'd have to love the Shannon Shamrock for its location, if nothing else: five miles from Shannon Airport, nine miles from Limerick, and just next door to Bunratty Castle. The Folk Park, the medieval banquet, and Durty Nellie's are all just a short walk away, and there's courtesy coach service to the airport upon request as well as to Limerick twice daily. There's much more than location, however, to recommend this lovely hotel. It's a sister to Fitzpatrick's Castle Hotel in Killiney (see Chapter III), and while the two bear no outward resemblance, they are both looked over with the same personal care and attention by the Fitzpatrick family. The exceptionally efficient and friendly staff reflects that same sort of personal concern.

The Shannon Shamrock, a low, rambling stone building, exudes low-key informality in a setting of pure luxury. The stone-floored lobby leads into a large lounge whose focal point is a huge stone fireplace (ablaze on cool evenings). Comfortable seating arranged for intimate groupings make this an inviting place to have morning coffee, afternoon tea, or late-night drinks. The pretty cocktail bar, with dark-blue velvet upholstering, skylights, and lots of dark wood and green plants, has music Wednesday through Sunday during summer months. Shades of soft green and rose dominate the dining room. There's an indoor heated swimming pool and a sauna on the premises and plenty of parking space.

The 110 guest rooms all come with private bath, radio, TV, and telephone. Decor and furnishings are outstanding in all, but for a sumptuous break from the rigors of travel, treat yourself to a stay in one of the beautiful and spacious River Suites—velvet chair and sofa coverings, king-sized beds, and windows with a view are featured in bed/sitting rooms for two, separate bedroom and bed/sitting room for four.

Depending on the season, rates range from £34 ($51) to £48 ($72) for singles; £47 ($70.50) to £66 ($99) for doubles; £49 ($73.50) to £63 ($94.50) for family rooms. River Suites for two are £60 ($90) and £68 ($102); £99 ($148.50) to £110 ($165) for four. Service charge is 10%.

Old Ground Hotel, Ennis, County Clare (tel. 065-21127)

Located in the middle of County Clare, 12 miles north of Shannon Airport, the Old Ground is a low, ivy-covered little haven that strikes a delicate balance between Irish country charm and modern hotel luxury. It has a special hard-to-define appeal—how many hotels are there mounting an iron cannon at the entrance with the muzzle pointing *toward* the building?

Inside, the place has an intriguing duality of period decor and contemporary streamlining. The dining room, for instance, sounds a luxuriously traditional note, with a huge fireplace bearing brass plates and sets of body armor and crossed swords on the wall. Yet right alongside runs a quick-service food bar—rare in Irish hostelries—where you get meals at prices well below those of the formal dinery.

The same contrast governs the 63 bedrooms. All come with private bath, direct-dial telephone, color TV, and tea- and coffee-makings, but the fittings vary considerably. Some are standard modern hotel rooms, pastel colored and plush. Others show a Victorian touch, with delicate occasional tables, oval mirrors on white walls, and drawers with ornate brass handles. Lighting ranges from miniature chandeliers to fluorescent tubes. entral heating keeps the place snug on chill nights, yet the public rooms have wonderfully convivial fireplaces. The Celtic Bar features Donegal hand-woven tweed seating and teak tables with inserts of woven rushwork. This pattern of contrasts may be the secret of the Old Ground's specially endearing effect on visitors.

Rates begin at £37 ($55.50) for singles, £52 ($78) for double rooms, including full Irish breakfast. Deduct one-third for children.

Hyland's Hotel, Ballyvaughan, County Clare (tel. 065-77037)

The Burren is an important part of the Shannonside area, and Ballyvaughan, on its northern reaches, is a convenient stopover point en route to Galway and points northwest or a handy touring base for both the Clare and Galway countryside. The medieval banquet at Dunguaire Castle (see Chapter XI) is a mere 15 miles away. On its main street, the Hyland Hotel dates back to the early 18th century—the present Hylands are the seventh and eighth generation of that family to own and operate this friendly small hotel.

This is country that draws botanists, painters, and fishermen in droves, and you'll likely find a congenial mix of all three plus a goodly portion of locals in the Hyland's public lounge bar. A turf fire is laid on every night, and spontaneous musical sessions erupt with amazing frequency. There's a fire, as well, in the cozy residents' lounge for relaxing away from the bar.

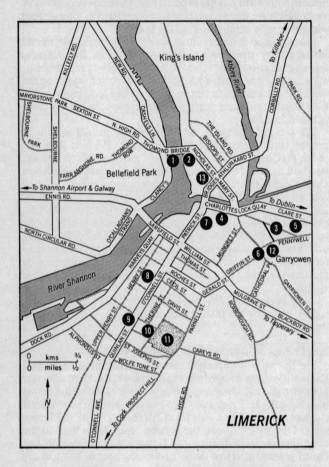

1. Treaty Stone
2. King John's Castle
3. City Walls
4. Tourist Office
5. Limerick Lace
6. Museum
7. Town Hall
8. General Post Office
9. O'Connell Monument
10. Museum & Art Gallery
11. People's Park
12. St. John's Cathedral
13. St. Mary's Cathedral

Rooms are simply, but comfortably, furnished, with attractive decor, and seasonal rates range from £16.50 ($24.75) to £20 ($30) for singles, £28 ($42) to £33 ($49.50) for doubles. Add £2 ($3) per person sharing for private bath. Children get a one-third reduction, and there's a 10% service charge.

The Smyth Village Hotel, Feakle, County Clare (tel. Feakle 2 or 6)

A quite remarkable concept in budget accommodations, the Smyth Village Hotel is located in the tiny village of Feakle, 20 miles from Shannon Airport, close to the foothills of the Slieve Aughty mountains and a few miles south of lovely Lough Graney.

Feakle is a Rent-a-Cottage town, meaning that the people have become shareholders in a group of traditional-style cottages with modern amenities which they rent to visitors to bring much-needed cash to the community. The hotel is an outcropping of the scheme.

Owned and operated by Mr. and Mrs. Con Smyth (she was born in Feakle; he, six miles away), who also own the general store, the hotel looks like three two-story, slate-roofed cottages linked together on a bluff overlooking the village. In hotel style, it is licensed to serve alcohol; accommodations, breakfast, and dinner are offered to all comers March to November; and there's a tennis court for guests. In guesthouse style, it provides lunch to residents only (upon request) and has no receptionist or porter to provide service. You dine family-style at large wooden tables and get no choice of menu. The cooking is home-style Irish, but "the very best quality done in the simplest way." The Smyths butcher their own beef; Mrs. Smyth bakes the bread and buns.

All the touches are traditional: Sugan chairs, cottage windows with tweed curtains, a hanging two-century-old lamp in the dining room, and the pub has a large open fireplace hung with iron implements. Every Thursday and Saturday nights local musicians hold forth on their pipes and fiddles for themselves and the visitors (no charge).

The 12 bedrooms, all with private bath and central heating, are white-walled, fresh, and attractive. The eight on the main floor have twin beds, shower, and toilet. The four upstairs are large family rooms, capable of sleeping two parents and three young children. These come with bath, shower, and toilet. Walls are white, the spreads of olive baineen woven in Connemara. Calf baskets hang below the dressing tables for use as wastebaskets.

And since nothing but indigenous materials is used, not even the shower curtain is plastic.

It's a simple place, a refreshing place, but also an amazingly inexpensive place. Rates are £11 ($16.50) single, £20 ($30) double, for bed and a full breakfast, with a 10% service charge and a one-third reduction for children.

Meals

In the Shannon area, you don't dine—you feast! Both the touted **Bunratty Medieval Banquet** and the historical banquet at **Knappogue Castle** are within easy driving distance of the airport and surrounding hotels. If you prefer something less formal, more rustic, opt for the farm meal in the barn at the Bunratty Folk Park. Details are given in the "Castle Banquets" chapter.

With such exceptional fun-and-food evenings available, there is little need for restaurant recommendations. But for that odd meal you might want without music and mead, there are several luxury-priced places nearby: **MacCloskey's, The Copper Room,** and the **Shannon Airport Restaurant.** And those watching pennies can pick from the varied menu at the swift-service **Airport Grill.** Or snack on pub grub under the rafters at **Durty Nelly's.**

MacCloskey's at Bunratty House, Bunratty, County Clare (tel. 061-74082)

Bunratty House (just back of the castle) is an elegant mansion whose age is more than a century-and-a-half. Its living quarters have seen comings and goings which would probably fill a book, but it's a sure bet that its arched-ceiling cellar has never before seen the likes of MacCloskey's gourmet restaurant. Gerry and Marie MacCloskey left West Cork and their award-winning Courtyard restaurant in Schull to bring their expertise to Shannonside, and the result is one of Ireland's most beautiful and appealing places to eat.

The low ceilings and foot-and-a-half-thick walls have been whitewashed to a pristine white as a background for delicate shades of pink and rose, which are punctuated by the deep blue of tall candles at each table. Original room separations make for intimate dining. The mansion's original wine cellar has been retained and behind its ironwork gates rests an excellent selection of good wines.

Main courses of the preset dinner change often to be sure that only the freshest produce, meats, and seafoods are served. A typical five-course offering might include such starters as snails in garlic butter, selection of melon with Kiwi fruit, and smoked salmon; cream of lettuce soup or salad with Stilton cheese dressing; main courses of sea trout with hollandaise sauce, rod-caught salmon baked with herbs, leeks, and mushrooms, or black sole on the bone; fresh garden vegetables; and dessert of iced lemon and lime soufflé, rhubarb tart, or stuffed chocolate-covered pears. Amazingly, the price for such a feast comes to only £19 ($28.50).

Hours are 6:30 to 10 p.m. every night except Sunday and Monday. If you have only one dinner in Shannonside, let this be it!

The Copper Room, Jurys Hotel, Ennis Road, Limerick, County Clare (tel. 061-55266)

The Cooper Room inside Jurys' large and bustling hotel is as intimate and serene as an executive dining room. The colors are autumnal and subdued. Wooden planters divide tables into private conversation areas. Deep-green easy chairs provide comfortable seating. Copper touches prevail—copper shades overhanging the round wooden tables, copper salt and pepper shakers upon them, a copper cornucopia with good things flowing forth on the far wall.

It is the good things that flow from the kitchen, however, that bring one to the Copper Room. French/Belgian chef Louis Lambert has added Gallic know-how to Ireland's first-rate fresh ingredients and come up with some very pleasing specialties. The filets de sole maison consists of fluffy poached sole stuffed with mushrooms, tomato, and lobster, and laced with white-wine sauce; the homard à la maison (in season) is lobster cooked in white wine and flamed with brandy at your table. Flaming goes on a great deal at the Copper Room. Also popular is the entrecôte au poivre façon du chef, pepper steak flamed with brandy, and you can order either bananas or peaches done flambé style for dessert.

Dinners from the à la carte menu average £17 ($25.50). Hours are 5 to 11:30 p.m., closed Sunday. Book ahead. The Copper Room seats only 42, and diners are invited to loiter.

Shannon Airport Grill

This is the kind of cafeteria that every American airport should have, but doesn't: large, streamlined, functional yet attractive, with mushroom-colored carpets and contemporary lights, plus decent food at very moderate prices. The carousel-type grill op-

erates from 7:30 a.m. to 10 p.m. in summer, to 7:30 p.m. the rest
of the year, and provides fast service laced with unhurried smiles
—a combination rare in any airport.

The choice varies according to the time of day. For breakfast
you can get scrambled eggs and bacon and excellent tea for about
£3.80 ($5.70). Lunch and dinner menus are remarkably exten-
sive. To mention a random sampling: cold meat salad plates,
roast chicken with potatoes and vegetables, Irish stew, priced
below £3 ($4.50); and soup or sandwiches at £2.50 ($3.75) or less.

The tea is the usual superb Irish brew, the coffee acceptable,
the milk fresher than you'd get anywhere in the U.S. For more
luxurious dining, there's the lovely **Lindberg Room,** which offers
gourmet delights at less than gourmet prices.

Other Attractions

While here, don't miss a visit to the **Bunratty Folk Park,** laid
out on the grounds of the castle. Seven country cottages encircle
the fresh, green lawn, each typical of an era. In one, a basket-
maker weaves Shannon reeds into everything from placemats to
a cradle (all for sale). In another, a candlemaker turns out the
long, smokeless candles and turned wooden candlesticks used at
the banquets. Visit the Golden Vale farmhouse with its spacious
parlor, peat fires, and 19th-century trappings. Stop in for tea and
hot scones in the sunny tea room. The folk park makes a peaceful
interlude.

At the same time, visit the museum rooms at **Bunratty Castle,**
filled with elaborately carved furnishings, tapestries, stained-
glass panels, church art, and one amazingly detailed four-poster
bed draped with valances embroidered with scenes from the
childhood of Christ. Hours: 9:30 a.m. to 5:30 p.m. daily.

Then wander to the arched bridge before the keep, and stop
into **Durty Nelly's** for a pint (see Chapter XIV). Or drive up the
road to **Dromoland Castle** in Newmarket-on-Fergus for a perfectly made cocktail in the lounge overlooking the private lake—
especially impressive at sunset. If it's too early for refreshments,
cross the road and inspect the items on sale at the **Bunratty Cottage International Fashion Shop** (details in Chapter XV).

In Limerick City, visit **King John's Castle** on the banks of the
Shannon. Built in the 13th century, it is a fine example of medieval architecture. Open Monday through Saturday from 10 a.m.
to 12:30 p.m. and 3 to 6 p.m., on Sunday from 2 to 6 p.m. Or
800-year-old **St. Mary's Cathedral,** which is free and contains a
wealth of historical treasures. Open daily from 9 a.m. to 1 p.m.
and 2:30 to 5:30 p.m.

A short drive out the Quin-Sixmilebridge road will bring you to **Craggaunowen Castle,** the fortified home John MacSheeda MacNamara built about 1550. On its grounds you'll find a ring fort with its man-made cave called a souterrain, and a reconstructed crannog (one of the most ancient Irish habitations) built on an artifical island in a lake. Replicas of the implements, weapons, and utensils of the late Bronze Age are among its furnishings. Close by is the leather boat *Brendan* in which an adventurous crew retraced St. Brendan's voyage from Ireland to Newfoundland. Craggaunowen is open daily from 9:30 a.m. to 5:30 p.m.

Also near Quinn, and well signposted, is **Knappogue Castle,** a 1467 residence of the MacNamara tribe that is today restored and furnished with a unique collection of antiques. For details of the medieval banquet here, see Chapter XI. Viewing hours are 9:30 a.m. to 5:30 p.m.

No one should leave the Shannonside area without having visited the majestic **Cliffs of Moher,** just beyond Ennistymon in County Clare. The spectacular cliffs of millstone, grit, and sandstone stretch for nearly five miles, and from **O'Brien's Tower,** perched almost 700 feet above the sea, there are marvelous views of the Clare coastline, the Kerry and Connemara Mountains, and the Aran Islands. There's no charge, and the well-equipped visitor center is open from 10 a.m. to 6 p.m. Monday through Saturday, noon to 6 p.m. on Sunday.

Chapter XVII

SPECIAL IRISH VACATIONS

Boats, Cottages, Farmhouses, and Caravans

SEVERAL DIFFERENT but distinctly inviting vacation possibilities can be worked in as part of your country tour or can constitute the whole of your stay. All are seductively peaceful, offering a refreshing pause from the turmoil of 20th-century life.

Boating on the Shannon

The lordly River Shannon is not only Ireland's longest waterway, but one of the most easily navigable in the world. Its 140 miles of navigable length are broken by only six locks and are nontidal for 128 miles of the way. Experience, while handy, is not essential in cruising this sparkling green-and-blue stream. In fact, it takes a certain amount of talent to hole or wreck your craft. Apart from the sheer joy of "messing around in boats" you can join the river festivities like the **Shannon Harbor Canal Boat Rally** (late June at Shannonbridge), the **Festival of the Shannon** (first two weeks in July at Carrick-on-Shannon), and the **Shannon Boat Rally** (end of July between Athlone and Carrick-on-Shannon).

You can rent cruising motor vessels from a number of firms whose boats have been inspected and approved by the Irish Tourist Board (which can furnish a complete listing). Some of these cruisers have showers, central heating, and refrigerators, and all are completely seaworthy. Charges range from £150 ($225) to £750 ($1,125) per week. Sample offerings are:

Carrick Craft in Carrick-on-Shannon, County Leitrim (tel. 078-20236)—has two- to eight-berth craft.

Emerald Star Line, St. James Gate, Dublin (tel. 01-720244)—has four- to eight-berth craft at two bases on the River Shannon.

FlagLine, Shancurragh, Athlone, County Westmeath (tel. 0902-2892)—has two- to eight-berth craft and sailing dinghies.

Rent an Irish Cottage

Scattered over some of the prettiest spots in the land is a unique network of villages built for *you*—small clusters of enchanted-looking cottages specially designed for a close-to-nature vacation, but minus any of the discomforts usually connected with such retreats. The whole project is known as **Rent an Irish Cottage Ltd.,** and fulfills a highly original dual purpose. It can, first, give you the most peacefully relaxed holiday you've ever known. And, second, it gives you a chance to really get to know the people of rural Ireland. Not as a passing tourist, but as an esteemed guest living among them.

The reason for this is that the villagers are shareholders in the scheme. You are *their* guest. The folks you'll meet in the local pub or at the grocery are your hosts. So what they'll extend to you on top of their traditional hospitality is the knowledge that the happier you are, the quicker you'll come back, and the greater their project will prosper.

But don't get the idea that you'll be roughing it. True, the cottages are thatched by hand—part of their special charm. They also have open fireplaces, traditional furnishings, rustic decor, and those village half-doors, designed for a neighborly gossip. But at the same time they boast central heating, electric lights, electric kitchens with refrigerators, bathrooms with showers, drapes, linen, kitchen utensils, built-in cupboards, dishes, cutlery, and even an immersion heater. So it's not what you might call a primitive existence. You do your shopping in the village store, your socializing in the pub, where *everybody* meets, including old ladies, children, and wayfarers from other villages.

Other pleasures are golfing, fishing, swimming, boating, pony trekking, or country walking. The banquets at three medieval castles lie within easy reach. So does Shannon Airport.

You'll find Rent-a-Cottage locations at:

Corofin, County Clare—dotted with fishable lakes, castles, underground caves, and rare flora.

Feakle, in East Clare—a district of lakes, rivers, and streams, surrounded by woodland, just 24 miles from Shannon Airport.

Knocklong, County Limerick—20 miles from Limerick City, close to historic ruins and amid outstanding beautiful scenery.

Puckane, North Tipperary—a picturesque village two miles from the Shannon River where you can fish, boat, waterski, and watch local craftworkers at their jigsaw wood art.

Kilfinane, County Limerick, at the foot of the Ballyhoura Mountains, 27 miles from Limerick City—lush valleys, horseback riding, trout angling.

Ballyvaughan, County Clare—a magical setting overlooking Galway Bay, with the Atlantic Ocean beach only three miles away.

Carrigaholt, County Clare—a seaside village at the mouth of the River Shannon, with magnificent cliff scenery, historic towers, and church ruins.

Holycross, County Tipperary—near the famous 12th-century Holy Cross Abbey; go pony riding, hunting, fishing.

Murroe, County Limerick, seven miles from Limerick—picnics in the nearby glens, historical castles, game angling.

Broadford, East Clare, 14 miles from Shannon Airport—jaunting car trips, superb scenic walks, plus game angling.

Renvyle, County Galway, on the bewitching edge of Connemara with the Atlantic washing the shoreline a mile away—uncrowded beaches, fine freshwater angling and sea fishing, golf, picnics on the offshore islands, pony trekking, exploring the glorious countryside.

Ballycastle, County Mayo, on the North Mayo Coast—beside a clean sandy beach, with good fishing and easy access to the scenic Mayo moors and the Yeats Country of Sligo to the north.

The four types of cottages available cost £150 ($225) to £260 ($390) per week in peak season, and can accommodate from five to eight. Off-season rates range as low as £80 ($120). For further information and application forms, contact Rent an Irish Cottage Ltd., Shannon Free Airport, County Clare, Ireland (tel. 061-61788).

Donegal Thatched Cottages, at Cruit Island on the coast of County Donegal, are perhaps even more special. For one thing, they are a group of eight traditional thatched cottages perched on a sheltered clearing on a clifftop overlooking some of Donegal's most spectacular seascapes. For another, while they are constructed and furnished entirely with Irish-made products and adhere faithfully to traditional styles, modern conveniences of a luxury nature have been carefully tucked in so as not to mar their old-world charm. For instance, there's central heat, in case you shouldn't want to bother with turf fires, and automatic washer and drier make laundry a breeze. Just below the clifftop (and a short walk down a rocky path) lies a perfect, crescent-shaped strand, and on the other side miles of safe, sandy beach line the incredibly blue waters of Kincasslagh Bay. Offshore can be seen the rugged outlines of Aranmore and Owey Islands. Swimming, boating, trekking, picnicking, and just plain loafing are perfect daytime activities, while the colorful local pubs and one outstanding nearby restaurant give you the nighttime option of enjoying your own company or that of others. Weekly rental rates of £105 ($157.50) to £285 ($427.50), depending on season, are remarkably reasonable on a per-person basis, since each cottage can comfortably accommodate seven adults. September through May, special midweek and weekend rates are also available. For full details and bookings, contact: Conor and Mary Ward, Rosses Point, County Sligo (tel. 071-77197).

Gold Coast Holiday Homes, Ballinacourty, Dungarvan, County Waterford (tel. 058-42249), sit on the edge of Dungarvan Bay along Ireland's beautiful southeast coast. Just minutes away, there are coastal drives through breathtaking scenery of tall cliffs, sheltered coves and sandy beaches; the historic marketing town of Dungarvan is your next-door neighbor; both Cork City and Waterford City are less than an hour's drive; and wherever you wander in the region you'll find rugged mountains (the Comeragh and Knockmealdown ranges are both within easy reach), cathedrals, castles, and some of the most verdant farmland in the country dotted with lush forests and rushing rivers. Angling and deepsea fishing are both very good here (boats and gear are available at the Holiday Homes); there are safe beaches nearby for swimming; and you can walk to the adjacent Dungarvan Golf Club, which extends playing rights to visitors. All in all, this is the perfect base for touring almost all of the Southeast.

The cottages are semi-detached, arranged in a semicircle, each with its own garden area. There's ample parking, and an outstanding restaurant and lounge bar are on the property (this is a favorite gathering spot for locals, with music in the lounge frequently during summer months). Inside, each cottage has an entrance hall, living room/dining room (with fireplace), kitchen (fully equipped), bath, and three bedrooms (two on the ground floor, one upstairs). They're carpeted throughout, have TV and are nicely furnished. Bedrooms feature built-in wardrobes and dressing tables, and beds consist of one double and four singles. Six people are accommodated very nicely, but even if you install a cot in the spacious upstairs bedroom, you won't feel cramped. All linens are included, although electricity is extra.

Weekly rates per cottage range from £92 ($138) to £252 ($378), depending on season. However, from January to May and October to December, they can be rented for less than a full week, with very attractive midweek and weekend rates.

Dun an Oir Cottages, Ballyferriter, Dingle, County Kerry (tel. 066-56133), look out over a sandy beach to Dingle Bay and the offshore Blasket Islands. There's no more romantic, wildly beautiful spot in Ireland than the Dingle Peninsula, and these cottages are at its very tip. Weeks could be spent exploring the surrounding archeological leavings of its history. There are mountain walks unlike any you've seen elsewhere, and the three bird sanctuaries attract seabirds from all over Western Europe. Fishermen will be in their glory, whether angling from the shore or shipping out on one of Dingle's many fishing boats. When self-catering palls, there's the luxury Dun an Oir Hotel (see Chapter XIII) right at hand with a gorgeous restaurant and a lounge bar that attracts the Irish-speaking natives for many an evening's fun, including traditional music and—if you're lucky—yarns that have come down over the generations. It's another world, this Dun an Oir, and a beguiling, spellbinding one, at that.

The self-catering complex surrounding the hotel has been planned with children in mind, and far from being a liability, they're cared for with affection. The play area holds swings, slides, climbers, and a variety of other equipment to keep them happily occupied. Even the swimming pool has a special toddlers pool. For teenagers, there's a game room, table tennis, and from time to time, a disco. Need a babysitter? Just give the hotel management a little notice and you're free for a night on your own.

Cottages come in two sizes: two bedrooms, which will accommodate four or five; and three bedrooms, which will sleep six comfortably. There's a fireplace in the living room, and for chilly nights, each bedroom has an electric heater. All kitchens are fully fitted out, with electric stoves for cooking.

From May to September, there's a minimum seven-day stay (running from Saturday to Saturday); other months, the cottages are available at special midweek and weekend rates. Seasonal rates range from £130 ($195) to £330 ($495), and you'll be asked to send a deposit of £75 ($112.50) per week of booking to confirm your reservation (returnable if cancellation is received 21 days in advance). The balance is due three weeks in advance of your arrival.

Rent an Irish Castle

Which of us has not, at one time or another, had fantasies of being lord or lady of a real-life castle! Well, in Ireland, you can be just that for a time. Since 1981 several castles have been available for weekly rental at rates that start around £250 ($375) and climb up into the £3,000 ($4,500) range—rates that become more manageable when prorated on a per-person basis. For a complete listing, write for the **Rent-an-Irish-Castle** leaflet from Bord Failte, Baggot Street Bridge, Dublin 2, Ireland. For full descriptions of each, and booking information, contact them directly at these addresses, and remember to inquire about the number of guests who can be accommodated (a party of 12, for instance, sharing, can reduce that weekly charge substantially):

Carraigin Castle (self-catering), Headford, County Galway
Cloghan Castle, Kilchreest, Loughrea, County Galway
Springfield Castle, Drumcollogher, County Limerick
Lismore Castle, Lismore, County Waterford

Farmhouse Holidays

If you're looking for the absolute top value in budget holidays for yourself and the kids—this is it! A vacation spent in an Irish farmhouse does more than rest the body. It recharges your psychic batteries, fills your lungs with God's pure air, your stomach with fresh, unadulterated country food, and your soul with an amount of tranquility and human warmth you probably never believed existed—quite apart from letting your children learn that milk isn't made in plastic containers and that eggs are laid by real live chickens.

You could write a volume about Irish farms as recuperation centers and their owners as restorers of faith in hospitality, good humor, and plain honest kindness. Out there the Great Rat Race may be run, but the sound of it hasn't yet wafted into those whitewashed cottages, farming castles, and neat, slate-roofed houses that open both their doors and their hearts to guests.

In the late 1960s an outfit called the Irish Farm Holidays Association (*Failte Tuaithe*) put country hospitality on an organized basis, simultaneously keeping a gimlet eye on the quality thereof. Now there are more than 1,000 such farmhouse rooms to choose from. The association insists that all *must* belong to working farms. Within that bracket you get a vast variety of homesteads to choose from. You'll find them listed, with photographs, plus amenities and prices, in **"Farm Holidays in Ireland,"** available from the Irish Tourist Board.

Herewith two of the more unusual spots within the selection:

Mrs. O'Hara, Coopershill, Riverstown, County Sligo (tel. 071-65108), offers a beautiful, three-story Georgian mansion dating to 1774 with 500 acres of farmland surrounding, threaded through by a river. The house is furnished with antiques including several vast and luxurious four-poster beds. Mrs. O'Hara's rates are: bed-and-breakfast, £20 ($30) to £24 ($36) a night; dinner, £14 ($21).

Hawthorn Farm, Kilgarvan, County Kerry (tel. 064-85326), is a modern farmhouse, the domain of charming Kitty Dineen and her family. The hospitality, however, harks back to the strictly old-fashioned type and Kitty's table is widely known for its magnificent farm fare. Just wait until you taste her traditional Christmas cake (served year round), brown bread, and scones! Located just 12 miles from the sea, Hawthorn Farm has seven bedrooms with hand basins and three with private facilities. There's central heating, and it's open April through September. Bed-and-breakfast rate is £11 ($16.50) per person, dinner is £10.50 ($15.75), and weekly half-board is £133 ($199.50) per person.

Many other, more modest, places exist but, as you can tell from reading through the above list, a "farmhouse" in Ireland can mean anything from a thatched-roof cottage to a modern bungalow furnished with formica and gleaming linoleum floors, to a stately home crammed with the portraits and collected artworks of ancestors. Yet, in almost every case, the term "ideal for children" would apply. Hospitality is always personal, and many houses even invite the locals in to meet guests and stage quite impromptu song-and-dance "hoolies."

Farmhouses can be utilized as places to park for a week or two or overnight accommodation stops on an Ireland tour. Some stay open year round, but most take guests only from Easter to October. All serve both hearty breakfasts and dinners; some supply a packed lunch by request.

Horse-Drawn Caravans

Traveling the roads of Ireland by horse-drawn caravan isn't the speediest way to see the country, but it certainly isn't the most expensive, either. And it can be mighty memorable to all the Mittys among us who are gypsies in our souls. For the 20th-century soul to convert to such a simple mode of living, even if only for a week, may take a certain amount of adjustment, however. We've talked to quite a few caravan tour returnees. Some have called it the most fun they've had in years. They got into the country homes and pubs and spent long nights drinking beer and exchanging songs with their new friends. The horse was the epitome of Irish goodwill and the countryside a bewilderment of beauties—or words to that effect. Others come back looking a bit haggard. It's a matter of temperament.

These are the things to consider. You can rent a caravan for a minimum of one week, usually starting on Saturday morning. You get a colorful, barrel-shaped, gypsy-style caravan and a gentle horse (they promise!). The caravan is fitted out with beds or bunks, all bedding and kitchenware, a small gas stove, and lamps. Bottled gas, and oats for the horse, are provided; insurance is included in the cost. You can't make much more than 16 miles a day, usually less, and probably won't cover more than 100 miles during the week. As the caravan companies are scattered over several scenic areas, your choice of company will be determined by the area you most want to explore. In any case, most of the fleets are quite small and are usually booked up during July and August, so you must make summer reservations well in advance. All the caravan companies promise to send you off well versed in horse management, after drilling you in harnessing, unharnessing, and other details. They all say you need no previous experience with horses and supply you with long lists of such instructions as "NEVER stand behind the horse" and "NEVER put the horse in an unfenced field, or you will discover how heavy the caravan is to pull."

Once you've picked up your caravan and been tutored in its care, you're on your own. You can drift around at will, parking at night on scenic lay-bys or requesting space on some farmer's land. Most of the companies will provide you with itineraries of their area, marked with locations of welcoming farmers, pubs, householders, or even little grocery shops where you can find space, toilet facilities, and grazing land for your overnight stop. The cost of "parking and grazing" privileges ranges from £4 ($6) to £5 ($7.50), and country folk who grant such privileges have been known to lend a hand with the harnessing and running after the horse and to unburden themselves of much local lore over a pint at the nearest hostelry. It's also a nice—and inexpensive— gesture to purchase your milk, eggs, and bread where you've spent the night. You sleep, eat, and travel in the caravan, so choose congenial companions. Many of the caravans are advertised as sleeping five, but they would have to be a very slender and tolerant five indeed; we suggest that, for comfort's sake, you go in a party of no more than four.

You will have to write to the companies personally to reserve a caravan, and send at least a quarter of the fee as a deposit. All the following are companies noted for their reliability. All charge £150 ($225) to £350 ($525) per week from mid-June through August. Some offer special weekend rates and lower rates during other months. Locations vary considerably, so pick an area you want to see in depth.

Slattery's Horse-Drawn Caravans, 1 Russell St., Tralee, County Kerry (tel. 066-21722). Base: Tralee.

Dieter Clissmann Horse-Drawn Caravans, Carrigmore Farm, County Wicklow (tel. 0404-8188). Base: Carrigmore Farm, Wicklow.

Ocean Breeze Horse Caravans (attention Mr. Jerry Desmond), Granreigh, Kilbritain, County Cork (tel. 023-49731). Base: Granreigh, County Cork.

Chapter XVIII

INTRODUCING NORTHERN IRELAND

What About the Troubles?
The Practicalities

ACROSS THE BORDER in the six counties of Northern Ireland lies a panorama of scenic splendors and cultural riches that present yet another face of Ireland.

It was here that many of the ancient epics tell of heroic deeds by the mighty Fionn MacCumhaill (Finn MacCoul) and his fighting *Fianna* band; the courageous Cuchulainn, who single-handedly defended Ulster's borders against Queen Medb's forces when she set her heart on capturing the famed Brown Bull of Cuailgne; and the romantic tragedy of *Deirdre o' the Sorrows*.

It is here that the soft accents of Scotland mingle with the lilting rhythms of Ulster amid a landscape that swings from a rugged, cliff-lined coastline dotted with small inlets to the lofty heights and lonely glens of the beautiful Mountains of Mourne sweeping down to the sea to the vastness of Lough Neagh, Ireland's largest lake, to the shipyards and smoky skyline of industrial Belfast. Indeed, the treasures of this region are legion, among them such world-renowned attractions as the Giant's Causeway, the Glens of Antrim, and the incredible Carrick-a-Rede rope bridge.

Americans will be particularly interested in the fact that six U.S. Presidents had Ulster ancestors on both sides—Jackson, Polk, Buchanan, Arthur, McKinley, and Wilson—while seven others sprang from at least one Ulster root. Four of their ancestral homes are open to the public and they are listed in the following chapters.

In short, the counties of Londonderry, Antrim, Down, Armagh, Tyrone, and Fermanagh add depth and extra dimension to any visit to Ireland. It's an experience not to be missed. Within the province's 14,120 square kilometers you'll meet with a warm welcome from any and all of the 1,578,500 Northern Irish who live in this unique corner of the country, and—as a visitor—you'll seldom, if ever, be touched by the "troubles" that many travelers misguidedly allow to keep them away. As is true in most of the world's troubled areas, the *informed* traveler can move about Northern Ireland with little more than occasional inconvenience.

What About the Troubles?

The entrenched bitterness between two strong religious and political factions in Northern Ireland is a direct result of all that history we told you about in Chapter I of this book. Unfortunately, no resolution appears on the immediate horizon—it is a complex situation and will require a complex solution. Meanwhile, northerners live out their daily lives under its pall, but chiefly concerned with inflation, unemployment, and those other problems with which the rest of us struggle. They are little interested in discussing politics with visitors—much more interested in seeing that you have a good time.

You will be most aware of "the troubles" when you cross the border through a military checkpoint, although in most cases you will be waved straight through after a cursory peek into your car assures guards of your noninvolvement in the internal situation. There's no passport inspection or visa to be stamped. One note of caution, however: It is advisable to enter the province at one of the approved checkpoints (clearly indicated on tourist maps), since it is at remote, unguarded points where trouble sometimes erupts suddenly. Once in the North, there are certain precautions with which the natives live and which you must accept as a part of contemporary life there. And on occasion you will pass armed patrols on some roads or be stopped and asked to show your identification.

In short, come prepared to observe the same rules and regulations as those who live here. Leave your own prejudices at home, and concentrate on enjoying the many delights Northern Ireland has to offer.

Of one thing you may be absolutely certain: The people of the North love their part of Ireland and will universally extend open arms to you as a visitor. They will welcome you to their homes, proudly display the physical charms of their land, and do everything in their power to make your time north of the border an experience you will recall with pleasure.

The Practicalities

CURRENCY: Until 1979, Irish pounds and the pound sterling held parity, but since then they have no longer been equal in value. The following listing is the sterling exchange rate against the American dollar as we go to press (£1 - $1.65) and all prices quoted are based on that figure. If you are coming from the Republic, you will be well advised to buy pounds sterling with dollars rather than Irish pounds, since the exchange rate is much more favorable.

1p	$ .02	£ 1	$ 1.65
5p	$ .08	£ 2.50	$ 4.13
25p	$ .41	£ 3	$ 4.95
50p	$ .83	£ 4.50	$ 7.43
75p	$1.24	£10	$16.50

If you plan to arrive on a weekend or bank holiday, be sure to buy pounds sterling before your arrival. And, as in the Republic, it is best to exchange money at banks or the Thomas Cook office (11 Donegall Pl., Belfast 1) rather than at hotels or department stores.

THOSE RULES AND REGULATIONS: You will see in most Northern Ireland towns and cities certain areas signposted "Control Zone." This means that cars must *at no time be left unattended,* and if you must leave your car parked and empty, even for a few minutes, you'd best look for a car park with an attendant. Unattended cars in Control Zones represent a security risk, and police are quite serious about violations of this regulation.

Certain public buildings, hotels, and shopping areas are in high-risk zones and will be surrounded by wire fencing. You'll sometimes—but not often—be asked to open your shopping bag or purse for a quick examination before entering. All such searches are carried out quickly and with courtesy and amount to not much more than a momentary nuisance.

ACCOMMODATIONS: As in the Republic, it is possible to select accommodations from a wide variety of style and price ranges. Hotels are inspected and graded on the same basis as those south of the border, and guesthouses, farmhouses, and bed-and-breakfast homes undergo the same rigid inspection. You'll find them in plentiful supply, and it usually isn't necessary to book ahead

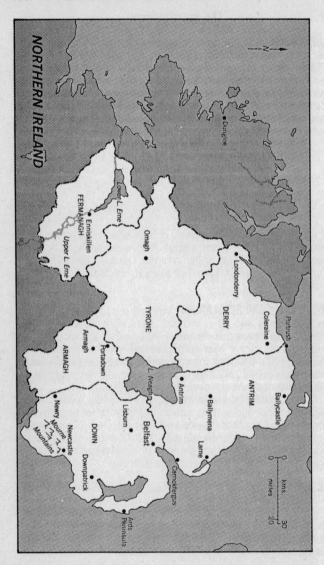

unless you have a definite choice in mind. In other words, the freewheeler should have no problem finding accommodations at the end of the day. In fact, the **Northern Ireland Tourist Board** has made it simple, with all approved accommodations listed in one handy booklet, **"All the Places to Stay,"** which you may obtain for 50p (83¢) at any Tourist Office or by writing ahead to Northern Ireland Tourist Board, River House, 48-52 High St., Belfast (tel. 0232-246609). Two other useful publications are: **"Farm & Country Holidays"** (illustrated listings of about 100 homes) and **"Town & Seaside House Holidays"** (over 50 homes illustrated). If you plan to camp, look for **"Caravan & Camp Sites,"** which lists over 100 approved sites.

MEALS: Tourist Offices and news agents carry a Tourist Board booklet, **"Let's Eat Out in Northern Ireland,"** which is well worth its £1 ($1.65) cost, since it lists eateries in every price range, as well as those pubs which serve food, in every location. In the better restaurants, it is almost always advisable to book ahead, especially over weekends or holidays. If you're traveling on a budget, look for restaurants and hotels which serve high tea at 6 p.m. (dinner is usually at 7 p.m. or later), which might include an Ulster fry of eggs, sausages, ham, or fish with chips plus scones and cakes at less cost than dinner prices. Another budget tip is to make your main meal at midday—and don't overlook pub grub, which can be quite good.

TOURIST INFORMATION: There are Tourist Information Offices in about 30 locations around the province, all prepared to give you up-to-the-minute information about their area, assist with emergencies, and help plan itineraries. The main **Northern Ireland Tourist Board** office is at River House, 48-52 High St., Belfast (tel. 0232-246609). Hours are 9 a.m. to 5:15 p.m. Monday through Friday, and 9 a.m. to noon on Saturday during the summer months. You'll also find Tourist Offices at the Belfast International Airport and Lane Harbor terminal. Look for their tourist guide, **"Northern Ireland,"** which is filled with specific information.

CAR RENTALS: Major rental firms in the North are **Avis** (tel. 08494-52333 at the Airport; 0232-240404 in the city), **Hertz** (tel. 08494-52533), and **Godfrey Davis Europcar** (tel. 08494-53444 at the Airport; 0232-773555 in the city). If you're driving up from the

Republic with a rental car, be sure to check to see that insurance covers you across the border. The same holds true if you drive from north to south. Also, if you plan to pick up the car in the North and drop it off in the South, or vice versa, check carefully about drop-off fees—it could be cheaper to do a round trip and drop your car off where you picked it up.

As in the Republic, driving in Northern Ireland is on the left, speed limits are 30 m.p.h. in towns, 70 m.p.h. on all other roads, including Motorways.

PUB HOURS: Pubs (and there are some particularly interesting ones in Belfast) are open from 11 a.m. to 11:30 p.m., with the last drinks served promptly at 11 p.m. They're closed on Sunday, so if you develop a thirst then, head for the nearest hotel or licensed restaurant.

PUBLIC TRANSPORT: There's an excellent network of rail and bus services throughout the six counties, with day tours available to almost all major points of interest. For information on Northern Ireland Railways services, go by the Travel and Information Centre in Belfast Central Station or call 230310 or 230671. NIR offers a seven-day, unlimited-travel Rail Runabout ticket from April through October which costs £18.50 ($30.53) for adults, £9.25 ($15.27) for children. Buy it at principal stations throughout the system. The three main rail routes run between Belfast and Londonderry via Ballymena and Coleraine; Belfast and Bangor; and Belfast and Dublin (about 2 hours). There's very good bus service between those towns not served by rail.

TAXIS: Taxis are the black, London-cab type which seat five, and there are ranks at main rail and bus stations, ports, and Belfast International Airport. Otherwise, you'll have to telephone (see the local directory). Many do not have meters, so be sure to settle the fare when you get in.

SPORTS: There are over 60 golf courses in Northern Ireland, with greens fees of £3 ($4.50) to £12 ($19.80). Fishermen will find course, game, and sea fish in good supply.

SHOPPING: Irish linen, Belleek pottery, and Tyrone crystal are just a few of the items shoppers will have on their lists. What fun to buy them where you've seen them being made, and you can do that at the following by telephoning ahead: Belleek pottery, Belleek, County Fermanagh (tel. Belleek 036565-501); and Tyrone crystal, Dungannon, County Tyrone (tel. Dungannon 08687-25335). For the thirsty, there's nothing like a visit to Old Bushmills Distillery, Bushmills, County Antrim (tel. Bushmills 02657-31521 to book a tour).

Chapter XIX

BELFAST AND LONDONDERRY

The North's Two Major Cities

THESE TWO CITIES are the largest in Northern Ireland, and a visit to the province can be centered in either, or both, with easy touring to outlying points of interest.

Belfast

In its circle of hills on the River Lagan, Belfast (whose name means "Mouth of the Sandy Ford") began life as an ancient fort. A small village had grown up around the fort by the Middle Ages, and in the early 17th century, village inhabitants were turned out to make room for Protestant settlers sent by the English Crown from Scotland and Devonshire. By the late 1600s, a linen trade was firmly established, and Belfast enjoyed a steady, though slow, growth right up to the late 1700s. It was here that the United Irish Society was founded in 1791 by Wolfe Tone when both Protestants and Catholics found the Penal Laws so restrictive that they came together and eventually led the abortive uprising of 1798. It was in 1791, too, that the first shipyard was established in the city. With the 19th-century Industrial Revolution came modernization of both the linen and shipbuilding industries and a dramatic upsurge in the population of Belfast which has produced a bustling capital city with more than 360,000 inhabitants.

While its chief aspect is that of a functional, industrial city, Belfast is compact enough for walking to its most interesting architectural sights in the city center. And the city's face in its center is that of Queen Victoria—every important structure bears the stamp of her era.

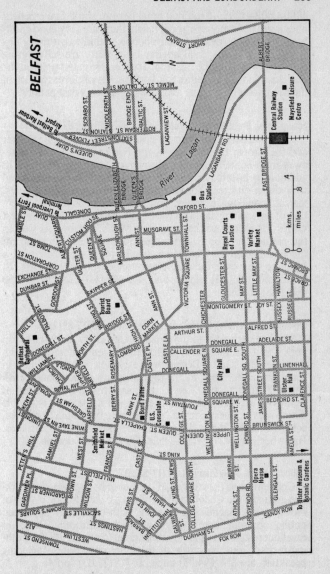

ACCOMMODATIONS: If you're a hotel person, you'll find excellent ones here. For a more personal touch, there are very good guest-houses as well as delightful farmhouses within easy driving distance. For a very special holiday base, there are self-catering cottages, owned by the National Trust and situated right on the sea, close enough to Belfast for day trips, yet within easy reach of the Mountains of Mourne and other sightseeing destinations.

Forum Hotel, Great Victoria Street, Belfast BT2 7AP (tel. 0232-245161)

Right in the heart of the city, close to shopping and the theater and the Crown Liquor Saloon, the Forum is a favorite home-away-from-home for visiting businessmen as well as tourists. In addition to tastefully decorated, comfortable rooms equipped with direct-dial telephones, color TV, refrigerated mini-bars, tea/coffee-making facilities, and radio, there is a good selection of bars and restaurants (one of which offers one of the best values for money in the city; see "Meals," below) as well as the casual Carriage Room coffeeshop. You can also top off the evening at the Penthouse nightspot, a nightclub with a stunning view over the city. Rates range from £49.50 ($81.68) to £54.50 ($89.93) single and £63.50 ($104.78) to £69.50 ($114.68) double.

Wellington Park Hotel, 21 Malone Rd., Belfast (tel. 0232-661232)

Situated very close to the Queen's University, the Wellington Park is in a quiet location, yet less than a ten-minute walk from the city center. One of Belfast's newest hotels, it is the ultimate in sophisticated comfort. Public rooms feature contemporary Irish painting and sculpture, and there's an attractive lounge bar as well as an excellent restaurant serving both à la carte and table d'hôte meals. Guestrooms all have private bathroom or shower, color TV, radio, direct-dial telephone, and tea-making facilities. Rates begin at £42 ($69.30) single, £62 ($102.30) double.

Culloden Hotel, Craigavad (tel. 02317-5223)

Convenient to the city center, yet set in its own wooded park-like grounds, the Culloden was built as a palace for the bishop of Down. It's a magnificent building, with beautifully appointed public rooms and luxuriously decorated guestrooms. There are excellent restaurants and nighttime entertainment. It's a refreshing respite from the bustle of the inner city. Rates, including breakfast, are £57 ($94.05) single, £77 ($127.05) double.

Dunadry Inn, Dunadry, County Antrim (tel. Templepatrick 32474)

The Dunadry is 15 miles from the city center, 4 from the airport, and 3 from the town of Antrim. It's an ideal touring base, and a restful place to end Belfast days. Its name means "The Middle Fort" (it was the center of three fortifications between Tara and Dunseverick), and it has been in turn a paper mill and linen mill, surrounded by a village of some 20 cottages. The inn now covers the site of the village, and its restaurant is built over the old mill stream. Perhaps the most striking room at the Dunadry is the Copper Bar, a two-story baronial hall with a fireplace at one end, exposed wooden rafters, and a wood-railed mezzanine leading off to second-story guest rooms. The copper-hooded bar is the scene of a lunchtime buffet and late-night drinks. One side of the courtyard is a wall of the old mill, built of stone and some two feet deep. All 64 bedrooms are equipped with color TV, radio, and direct-dial telephone, and many have French windows leading out to the garden or courtyard. Bedspreads are of locally woven tweeds. A special feature is their car-hire service, which allows you to pick up and leave your car at the inn (there's also airport transfer service with advance notice). The river out back is amply stocked with trout and fishing is free to guests. Rates begin at £49 ($80.85) single, £60 ($99) double. There's a special weekend with lower rates, covering two nights (sharing), full breakfasts, Saturday dinner-dance (September–May), and Sunday lunch.

Liserin Guest House, 17 Eglantine Ave., Belfast BT 9 6DW (tel. 660769)

Mrs. Joan Walker presides over this 1893 Victorian townhouse close to the Queens University campus. A warm, gracious lady, she creates a homey atmosphere, serving tea at 10 p.m., and prepared to serve a simple evening meal for under £6 ($9.90) on request. The house itself has high ceilings (with original, ornate medallions) and much of its original woodwork. There are five single rooms and two doubles, all attractively furnished and all with hot and cold sinks. Back rooms get longer sunlight, but none is dark or gloomy. The pleasant location on lime-tree-lined Eglantine Avenue affords a good view of the Belfast hills, yet is convenient to the center city, either via bus (at the end of the block) or a 15-minute walk. There's also good shopping and a moderately priced restaurant just a block away. Rates for bed-and-breakfast are £10 ($16.50) single, £18 ($29.70) double.

Camera House, 44 Wellington Park, Belfast (tel. 0232-660026 or 667856)

Mrs. Angela Drumm, a native of County Meath who has lived in Belfast for many years, is the attractive and gracious hostess at this lovely guesthouse located within a few minutes' walk of the city center. The red-brick Victorian-style house has bay windows in the guest lounge and dining room, giving a light, airy look to both. All rooms, in fact, are quite bright. There are four with showers and toilet, seven with hand basin only, and of the eleven, four are single. Bed-and-breakfast rates range from £16 ($26.40) single, £24 ($39.60) double for rooms with hand basins, more for those with private facilities.

The Cottage, 377 Comber Rd., Dundonald, County Down (tel. Comber 878189)

Your enchantment with The Cottage is likely to begin even as you drive into the parking area out back, for the driveway brings you into full view of a lovely lawn and colorful flowerbeds that beckon the traveler to sit awhile and enjoy such outdoors beauty. There is also a conservatory at the back of the cottage. Once inside the traditional, sparkling white cottage, however, you'll be sorely tempted never to set foot outside again. Mrs. Elizabeth Muldoon has realized every cottage-lover's dream—she has lovingly retained (and even enhanced) all the original charm of the house at the same time she installed every modern convenience. The living room is picture pretty, as is the rustic dining area, and bedrooms are beautifully furnished with many antique furnishings scattered about. Decor throughout is in keeping with a traditional country home. Just a short drive from Belfast, The Cottage is one of the most inviting accommodations in the area. Bed-and-breakfast rates are £10 ($16.50) single, £19 ($31.35) double.

Greenlea Farm, 48 Dunover Rd., Ballywater, County Down (tel. 02477-58218)

Farmhouse devotees will delight in this modernized farmhouse perched on a hill with marvelous views of the Ards Peninsula countryside and the Scottish coastline and the Isle of Man across the water. Even more delightful is Mrs. Evelyn McIvor, its friendly hostess. Large windows in the lounge and dining room (beautifully furnished with antiques and much silver and crystal) look out on those views, and every bedroom is also made light and airy with picture windows. There are tennis courts and outdoor bowling. Mrs. McIvor can accommodate single travelers and couples, and has one family room which will sleep parents and two children (on bunk beds). A lively, interesting teacher of crafts, she will happily help with touring plans and background information on the immediate vicinity and Belfast, some 20 miles away. Rates for bed-and-breakfast are £8 ($13.20) per person for a single night's stay, £7.50 ($12.38) per person for a longer stay. Deduct one-fourth for children under 12, one-half for those under 8.

Self-Catering Facilities, Kearney Village, County Down

Kearney is a charming old fishing village on the Ards Peninsula, about 35 miles from Belfast off the Portaferry–Cloughy road, which has been taken over by the National Trust to ensure its preservation. Three houses are available for weekly rental and make an ideal holiday base, with views across to Scotland, the Isle of Man, and the Mountains of Mourne, and a lovely two-mile coastal walk. Golf and swimming are within easy driving distance. Nos. 6 and 8 are pretty cottages overlooking the sea which sleep four and rent for about £100 ($165); no. 11 also overlooks the sea and sleeps six at a rental of about £120 ($198). These are weekly rates during the high season of June through September; lower rates are available at other times. For full particulars, an illustrated booklet, and booking information, contact: The National Trust, Holiday Cottage Bookings Secretary, Rowallane, Saintfield, Ballynahinch, County Down (tel. Smithfield 510721).

MEALS: Belfast is rich in good places to eat that range from pub grub to elegance, at prices to fit every purse. Pick up a copy of **Let's Eat Out** for selections to supplement those below.

The Carvers' Table, Forum Hotel, Great Victoria Street (tel. 245161)

As we've said before, this is one of the best eateries in town, and one of the most popular. Large, juicy joints of roast beef (hot and cold), lamb, and pork are carved to suit your appetite, and come as part of the three courses plus coffee or tea for £9 ($14.85) to £14 ($23.10). Vegetables are fresh and well prepared, and desserts include freshly baked apple pie. Hours are 12:30 p.m. to 10:30 p.m.

Thompsons Restaurant, 47 Arthur St., Belfast (tel. 223762)

Thompsons is one of those unobtrusive little places you sometimes—if you're very, very lucky—stumble across right in the heart of the city simply going about the business of supplying good food in ample portions at reasonable prices in a friendly, unpretentious setting. Because its front room is a pub, it might, in fact, be listed under the Pub Grub section below; but because its food goes so far beyond the usual, it warrants much more attention. Food service is in a room just beyond the bar, but you're likely to spend at least one drink's time out front waiting to be seated, for this is a popular place with Belfast natives who work in the inner city. Cordiality reigns, however, in both the pub and the restaurant sections, and any wait is bound to be a pleasant one.

The extensive (and surprising) menu, concentrating mainly on such Irish offerings as seafoods, steaks, ham, and chicken, covers just about anything you could want, and far more than you could expect in this kind of eatery. There's plaice or sole poached with fresh prawns in cheese and wine sauce or in a mornay sauce or fried in breadcrumbs with banana and chutney (as well as less exotic choices); scampi that comes in several forms (Newburg, provençale, grilled, or deep-fried); fresh Irish trout baked or grilled; prime filet steaks (au poivre or tournedos Rossini); sirloin steaks; etc., etc., etc. À la carte prices for main courses range from £5 ($8.25) to £10 ($16.50), with omelets and appetizers (from which I happily assembled an excellent lunch) running under £5 ($8.25). All come with homemade Ulster wheaten bread and butter. Hours are 12:15 to 3:15 p.m. and 6 to 9:30 p.m. Monday through Saturday. As you may have guessed, this is a personal favorite and one I wouldn't want you to miss!

Pub Grub

Among pubs serving better-than-average pub grub for an average of £3 ($4.95) to £4 ($6.60) between the hours of noon and 2:30 p.m. are the following: **Crown Liquor Saloon,** 46 Great Victoria St. (tel. 225368); **White's Tavern,** Winecellar Entry (tel. 243080); **Queen's Lounge,** 4/6 Queen's Arcade (tel. 221347); **Kelly's Cellars,** 30 Bank St. (tel. 224835); **Linenhall Bar,** 9 Clarence St.; **Rumpoles,** 81 Chichester St.; **Beaten Docket,** 48 Great Victoria St.; **Elbow,** 49 Dublin Rd.; **Garrick,** 11 Montgomery St.; **Harper's Bar** (Forum Hotel), Great Victoria Street; **Botanic Inn,** 23 Malone Rd. (university area); and on the outskirts of town, **King's Head,** Lisburn Road, Balmoral (opposite King's Hall).

THINGS TO SEE AND DO: Before beginning any sightseeing, go by the **Northern Ireland Tourist Board Information Office** in River House, 48 High St. (tel. 246609), and pick up informational booklets and a calendar of events, as well as brochures on guided bus tours and guides to fishing, golfing, cruising, etc., for future use.

City Hall: Belfast's most impressive building is an ornate edifice of Portland stone with a copper dome which took some ten years to complete (finished in 1906). There is much green and Italian marble inside, and a large mural depicting the city's industrial history. It's on Donegall Square. Look for the bust of Queen Victoria, who visited Belfast in 1846. On the west side is a Great War Memorial, and on the east a sculpture commemorating those who died on the *Titanic* (a Belfast-built ship) in 1912.

Albert Memorial: At the river end of High Street, this ornate clock tower has a slight tilt which has earned it the nickname of Belfast's leaning tower.

Belfast Cathedral (St. Anne's): On Lower Donegall Street, the Hiberno-Romanesque cathedral was begun in 1899 and consecrated in 1904. There's a fine mosaic over the Chapel of the Holy Spirit entrance which depicts St. Patrick's landing at Saul in A.D. 432.

Harbour Office: Located on Corporation Square, this building holds an interesting collection of paintings, sculpture, and stained glass relating to the city's seafaring history. By telephoning the administration officer at 234422, ext. 206, you can arrange to visit it on weekdays from 9:30 a.m. to 4:30 p.m.

Belfast Zoo: Located on Antrim Road, in a mountain park overlooking the city and the lough, the zoo is open seven days a week (except Christmas Day) from 10 a.m. to 5 p.m. March through October, to 3 p.m. other months. An adjoining 45 acres overlooking the city and the lough are being developed as a new zoo. Check with the Tourist Office for details.

Grand Opera House: This lovely, roccoco theater was designed by noted theater architect Frank Matcham, and its interior is richly decorated in gold and maroon, with some 24 gilt elephant heads flanking canopied boxes and a fair sprinkling of Buddhas on draperies. No matter what performance is on when you're in Belfast, it's worth the price of admission to see the restored building. You are, incidentally, apt to see very good touring companies of hit plays in performance here.

Ulster Folk and Transport Museum: Some eight miles from the city on the road to Bangor, this unique folk museum is set on 136 acres of the Cultra Manor estate. The manor house holds exhibitions of historical artifacts and a tea room, as well as an interesting museum shop. But it's in the cottages and houses moved here from all parts of the province and restored to their original condition that you'll get a sense of rural life in Northern Ireland over the centuries. There's a farmhouse with cow byre in one end, a weaver's house, forge, spade mill, flax scutching mill, and a 1790 church. Plan at least a half day in this enchanting place. Hours are

11 a.m. to 6 p.m. on weekdays, 2 to 6 p.m. on Sunday, and admission is 50p (83¢) for adults, 20 p (33¢) for children.

Crown Liquor Saloon: Located on Great Victoria Street, just across from the Forum Hotel, this prime example of Belfast's Victorian pubs is a marvel to behold! Adorned with colorful ceramic tiles, miles of carved woodwork, a solid row of snugs along one entire wall, and flickering gaslights, it suffered the effects of "modernization" for a period of years, but fortunately the National Trust people got hold of it in time to restore it to its original, florid character. Stop in for a pint, or come for pub grub in the middle of the day, but don't miss the Crown!

Tracing Your Roots: For help in tracking down Ulster ancestors, contact the **Irish Genealogical Association,** 162a Kingsway, Dunmurry, Belfast BT17 9AD (tel. 0232-629595), who will do research on a mail-order basis or provide a professional to help while you're in Ireland, both north and south of the border. They also can arrange personal "roots" tours for individuals or groups.

Londonderry

In the Republic it's called simply Derry, the English form of *Doire,* which means oak grove in Irish, and the arrival of St. Columba in A.D. 546 to found his abbey in this "place of oaks" signalled the first settlement. It wasn't until the early 17th century, when the City of London sent a work force over to build thick walls enclosing the town, that Derry became Londonderry, and indeed the shorter form is used affectionately by many of its residents. Its history includes siege after siege by opposing forces, the most famous of which occurred in 1689 and lasted for 105 days, when supporters of William of Orange held out against troops of King James II despite starvation and disease. Those sturdy city walls were never breached, and you may walk them today to get a graphic picture of the old and newer parts of the city. The original town lies on the western side of the River Foyle, and its charming old streets make up the main shopping and business section. Modern Londonderry is ten times the size of the old, and extends to both sides of the river, which is spanned by Craigavon Bridge. It makes an ideal touring base for the Antrim Coast, including the Giant's Causeway, to the east or County Donegal to the west.

ACCOMMODATIONS: Accommodations are somewhat limited in Londonderry itself, but there is one excellent hotel we can recommend, and one just four miles outside the city. One guest-house within city limits and an equally good farmhouse in the area are to be found in the Tourist Board's **Farm & Country Holidays** booklet.

Everglades Hotel, Prehen Road, Londonderry BT47 2PA (tel. 0504-46722)

True to its name, the Everglades sports live tropical trees and plants, creating an atmosphere of unabashed luxury. Guest rooms are attractively furnished with cane chairs, tables, and beds, and have color TV, in-house movies, radio, direct-dial telephone, tea-making facilities, and private bath. There's an inviting cocktail bar, the Seminole Restaurant for full meal service, and the Buttery Bar for quick meals and snacks. Rates begin at £30 ($49.50) for singles, £40 ($66) for doubles.

White Horse Inn, 68 Clooney Rd., Londonderry, County Londonderry (tel. 0504-860606)

Only four miles out (on the road to Limavady), the White Horse is a hotel/motel which offers a block of rooms which permit parking just outside your room door. It is an attractive, rather sophisticated place, and owners Alwyn and Iris Kydd have settled on a *per-room* pricing policy, furnishing a double bed in each so that, in effect, two can stay at the same price as one—an innovative and money-saving feature. All rooms have tea-/coffee-making facilities, color TV, radio, direct-dial telephone, and alarm clock. The motel rooms (called chalets) also having cooking facilities and a fridge. The Carousel restaurant, Yesterdays grill room, and attractive bar and lounge in an open, two-story lobby make this a complete-service establishment. Moderate rates begin at £23 ($37.95) single, and £28 ($46.20) double.

Clarence House, 15 Northland Rd., Londonderry, (tel. 0504-265342)

Mrs. Eleonara C. Slevin offers bed-and-breakfast in the inner city for £9 ($14.85) per person. There are single rooms, doubles, twin rooms, and family rooms available.

Ballycarton Farm, Bellarena, Limavady BT49 0HZ (tel. Ballarena 50216)

On 50 acres in the midst of lovely coastal and mountain scenery, Ballycarton is about 17 miles from Londonderry, and has been named the "best farmhouse in Northern Ireland." Mrs. Emma Craig is the charming hostess, who will steer you to nearby points of interest and sandy beaches. The farm is on the coast road, making it convenient for sightseeing. Rates are £7 ($11.55) for bed-and-breakfast and the same for the evening meal, which she will prepare for nonresidents with advance booking. Rooms are all of good size and comfortably furnished. Babysitting is available, and Mrs. Craig welcomes dogs.

MEALS: For restaurant meals, we suggest either the **Everglades Hotel** or **White Horse Inn** (see above), and especially recommend **Yesterdays** grill room at the White Horse. Lunch entrées are in the £5 ($8.25) range, and dinners will run over £15 ($24.75). The lunch menu is in effect from 11:30 a.m. to 7:30 p.m.; after that, dinner is served until 10:30 p.m.

Among the pubs serving food, usually between noon and 2:30 p.m., at prices in the £3 ($4.95) to £5 ($8.25) range are: **Duffy's Tavern,** 17 Foyle St. (tel. 261362), and the **Anchor Inn,** 38 Ferryquay St. (tel. 268601).

THINGS TO SEE AND DO: The **Tourist Information Office** is in Foyle Street (tel. 269501), and is open year round Monday through Friday from 9 a.m. to 5 p.m., also from 10 a.m. to 5 p.m. on Saturday May to September. Closed 1 to 2 p.m. October to April. They'll furnish exhaustive information on the city, including a marvelous "Walk About Derry."

City Walls: The best view of the city is from the old city walls, most of which may be walked today, with access at Magazine Gate. They are the only complete and unbroken fortifications of any city in the British Isles, and are believed to be the last city walls built in Europe. The Tourist Office books marvelous guided tours at no charge.

The Guildhall: This imposing Gothic structure was built in 1890, but suffered a disastrous fire in 1908, which left it with only the main walls standing. Reconstruction saw beautiful oak panels and stained-glass windows made by local artisans, and in the marble vestibule, one window which is a reproduction of Follingby's *The Relief of Derry* painting (the original painting is also in the Guildhall). City regalia, such as the sword and mace, are also kept there. It's open for guided tours from 9 a.m. to 4 p.m. Monday through Friday. For further information, call the Information and Civics Office at 265151.

St. Columb's Cathedral: One of the most prominent landmarks within the Old City, the Gothic cathedral was built in 1633, but has been much added to since. The siege memorial window vividly depicts the relief of Londonderry in 1689. In the chapter house are many siege mementos, as well as part of Macauley's *History of England*. It's open daily from 9 a.m. to 12:30 p.m. and 2 to 5 p.m., and there's no admission charge.

   City Streets: Many of Londonderry's streets are steep and narrow, with striking examples of Victorian and Georgian buildings. Don't miss streets like Albert and Nailor Row, outside the walls, filled with rows of charming little houses

Chapter XX

SEEING THE SIX COUNTIES

Highlights, County by County

THE SIX COUNTIES which make up Northern Ireland hold some of the island's true scenic wonders, as well as a wealth of sightseeing attractions. We'll take them county by county.

County Antrim

THINGS TO SEE AND DO: Back in the late 18th and early 19th centuries, residents along the coast of County Antrim were often isolated for months at a time for the lack of a proper road to the outside world during rainy or winter spells. Finally, in the 1830s, the coast road was constructed when the principal engineer, William Bald, a Scot, worked out a way of blasting the cliffs so that a foundation was formed from huge blocks of rock which came to rest at the water's edge. The miraculous road not only freed Antrim folk, but opened up a whole new world for tourists, for it is along the Antrim coast that some of Northern Ireland's most exciting natural wonders are to be seen. The scenic road follows the coastline from Larne to Portrush, and many of the sights described below lie along its route.

The Glens of Antrim: There are nine of the famous glens which open to the sea, and our best advice to the traveler is to drive slowly so as not to miss the beauty of rocky cliffs, verdant enclosures, and tumbling waterfalls.

The Giant's Causeway: Possibly the most famous of Ireland's natural wonders, the Giant's Causeway lies 12 kilometers east of Portrush and 15 kilometers west of Ballycastle. It's an awe-inspiring collection of basalt columns, about 37,000 of them, which are packed closely together along this stretch of coast out into the sea, disappearing under water, then reappearing on the island of Staffa, in the Hebrides opposite. Legend says that the giant Finn MacCoul built a road to connect the two countries, but scientists stubbornly cling to the theory that they were formed some 60 million years ago when molten lava from a vast volcanic eruption cooled and shrank into these curiously geometric shapes. However they came into being, they're there for us to visit today via a walk down the cliffside. There's no admission charge, and for nonwalkers, there's minibus transportation down to sea level for a small charge.

Carrick-a-Rede Rope Bridge: Just eight kilometers northwest of Ballycastle, there's an amazing bridge suspended between the cliffs and a salmon fishery on a steep island. Made of planks strung between wires, with wire handrails, the bridge is assembled in May and dismantled in September (when weather and wind make crossing the 80-foot sea chasm too hazardous). There's no charge to descend the footpath from a roadside car park and cross the bridge—the only inhibition is the degree to which you are fainthearted.

Carrickfergus Castle: Northern Ireland's largest and best preserved medieval castle squats on the waterfront at Carrickfergus. It was built between the late 12th and early 13th centuries. Inside, a museum in the castle keep holds mementos of the Inniskilling Dragoons, the Irish Hussars, and the North Irish Horse Regiments. It was just below these walls that John Paul Jones captured the British ship *Drake* in 1778. It is open from 10 a.m. to 6 p.m. Monday through Saturday, and 2 to 6 p.m. on Sunday during summer months at a charge of 50p (83¢) for adults, 15p (25¢) for children.

Dunluce Castle: The romantic ruin of Dunluce sits on a rocky headland three miles east of Portrush. One translation of its name is "mermaid's fort," which certainly seems appropriate in view of the cave which goes right through the rock underneath the castle to the sea. There are many legends attached to the place, some of which are recounted in the official guide on sale at the entrance. Dunluce is open year round from 10 a.m. to 1 p.m. and 2 to 6 p.m. Monday through Saturday, and from 2 to 6 p.m. on Sunday. Closing times are extended to 7 p.m. April through September. There's a 40p (66¢) admission for adults, 15p (25¢) for children.

Round Tower: One of Ireland's most perfectly preserved

round towers is in the town of Antrim. It rises more than 90 feet from a base 49 feet around. No charge for the viewing.

Old Bushmills Distillery: The world's oldest licensed distillery is located in the little town of Bushmills, and you can see the entire process of distilling by booking for one of the free tours conducted Monday through Thursday every morning and afternoon and on Friday morning. Telephone ahead for exact times; call Bushmills 31521.

Arthur Ancestral Home: At Dreen, near Cullybackey, Ballymena, a thatched, whitewashed cottage was the home from which Chester Alan Arthur's father departed for America in 1816. His son later became the 21st president. The home is open Monday through Friday from 2 to 6 p.m. mid-April to mid-September, and there's a 20p (33¢) admission fee.

ACCOMMODATIONS: There are several outstanding hotels and one very good guesthouse we'd like to tell you about in County Antrim. The **Londonderry Arms Hotel,** Carnlough, County Antrim (tel. 0574-85255, 85458, or 85459), was built in 1854 as a coaching inn right across from the harbor. It's a charming, ivy-covered structure which has been owned by Frank O'Neill's family since 1947. Old-style graciousness reigns supreme in a country-home atmosphere that's reflected in both decor and hospitality. Antiques are everywhere; the tavern-type bar is a den of conviviality for locals and travelers alike, and the lounge with its hooded fireplace is an inviting gathering place. Rooms are handsomely decorated, with hand-woven Avoca bedspreads. Rates (including full Irish breakfast) are £18 ($29.70) single, £32 ($52.80) double from May 1 through December, lower other months. All rooms have private bath, telephone, radio, and TV.

Glenbay Hotel, Carnlough, County Antrim (tel. 0574-85248 or 85455)

Just next door to the Londonderry Arms, the Glenbay is also owned and operated by the O'Neill family. Although the sparkling black-and-white hotel faces Carnlough's main street (which is really a section of the Antrim Coast Road), its reception area encompasses what was once Whistle Cock Lane, a tiny road which led back to small cottages in years past. In fact, the kitchen of one of those cottages is now the hotel's Cottage Bar, complete with its original smoky fireplace, low ceiling and thick walls. During summer months, a very good bar lunch is served there for about £3 ($4.95). There's also a Grill Room for meals under £5 ($8.25) and a restaurant featuring seafood, steak, and chicken for under £10 ($16.50). Guest rooms all have private bath, telephone, TV, and radio. Rates are £17 ($28.05) single, £31 ($51.15) double. Open May to mid-October.

O'Malley's Edgewater Hotel, 88 Strand Rd., Portstewart, County Antrim (tel. 026-5832224 or 5833688), is the kind of oldstyle hotel you dream of finding and seldom do. There's a fire burning in the small, homey lobby and huge windows overlooking the sea in a lounge filled with deep, comfortable chairs. The dining room also looks out on sea views. A mini-leisure center holds a sauna, sun bed, and a Jacuzzi. There's a stained-glass window on the staircase landing leading up to the second-floor guestrooms, which are equipped with private bath, TV, and radio. Bed-and-breakfast rates are £18.50 ($30.53) single, £34 ($56.10) double, during summer months, lower in winter. Children under 12 are one-third less.

In nearby Portballintrae, the **Bayview Hotel,** Portballintrae, Bushmills, County Antrim (tel. Bushmills 31453), also faces the sea and provides old-time comfort at moderate prices. Its Porthole Lounge Bar and luxury Watch House Restaurant are local favorites. In a brilliant concept of renovation, the hotel's owners have given all guestrooms a front view of the curving bay front, and all are nicely furnished and decorated. Bed-and-breakfast rates begin at £20 ($33) for singles, £36 ($59.40) for doubles.

Within easy reach of the Glens of Antrim, airport, boats, and trains, **Mrs. Catharine Scally**'s Tudor farmhouse at 185 Torr Rd., Cushendun BT44 (tel. Cushendun 252), has an inviting and old-fashioned air, with stained-glass windows and antiques. The house has five bedrooms very comfortably furnished with beautiful views overlooking Cushendun. Bed-and-breakfast rates are £9 ($13.50) and the charge for bed-and-breakfast and dinner is £15 ($22.50). Children 25% reduction.

MEALS: By all means, plan your coast-road drive so that lunchtime will arrive with the **Londonderry Arms** (tel. 0574-85255) at Carnlough. Or end up there for dinner. Either way, you're in for a treat in the antique-filled dining room looking across at the water. An excellent table d'hôte lunch is just £6.50 ($10.73); dinner, £9.50 ($15.68).

County Armagh

Derrymore House: This 18th-century thatched manor house is two miles from Newry on A25 (the Newtownhamilton road), and in its drawing room the Act of Union of Great Britain and Ireland is supposed to have been drafted. You can get a glimpse inside by telephoning Saintfield 510721 to book. Admission is 50p (83¢).

Cathedrals: Catholic and Protestant cathedrals face each other on opposite hilltops in the town of Armagh. The Church of Ireland cathedral was restored in the 18th and 19th centuries, and on its north side is a tablet purporting to mark the grave of Brian Boru. The Gothic-style Catholic cathedral was built between 1840 and 1873, and it holds red hats of all the cardinal archbishops of Armagh, as well as medallions of the saints of Ireland.

County Down

THINGS TO SEE AND DO: The **Mountains of Mourne** are the mountains that "sweep down to the sea" in story and song, and are much loved by walkers as well. Highest is Slieve Donard (2,840 feet). One of the best views of the Mournes is from **Newcastle,** a major seaside resort nestled at their feet.

Ards Peninsula: The 60-mile-long Ards Peninsula is an unspoiled strip of land peopled with charming shore villages, windmill towers, and ruined hilltop forts. Especially interesting is the 19th-century fishing village of **Kearney,** near the tip of the peninsula, which has been restored by the National Trust, which offers three of the old homes for rent (see Chapter XIX). A car ferry connects Portaferry and Strangford, running every half hour from 7:30 a.m. to 8:30 p.m. and crossing in about four minutes, with marvelous views out to sea if you don't blink.

St. Patrick's Grave: Down Cathedral in Downpatrick is built on what is believed to be the site of St. Patrick's first stone church. It is also believed that the saint's remains rest under a huge stone slab in its churchyard, along with those of St. Brigid and St. Columba. Whether or not *you* believe all that, the cathedral is worth a visit, and you've a hard heart, indeed, if you don't fall under its peaceful spell and leave at least a *half* believer!

ACCOMMODATIONS: At the **Slieve Donard Hotel,** Newcastle, County Down (tel. Newcastle 23681), you can look across Dundrum Bay to where the Mountains of Mourne sweep down to the sea and walk along the four-mile curving sandy strand to their very feet. You can also live out any latent Victoriana fantasies in the turreted, red-brick hotel set in its acres of green lawn. When it was built, back in 1897, there were coal fires in every bath. These days, every modern convenience is incorporated into public and guestrooms alike (including an indoor swimming pool), somehow leaving intact a genteel atmosphere that evokes an era of sweeping long skirts and frock-coated gentlemen. Front rooms overlooking the bar are especially nice, and our own favorites are nos. 103 and 104, which are singles with curved windows and the bath up a short flight of steps, a perfect retreat for the single traveler. The Dogs Head pub and restaurant at the entrance of the grounds is a whitewashed gate lodge which offers good food at extremely moderate prices. Rates begin at £28 ($46.20) single, £45 ($74.25) double, and it's a good idea to book ahead.

Just on the edge of Newcastle (off the Bryansford–Newcastle road—B180) you'll find the modern bungalow presided over by **Mrs. Jean Hart,** Grasmere, 16 Marguerite Park, Bryansford Road, Newcastle BT33 OPE (tel. Newcastle 03967-22450). This charming lady has two double rooms and one single, all with hand basins. Surrounded by green fields, Grasmere is only a 10-minute walk from the beach. Bed-and-breakfast rates are £9 ($13.50).

County Fermanagh

THINGS TO SEE AND DO: Don't miss **Lough Erne.** Upper and Lower Lough Erne constitute the most dominant feature of County Fermanagh. Stemming from the River Erne, the lough wanders in a northwestern direction from County Cavan and provides one of the principal attractions of midland Northern Ireland, cruising and fishing. For information on boat rentals, conducted cruises, and fishing regulations, go by the **Lakeland Visitor Centre,** Shore Road, Enniskillen (tel. Enniskillen 0365-23110). They will help you with accommodations reservations (no charge), as well as activities on the lough.

The Belleek Pottery Ltd.: Visit the Belleek chinaware factory in the little town of Belleek on the Donegal border, where you can purchase items you've actually watched being made. Call ahead (Belleek 501) to check on hours the factory is open and to book for conducted tours.

ACCOMMODATIONS: Only a little more than one mile from the heart of Enniskillen, the lovely **Killyhevlin Hotel,** Dublin Road, Enniskillen, County Fermanagh (tel. Enniskillen 0365-23481), sits on the shore of Logh Erne. Its lounge and most guest rooms look out onto the gardens and lough (rooms have balconies reached through floor-length glass walls). All rooms have color TV, double and single beds, and radio. Also available are luxury self-catering chalets. Rates for bed-and-breakfast are £30 ($49.50) single and £47 ($77.55) double. There are weekend specials as low as £45 ($74.25) for two nights bed-and-breakfast, dinner and lounge entertainment on Saturday, and lunch on

Sunday. Chalets start at a weekly rate of £150 ($247.50) and vary according to season. Early booking is advised.

MEALS: In the little town of Ballinamallard, a short drive from Enniskillen, the **Encore Steak House** on Main Street (tel. Ballinamallard 606) was the scene of perhaps our best meal in Northern Ireland. In a 200-year-old building, Cyril Evans and Roger Davies have created a jewel of a restaurant, with a warm, intimate interior cozy bar / lounge and superb cuisine. Steak is, of course, a specialty, but the seafood (scampi, trout, plaice, etc.) is cooked to perfection, and the beef curry outstanding. Pork and chicken dishes round out the menu. There's an extensive and very good wine list and a selection of liqueur coffees (including Irish, Highland, Russian, Caribbean, French, and Calypso) to bring a perfect meal to a perfect close. The Encore is open seven days a week from 5 to 11 p.m., and booking is not usually necessary. Complete dinner prices range from £8 ($13.20) to £12 ($19.80).

County Londonderry

Bellarena Smokery: To see how traditional oak smoking is done, and perhaps pick up smoked fish delicacies for a picnic, go by the Bellarena Smokery at Limavady (tel. Bellarena 50481) from 8:30 a.m. to 4:30 p.m., Monday through Friday.

County Tyrone

Ulster-American Folk Park: Three miles north of Omagh, on the Newtownstewart road, this park depicts the rural life in Ulster of those who left for America and their life in the New World. Endowed by the Mellon family of Pittsburgh, it includes their ancestral home, a colonial village, and an Indian settlement. Open daily from 11 a.m. to 6:30 p.m. April through August, 10:30 a.m. to 5 p.m. Monday through Friday other months; closed major holidays in winter months. Adults pay £1.25 ($2.07); children, 50p (83¢).

Woodrow Wilson Ancestral Home: Members of the Wilson family still live on the farm at Dergalt, near Strabane, from which our 28th president's family emigrated to America. The white-washed single- and double-story home contains some of its original furnishings, and is open to visitors for a 25p (42¢) admission fee.

ACCOMMODATIONS: Convenience, comfort, and a friendly, accommodating staff make **The Royal Arms Hotel,** Main Street,

Omagh, County Tyrone (tel. 0662-2119) an ideal base. Family owned and operated, it exudes a homey warmth, and there's an Old World charm about its Tavern Lounge and the adjoining dining room. There's also an attractive lounge, a coffeeshop, and residents' games room. All 21 bedrooms are nicely appointed and comfortably furnished, and all have telephone, TV, radio, and private bath. Rates for bed-and-breakfast start at £16 ($26.40) single, £28 ($46.20) double.

Chapter XXI

TOURIST TIPS

From A to Z

HERE'S A HANDY, quick-reference list covering all those details tourists always need to know, such as whom to tip and how much, what time the pubs open and close, where to find a hairdresser or medical attention, plus a few items of interest on Ireland we couldn't fit in elsewhere.

AMERICAN EMBASSY: The American Embassy is located in Dublin at 42 Eglin Road (tel. 01-688777). Hours are 8:30 a.m. to noon and 1 to 5 p.m., Monday to Friday. In Northern Ireland, the American Consulate General is at Queen's House, Queen Street, Belfast (tel. 0232-228239).

AMERICAN EXPRESS: The American Express office in Dublin is just off College Green at 116 Grafton St. (tel. 01-772874). The office changes money, sells traveler's checks, operates a travel agency, and accepts mail for clients. Hours: 9 a.m. to 5:15 p.m. Monday through Friday, 9 a.m. to noon on Saturday. In Belfast, the address is Hamilton Travel, 23 Waring St. (tel. 084-230321).

BANKING HOURS: Throughout the Republic of Ireland, banks are open from 10 a.m. to 12:30 p.m. and 1:30 to 3 p.m. weekdays (to 5 p.m. on Thursday in Dublin); closed Saturday, Sunday, and holidays. In Dublin International Airport, the bank is open daily, except Christmas, from 7:30 a.m. to 11 p.m. In Northern Ireland, hours are the same.

ELECTRIC CURRENT: The electric current most commonly used in Ireland is 220 volts A.C., but you will find that almost every place of accommodation, however humble, has shaver points available for 110-volt electric shavers. It's best to leave your other appliances at home as plug prongs vary and you would need to equip yourself with several converter/adapters.

EMERGENCY: To contact an ambulance, the police, or firemen, dial 999.

HOLIDAYS: National holidays are: January 1; March 17, St. Patrick's Day (which is more flamboyantly celebrated almost anywhere else); Good Friday; Easter Monday; first Monday in June; first Monday in August; last Monday in October; Christmas Day and the day after, St. Stephen's Day. All banks, public offices, and most shops are closed on those days. Holidays are the same in Northern Ireland except that the bank holiday is the first Monday in September, and July 12 commemorates the Battle of the Boyne.

MAIL DELIVERY: You may have your mail sent to **Poste Restante** (General Delivery), General Post Office, O'Connell Street, Dublin (tel. 748888), where you can pick it up any time between 8 a.m. and 8 p.m. Monday through Saturday, 9 a.m. and 8 p.m. on Sunday. *Poste Restante* facilities are also available at Head Post Offices in all the major towns between the hours of 9 a.m. and 5:30 p.m., Monday through Saturday. Foreign mail is held for a maximum of two months. **American Express** (see above) also accepts mail—but for clients only. You are required to show your American Express traveler's check or credit card.

MEDICAL ATTENTION: Most hospitals, dentists, and doctors in Ireland are equipped to give first-class care. For a reference to a doctor in your area, contact the **Irish Medical Association,** 10 Fitzwilliam Place, Dublin (tel. 762550). For dental matters, contact the **Irish Dental Association,** 29 Kennilworth Square, Dublin 6 (tel. 978435). Drugstores are known as *chemists* and are open weekdays during regular shopping hours. In most city suburbs, one chemist shop is open on Sunday and bank holidays from 11 a.m. to 1 p.m.

NEWSPAPERS: The four major national dailies are the *Irish Times* (not published on Sunday), the *Irish Independent,* the *Irish Press,* and the *Cork Examiner.* All are morning newspapers, and the best international coverage is given in the *Times.* Evening newspapers include the *Evening Press* and the *Evening Herald.* Papers are on sale everywhere in the Republic and you can pick up the Paris edition of the *International Herald Tribune* at some of the larger hotels. Foreign newspapers can be purchased at **Eason & Son Ltd.**, 40 Lower O'Connell St., Dublin, and **Ray's,** 13 St. Stephen's Green, Dublin (tel. 773661). Northern Ireland's leading newspapers are the *Belfast Telegraph,* the *Belfast News-letter,* and the *Sunday News.*

POLICE: The Irish police are actually civil guards. They wear blue uniforms and are unarmed. Their Gaelic name (and nobody calls them anything else) is *Garda Siochana,* which is literally translated as "protector of the peace." A single policeman is a *Garda*; in plural, they're *Gardai* (gard-ee). In Northern Ireland, police are called the Royal Ulster Constabulary. In emergency, you can reach the police anywhere in Ireland by phoning 999.

POSTAGE: In the Republic, the cost of postage between Ireland and the States is as follows: airmail letters are 46p (69¢) for the first half ounce, 17p (26¢) for each additional half ounce; air letters are cheaper at 40p (60¢) per letter; postcards cost 30p (45¢). Stamps can be purchased at hotels, post offices, news agents, and card shops. Mailboxes are easy enough to spot: they're painted Kelly green. Northern Ireland uses United Kingdom stamps, and mailboxes are painted a bright red.

PUB HOURS: Pubs are open from 10:30 a.m. to 11 p.m. in winter and to 11:30 p.m. in summer. Sunday hours throughout the year are from 12:30 to 2 p.m. and 4 to 10 p.m. In Dublin and Cork, the pubs close between 2:30 and 3:30 p.m. on weekdays, a time irreverently referred to as "The Holy Hour." In the North, pubs are closed on Sunday, but licensed restaurants and hotels may serve alcohol.

RADIO AND TELEVISION: Ireland has its own radio and television system, **Radio Telefis Eireann.** The three radio stations transmit from 7:30 a.m. to midnight and start at 8 a.m. on Sunday. The two television stations are on the air from about 5:30 p.m. to 11:30 or midnight, with special sports events on Saturday and Sunday afternoons and a half hour of school programs on Monday, Wednesday, and Friday mornings and afternoons. The **BBC** and the **British Independents (UTV Harlech)** are also received in some locations in the Republic.

RESTROOMS: You will find public restrooms located centrally in the cities (in Dublin, there's one next to the O'Connell Street Bridge) and in parks. You may also use restrooms in department stores, theaters that have public restaurants, and in pubs. When you're touring, you may use the facilities at any pub or hotel along the road; gas stations are seldom equipped with public restrooms. Keep a couple of pennies on hand to insert in the cubicle doors; the cover term is "going to spend a penny" (only these days it will cost you 2p—inflation is everywhere!). The word for women in Gaelic is *Mna;* for gentlemen, it's *Fir*—but such signs are usually bilingual.

SHOPPING HOURS: Major shops in Dublin are open from 9 a.m. to 5:30 or 6 p.m. Monday through Saturday. Smaller shops often close at 1 p.m. on either Wednesday or Saturday. Some stores close all day Monday; almost all are shuttered on Sunday and bank holidays. Similar hours pertain to country shops, with early-closing days varying from town to town. The same hours prevail in Northern Ireland.

TAXIS: In Ireland, taxis can seldom be hailed on the streets. Instead, they line up at ranks outside major hotels, bus or rail stations, or in the center of towns. You can either pick up a taxi at the rank or phone the rank for the taxi to pick you up (fares are metered from the moment the cab leaves the rank). Cab phone numbers are listed under "Taxi-cab Ranks and Shelters" in the telephone directories. In rural areas it is often necessary to make advance arrangements with the local cab driver.

TELEGRAMS: Telegrams can be sent through post offices. You can either go to the post office directly, or call in your telegram from your hotel. Calling from a coinbox is awkward, as you need a bushel of coins to feed into the slots. The number to call in order to send a telegram is listed in the front of the telephone directory (all the Republic is captured between the covers of two phone books—one for the Dublin area, the other for the rest of the country). Telegraph services are usually available for at least several hours on Sunday.

TELEPHONES: Telephone coin boxes take two-pence, five-pence, and ten-pence pieces. Local calls cost 15p for three minutes and you can't extend your call by feeding more coins. To make a local call at a coin box, put in your 15p, dial the number, and wait till it has been answered. At that point you will hear a shrill beeping noise. Press the button labeled "A" and your money will fall down into the box and the call will be connected. The party on the other end cannot hear you until you press button "A." If there is no answer, press button "B" and your money will be returned. If you want to make a long-distance call, dial the operator (at "0" or "10," depending on local instructions), and she will put through your call and instruct you on the amount to deposit. The telephone system in Ireland is in the process of being upgraded and perfected.

TIPPING: As ever, it's tricky and you can feel free to tip someone who's given you extra service and not to tip someone who doesn't deserve it—but the following are guides to custom: Most hotels and restaurants include a 10% to 15% service charge on the bill, and it is not necessary to leave more. In hotels, you might tip a minimum of 50p (83¢) per bag to porters carrying bags. Guesthouses seldom levy a service charge and you are not expected to tip members of the family that own the guesthouse. But you may tip the staff, such as a waitress, 50p (83¢) or more per meal. Taxi drivers are tipped 10% to 15% of the fare. Tip carpark attendants 50p (83¢)—these are usually elderly, uniformed men who make their living by directing people to parking spaces along the streets and guiding the car into place. Hairdressers and barbers receive a minimum 10% to 15% of the bill. You are not expected to tip sightseeing tour operators, but spontaneous gifts can be accepted. You are also not expected to tip theater ushers or gas station attendants, policemen, or Customs officials. Barmen are tippable (but it's not customary), and it is often handled with a suggestion that he "have one" himself, while slipping the cost of a Guinness across the bar. But you'll find that, in Ireland, a friendly "thank you" still goes a lot further than any ostentatious show of cash.

TRANSPORTATION: In the Republic, all trains and long-distance buses, as well as most local buses and sightseeing tours, are operated by the state-run **Coras Iompair Eireann (CIE).** If you are traveling the country by public transportation, it is best to purchase a **Train Timetable** and a **Provincial Bus Timetable,** available at news agents and terminals. If you are traveling for 8 to 15 days, you can almost halve your transportation costs by equipping yourself with a **Rambler** ticket, which gives you unlimited transportation throughout the Republic except on local and sightseeing buses. An eight-day rail-and-road ticket costs £70 ($105) for adults, half that for children; a 15-day rail-and-road ticket, £101 ($151.50) for adults, half that for children, in 1986. Rail-only Ramblers are less expensive and there are discounts for families and groups. Handy CIE numbers in Dublin are: 778777 for information on passenger trains and buses, 300777 for advance bookings on sightseeing tours. In Northern Ireland, a seven-day **"Rail Runabout"** costs £18.50 ($30.53) for adults, half that for children, from April through October.

YOUTH HOSTELS: Ireland is excellently provided with a full 54 well-distributed, simple but adequately equipped hostels for use of members of the **International Youth Hostel Association.** The Irish hostel association is called **An Oige,** and its head office is at 39 Mountjoy Square, Dublin 1 (tel. 01-745734). Your home association should be able to provide you with an An Oige handbook giving hostel locations and prices, or you can pick one up upon arrival in Dublin. All hostels supply pillows and blankets plus cooking gear, but you are required to bring a sheet, sleeping bag, cutlery, and towels. In Belfast, contact the **Youth Hostel Association of Northern Ireland,** 56 Bradbury Place, BT7 1RU (tel. 0232-224733).

NOW, SAVE MONEY ON ALL YOUR TRAVELS!
Join Arthur Frommer's $35-A-Day Travel Club™

Saving money while traveling is never a simple matter, which is why, over 26 years ago, the **$35-A-Day Travel Club** was formed. Actually, the idea came from readers of the Arthur Frommer Publications who felt that such an organization could bring financial benefits, continuing travel information, and a sense of community to economy-minded travelers all over the world.

In keeping with the money-saving concept, the annual membership fee is low—$18 (U.S. residents) or $20 U.S. (Canadian, Mexican, and foreign residents)—and is immediately exceeded by the value of your benefits which include:

(1) The latest edition of any TWO of the books listed on the following pages.

(2) An annual subscription to an 8-page quarterly newspaper *The Wonderful World of Budget Travel* which keeps you up-to-date on fastbreaking developments in low-cost travel in all parts of the world—bringing you the kind of information you'd have to pay over $35 a year to obtain elsewhere. This consumer-conscious publication also includes the following columns:

   Hospitality Exchange—members all over the world who are willing to provide hospitality to other members as they pass through their home cities.

   Share-a-Trip—requests from members for travel companions who can share costs and help avoid the burdensome single supplement.

   Readers Ask . . . Readers Reply—travel questions from members to which other members reply with authentic firsthand information.

(3) A copy of *Arthur Frommer's Guide to New York*.

(4) Your personal membership card which entitles you to purchase through the Club all Arthur Frommer Publications for a third to a half off their regular retail prices during the term of your membership.

So why not join this hardy band of international budgeteers NOW and participate in its exchange of information and hospitality? Simply send $18 (U.S. residents) or $20 U.S. (Canadian, Mexican, and other foreign residents) along with your name and address to: $35-A-Day Travel Club, Inc., Gulf + Western Building, One Gulf + Western Plaza, New York, NY 10023. Remember to specify which *two* of the books in section (1) above you wish to receive in your initial package of member's benefits. Or tear out the next page, check off any two of the books listed on either side, and send it to us with your membership fee.

Date_____

FROMMER BOOKS
PRENTICE HALL PRESS
ONE GULF + WESTERN PLAZA
NEW YORK, NY 10023

Friends:

Please send me the books checked below:

FROMMER'S $-A-DAY GUIDES™
(In-depth guides to sightseeing and low-cost tourist accommodations and facilities.)

☐ Europe on $30 a Day $13.95	☐ New Zealand on $40 a Day $11.95
☐ Australia on $30 a Day $12.95	☐ New York on $50 a Day............. $10.95
☐ Eastern Europe on $25 a Day $10.95	☐ Scandinavia on $50 a Day........... $12.95
☐ England on $40 a Day............... $12.95	☐ Scotland and Wales on $40 a Day..... $11.95
☐ Greece on $30 a Day............... $11.95	☐ South America on $30 a Day $12.95
☐ Hawaii on $50 a Day............... $11.95	☐ Spain and Morocco (plus the Canary
☐ India on $25 a Day $10.95	Is.) on $40 a Day $12.95
☐ Ireland on $30 a Day............... $12.95	☐ Turkey on $25 a Day............... $10.95
☐ Israel on $30 & $35 a Day $11.95	☐ Washington, D.C., & Historic Va. on
☐ Mexico (plus Belize & Guatemala)	$40 a Day $12.95
on $20 a Day..................... $10.95	

FROMMER'S DOLLARWISE GUIDES™
(Guides to sightseeing and tourist accommodations and facilities from budget to deluxe, with emphasis on the medium-priced.)

☐ Alaska $13.95	☐ Cruises (incl. Alaska, Carib, Mex,
☐ Austria & Hungary $11.95	Hawaii, Panama, Canada, & US) $13.95
☐ Belgium, Holland, Luxembourg $11.95	☐ California & Las Vegas $11.95
☐ Egypt....................... $11.95	☐ Florida....................... $11.95
☐ England & Scotland $11.95	☐ Mid-Atlantic States $12.95
☐ France....................... $11.95	☐ New England.................... $12.95
☐ Germany..................... $12.95	☐ New York State $12.95
☐ Italy....................... $11.95	☐ Northwest..................... $11.95
☐ Japan & Hong Kong $13.95	☐ Skiing in Europe $12.95
☐ Portugal, Madeira, & the Azores $12.95	☐ Skiing USA—East $11.95
☐ South Pacific................... $12.95	☐ Skiing USA—West $11.95
☐ Switzerland & Liechtenstein $12.95	☐ Southeast & New Orleans........... $11.95
☐ Bermuda & The Bahamas........... $11.95	☐ Southwest..................... $11.95
☐ Canada $12.95	☐ Texas....................... $11.95
☐ Caribbean $13.95	

FROMMER'S TOURING GUIDES™
(Color illustrated guides that include walking tours, cultural & historic sites, and other vital travel information.)

☐ Egypt........................... $8.95	☐ Paris $8.95
☐ Florence $8.95	☐ Venice $8.95
☐ London $8.95	

TURN PAGE FOR ADDITIONAL BOOKS AND ORDER FORM.

NOW!
ARTHUR FROMMER LAUNCHES HIS SECOND TRAVEL REVOLUTION
with

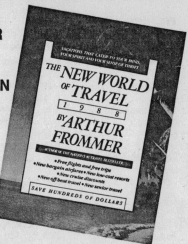

The New World of Travel

The hottest news and latest trends in travel today—heretofore the closely guarded secrets of the travel trade—are revealed in this new sourcebook by the dean of American travel. Here, collected in one book that is updated every year, are the most exciting, challenging, and money-saving ideas in travel today.

You'll find out about hundreds of alternative new modes of travel—and the many organizations that sponsor them—that will lead you to vacations that cater to your mind, your spirit, and your sense of thrift.

Learn how to fly for free as an air courier; travel for free as a tour escort; live for free on a hospitality exchange; add earnings as a part-time travel agent; pay less for air tickets, cruises, and hotels; enhance your life through cooperative camping, political tours, and adventure trips; change your life at utopian communities, low-cost spas, and yoga retreats; pursue low-cost studies and language training; travel comfortably while single or over 60; sail on passenger freighters; and vacation in the cheapest places on earth.

And in every yearly edition, Arthur Frommer spotlights the 10 GREATEST TRAVEL VALUES for the coming year. 384 pages, large—format with many, many illustrations. All for $12.95!

ORDER NOW
TURN TO THE LAST PAGE OF THIS BOOK FOR ORDER FORM.

THE ARTHUR FROMMER GUIDES™

(Pocket-size guides to sightseeing and tourist accommodations and facilities in all price ranges.)

☐ Amsterdam/Holland	$5.95	☐ Mexico City/Acapulco	$5.95
☐ Athens	$5.95	☐ Minneapolis/St. Paul	$5.95
☐ Atlantic City/Cape May	$5.95	☐ Montreal/Quebec City	$5.95
☐ Boston	$5.95	☐ New Orleans	$5.95
☐ Cancún/Cozumel/Yucatán	$5.95	☐ New York	$5.95
☐ Dublin/Ireland	$5.95	☐ Orlando/Disney World/EPCOT	$5.95
☐ Hawaii	$5.95	☐ Paris	$5.95
☐ Las Vegas	$5.95	☐ Philadelphia	$5.95
☐ Lisbon/Madrid/Costa del Sol	$5.95	☐ Rome	$5.95
☐ London	$5.95	☐ San Francisco	$5.95
☐ Los Angeles	$5.95	☐ Washington, D.C.	$5.95

SPECIAL EDITIONS

☐ A Shopper's Guide to the Caribbean	$12.95	☐ Motorist's Phrase Book (Fr/Ger/Sp)	$4.95
☐ Bed & Breakfast—N. America	$8.95	☐ Swap and Go (Home Exchanging)	$10.95
☐ Guide to Honeymoon Destinations (US, Canada, Mexico, & Carib)	$12.95	☐ The Candy Apple (NY for Kids)	$11.95
☐ Beat the High Cost of Travel	$6.95	☐ Travel Diary and Record Book	$5.95
☐ Marilyn Wood's Wonderful Weekends (NY, Conn, Mass, RI, Vt, NH, NJ, Del, Pa)	$11.95	☐ Where to Stay USA (Lodging from $3 to $30 a night)	$10.95

☐ Arthur Frommer's New World of Travel (Annual sourcebook previewing: new travel trends, new modes of travel, and the latest cost-cutting strategies for savvy travelers) $12.95

SERIOUS SHOPPER'S GUIDES

(Illustrated guides listing hundreds of stores, conveniently organized alphabetically by category.)

☐ Italy	$15.95	☐ Los Angeles	$14.95
☐ London	$15.95	☐ Paris	$15.95

ORDER NOW!

In U.S. include $1.50 shipping UPS for 1st book; 50¢ ea. add'l book. Outside U.S. $2 and 50¢, respectively.

Enclosed is my check or money order for $_____

NAME _____

ADDRESS _____

CITY _____ STATE _____ ZIP _____